# Catalyzing Transformation

# Catalyzing Transformation

*Making System Change Happen*

Sandra Waddock

BUSINESS EXPERT PRESS

*Leader in applied, concise business books*

*Catalyzing Transformation: Making System Change Happen*

Copyright © Business Expert Press, LLC, 2024

Cover design by Charlene Kronstedt

Interior design by Exeter Premedia Services Private Ltd., Chennai, India

First published in 2023 by
Business Expert Press, LLC
222 East 46th Street, New York, NY 10017
www.businessexpertpress.com

ISBN-13: 978-1-63742-508-4 (paperback)
ISBN-13: 978-1-63742-509-1 (e-book)

Business Expert Press Human Resource Management and Organizational Behavior Collection

First edition: 2023

10 9 8 7 6 5 4 3 2 1

*For*

*The extended Bounce Beyond Team, especially founder, Steve Waddell, and
Ian Kendrick, Peter Jones, Indra Adnan, Karen Downes, Jonny Norton,
Lesley Southwick-Trask, Zenda Ofir, and others.
Because you are the coauthors of these ideas.*


*For*

*All who would make the world a better place, system transformers
and musicians!*


*For*

*My mentors: Dave Brown, Stan Davis, and, most of all, Jim Post*


*For*

*Alan and Ben: You light up my life.*

# Description

**Here's how to make purposeful system change happen!**

The world faces a multitude of crises that demand transformative changes in how we live and do business. Yet a core question is, ***how to make purposeful transformation happen?*** *Catalyzing Transformation* shows the way through the following:

- Innovative *organizing* **processes** that anyone can use to catalyze purposeful whole system transformational change for a better world.
- How **transformation catalysts** work to organize purposeful, self-aware **transformation systems** that can tackle complex systemic challenges.
- Three processes: **connecting** (seeing, understanding, and making sense of the system), **cohering** (cocreatively developing shared goals and action plans), and **amplifying** (implementing, evaluating, and elaborating effective transformative action).
- **Design guidelines** for leaders **stewarding change efforts** in context-appropriate ways.

Whether you catalyze social change, responsible businesses, activists, policymakers, or students of change, *Catalyzing Transformation* can help!

# Keywords

transformation; system change; catalyzing system transformation; change agent; leading system change; stewarding change; flourishing; social imaginaries; ecological civilization; processes for system change

# Contents

*Testimonials* ......................................................................... xi

*Foreword*............................................................................. xv

*Acknowledgments*................................................................ xix

Chapter 1    A New Social Imaginary ..................................... 1

Chapter 2    Core Concepts for Transforming System
             Transformation ............................................... 19

Chapter 3    A Context of Cultural Myths............................. 35

Chapter 4    The Values Proposition ..................................... 49

Chapter 5    *What* Needs to Change in System Transformation ......... 69

Chapter 6    Transformation Catalysts: Connecting, Cohering,
             and Amplifying Transformation Systems' Work .............. 81

Chapter 7    Catalyzing Transformation (T-) Systems ....................... 103

Chapter 8    Design Guidelines and Principles for *Catalyzing
             Transformation* ............................................. 123

Chapter 9    Stewarding and Catalyzing Systemic Change ............... 147

Chapter 10   Synthesis: Transforming System Transformation .......... 167

*Notes*................................................................................. 187

*References* ......................................................................... 199

*About the Author*............................................................... 215

*Index* ............................................................................... 217

# Testimonials

*"For those becoming aware of our society's need for deep transformation, it's easy to get overwhelmed by the enormity of the challenge and confused as to how to engage most effectively. This book sheds much-needed light on the fog of our great transition, showing how the very process of transformation itself needs to be transformed in our current crisis. By explaining various categories of change agents, crystallizing concepts such as a 'transformation catalyst,' and distinguishing between different forms of leadership, Waddock helps illuminate the terrain that might just lead to a life-affirming civilization."*—**Jeremy Lent, Author of *The Patterning Instinct* and *The Web of Meaning***

*"This is a must read for anyone who is serious about supporting change toward achieving a better world. Sandra Waddock masterfully provides an accessible account of important concepts that together will reshape your thinking about how meaningful change comes about. The book challenges us to take systemic change seriously and will be an important guide for change makers for many years to come."*—**Dr. Ioan Fazey, Professor of the Social Dimensions of Environment and Change, University of York, UK**

*"It is increasingly clear that the next decade must be one of systemic change if we are to avert climate catastrophe and ascending authoritarianism in the world. Sandra Waddock provides the requisite roadmap for change makers everywhere to realize the transformational change required."*—**Stuart L. Hart, University of Vermont, author of *Capitalism at the Crossroads***

*"Our world is wracked by interconnected polycrises—ecological, economic, political, social, and spiritual.* Catalyzing Transformation *is more than an urgent call for action across these fronts; it is a playbook on how to think about and undertake systemic social change. Sandra Waddock draws from her multidisciplinary scholarship and practical experience to build a coherent and compelling model of transformational change and then gets into the*

*nitty-gritty of how to bring it to life. Whether you are a student or professor, manager or consultant, change designer or doer, there's gold herein. Reading and reflecting on this book will variously challenge assumptions, stretch your mind, stir your heart, and ultimately equip and embolden you to take a more comprehensive and creative approach to what you do to make a better world."*—**Dr. Philip Mirvis, Babson Institute for Social Innovation, and coauthor of** *Sustainability to Social Change: Lead Your Company from Managing Risk to Creating Social Value*

*"This book is so very timely. Sandra Waddock offers guidance on how to transform systems for a better world— at a time when there are so many systemic crises. This book offers sage advice for anyone who believes that a better future is possible and wants to make it a reality."*—**Dr. Tima Bansal, Canada Research Chair in Business Sustainability, Ivey Business School**

*"Sandra Waddock has done it again! In this book, she has isolated a key issue on sustainability and tackled it with gusto. While many talk of the need for transformative system change to bring about an equitable and flourishing world, there is not enough follow-on conversation about what exactly that change means and, importantly, how to bring it about. This book fills that enormous gap. In her usual blend of rigorous and yet accessible style, Sandra maps out a comprehensive handbook for anyone who wishes to play a role in "catalyzing" a new route for organizations and humankind, a route aimed at truly solving our sustainability challenges. Add this book to your toolkit for leading in a climate-changed world."*—**Professor Andrew J. Hoffman, PhD, Holcim (U.S.) Professor of Sustainable Enterprise, Ross School of Business/School for Environment and Sustainability, University of Michigan**

*"*Catalyzing Transformation *presents a state of the art, values-based, life-centrred perspective on systems transformation toward wholeness, justice, and a flourishing natural world. A must-read book for anyone looking to be an effective agent of fundamental change."*—**Reverend Professor Jasper Kenter, PhD, Ecological Economist and One Spirit Interfaith Minister**

*"Conscious, deliberate transformation toward a thriving, ecological civilization is the challenge that will define the 21st century. For those seeking to catalyze transformative change, Sandra Waddock's new book is the best manual we have so far for getting started."*—**Dr. Chris Riedy, Professor of Sustainability Transformations, University of Technology Sydney**

*"Sandra Waddock is a leading scholar in both organizational change theory and systems transformations, and she is the perfect guide to the field of Transformations, which can be difficult to encompass because of its broad transdisciplinary scope. Waddock interweaves the core insights and practical wisdom of this emerging field with prose that is both elegant and comprehensible. Her compelling narrative provides us with a way to make sense of the complexity of the challenges we face and the urgency of action, and inspires us with the possibility that we can be effective agents for deep systems change."*
—**Dr. Bruce Evan Goldstein, Environmental Design, University of Colorado Boulder**

# Foreword

"Change the system, not the climate." We've all seen the posters at climate rallies, and it's hard to disagree. After all, climate change, biodiversity loss, marine pollution, and other sustainability challenges are already contributing to the end of the world as we know it. Yet how do we equitably and sustainably transform systems in response to urgent and complex global challenges? The answer is in your hands!

In the pages ahead, Sandra Waddock will help you understand how to make systems change happen. Her theory of whole system change brings together a wide range of frameworks, ideas, and experiences that can be used to generate purposeful transformations. You will be introduced to a language and approach to systems change that is grounded in shared visions and values. This is no wishful thinking. It's a strategic approach, and your role is critical. Let me explain.

A catalyst is someone or something that causes a change. *Catalyzing Transformation* involves the processes of connecting, cohering, and amplifying the work of one *and* the work of many. In chemistry, the catalyst itself does not get consumed in the process. In other words, it does not change. In whole systems change, the catalyst of transformation is part of the system, and it can and often does change. In fact, *you* may very well change after reading this book, in at least three possible ways.

First, you will recognize the important role that you play in telling new stories. New narratives help to *disrupt cultural myths*, including those that prioritize competition over cooperation and self-interest over the common good, or those that separate us from nature. Without self-awareness, we perpetuate these myths and wonder why we are not seeing the changes we would like to see. Alternatives exist, and many of them are right in front of you, waiting to be seen. Seeing, however, often takes imagination and practice.

Second, you will understand the importance of actions based on *life-affirming values*, or values that are intrinsic to all of life. Values such as equity, inclusion, and integrity—or wholeness—are foundational to system change. They are reflected in your stories, narratives, and choices, and they form the basis of principles that support your purpose and goals. When a change process is value-driven, it affects not just one relationship, but many.

Third, with an awareness of how change happens, you will unleash your *collaborative capacity* and discover ways that you can connect with others and create coherence, or in other words, an alignment and resonance that amplifies your actions and impacts. This is a different way of engaging with and organizing change. As Sandra Waddock emphasizes, it is about *stewarding* transformative change.

This book provides you with a vocabulary, a framework, and tools to start you on your journey to redefining the very nature of change itself. As a catalyst for transformation, you contribute to what I describe as "quantum social change"—a conscious, nonlinear, and nonlocal approach to transformations that is grounded in our inherent oneness. Putting these tools into practice, you will recognize that no matter which sector, community, or issue you are engaged with, your values, choices, and actions are vital to the transformations needed for global sustainability. When it comes to catalyzing systems change, you matter more than you think.

—Karen O'Brien,[*]
Professor of Sociology and Human Geography
University of Oslo, Norway and Co-Chair,
IPBES Transformative Change Assessment

Having just finished *Catalyzing Transformation: Making System Change Happen*, I now face the challenge of introducing you to it. The best way to write a helpful foreword is to encourage readers to start reflecting on

[*] Karen O'Brien is Professor—Institutt for sosiologi og samfunnsgeografi at the University of Oslo. Her recent books include You Matter More Than You Think: Quantum Social Change for a Thriving World and Climate and Society: Transforming the Future (with Robin Leichenko). Karen has been named by Web of Science as one of the world's most influential researchers of the past decade. Karen is currently co-chair of the International Science-Policy Platform for Biodiversity and Ecosystem Services (IPBES) transformative change assessment.

the most important question that will arise for them as soon as they begin reading: *what is it about Sandra Waddock's insights in this book that inspire hope?*

For that's what these pages do. One can't make it through more than a few pages into the first chapter without feeling that, even with the insanely difficult challenges before humanity, *we are not stuck, and we are not doomed.* Dr. Waddock does not force readers to optimistic conclusions. Instead, with her calm style and careful analysis, she shows why we desire in the end to live in a thriving, just, sustainable society—what she calls an *ecological civilization.*

Then, one by one, step by inexorable step, she pulls the necessary pieces into place: Change agents exist. Systems are changeable; they can be transformed. The persons and organizations that change them are *transformation catalysts.* And we can indeed study, comprehend, and therefore increase the frequency and power of their catalytic effects. Before readers even leave the first chapter, they will already see the book's trajectory unfolding.

In short, *Catalyzing Transformation is a large-scale roadmap for systemic change.* Sandra Waddock rightly describes the long-term target as an "ecological civilization," a way of organizing human society that is fundamentally based on fully ecological principles. Humanity will not get there by means of "incremental changes," or even using "reformative" ones, but only by bringing about the transformation of human society— through civilizational change. This is a highly significant and ambitious thesis, one that deserves our closest attention. Suffice it here to say: the evidence fundamentally supports Sandra's case.

What makes these pages worthy of widespread attention is that, unlike most books about systemic change, the author does not just vaguely wave her hands in the direction of something greater. These pages offer a specific, detailed, plausible, and, I believe, reliable roadmap to get us to that destination. At EcoCiv.org, where Sandra is a board member, we call it the VBR method: Sandra starts with a *vision* of the final outcome, a new social imaginary. She then *backcasts* to the present, spelling out the cultural myths that have produced the global climate crisis. She tells us what needs to change in our approach to economic systems, and what are the broader dimensions (including even the metrics) that have to change.

Finally, her *roadmap* presents the details of how the necessary changes are achieved: the catalysts for change; who and what the "transformation catalysts" are and how they work; the values that undergird their policies and actions; and the methods they use. Rarely have I read a book driven by a breathtaking vision that is so concrete and specific about the means for achieving it.

Please take them seriously; these principles really work. Over the past eight years, I have led an international organization that seeks to be a transformational catalyst in Sandra's exact sense. The guidelines she offers in her closing chapters are the ones we have followed in dozens of events in 10 different countries around the world. *Connect, cohere, and amplify* are not abstract ideals for us; they are the daily bread of our work. Of course, much more needs to be said about these crucial transformational activities to make them maximally useful for leaders in specific regions and sectors. But she is right: on the ground in Beijing and Berlin, in South Africa and South Korea and South Sudan, what you will read here is exactly what transformational catalysts do, and do well, when we are most successful.

It is rare that a single book offers *both* a comprehensive vision *and* specific guidelines for action. Sandra Waddock's book does precisely this. Please read it carefully, share it with your friends, and mail it to leaders of organizations that you believe can really make a difference. Humanity really can make the transition: from a civilization characterized by unsustainable consumption to a sustainable civilization based on genuinely ecological principles. You hold the framework in your hands.

—Philip Clayton, PhD[†]
President, Institute for Ecological Civilization

---

[†] Philip Clayton is President of EcoCiv, the Institute for Ecological Civilization. He holds his PhD from Yale University; has held guest professorships at Harvard, University of Cambridge, and University of Munich; and is the author or editor of several dozen books and some 300 articles on science, ethics, and religion.

# Acknowledgments

This book would not exist at all without Steve Waddell's imagination, ideas, insights, and community organizing skills as well as the contributions of the rest of the extended Bounce Beyond team. I am forever grateful for his inclusion of me in these ways of thinking, and want to acknowledge Steve's deep contributions to whatever is good about this book (and, of course, any problems or flaws in thinking here rest entirely with me). Steve is the founder of Bounce Beyond (www.bouncebeyond .global), the former SDG Transformation Forum, and Networking Action. He is an undisputed global thought leader around system transformation. When the global pandemic brought about by COVID-19 and the lock-ins began, Steve used all of his community organizing skills and insights about system transformation to bring together an eclectic group to begin thinking about how the world's economic systems might "bounce beyond" today's flawed economics toward more pluralistic and well-being/flourishing-oriented economics.

That insight combined with Steve's deep understanding of large system change processes, ideas on which we have been collaborating over many years, has resulted in a plethora of coauthored and individually authored papers on which the present book relies. Steve's genius was to bring together a group of transformational change agents, who each in their own ways contributed to the content of this book. Since no one truly writes a book alone, I want to sincerely acknowledge all of the intellectual contributions of the Bounce Beyond team (and beyond) to this book right up front. It would not have been possible without Steve and the rest of the Bounce Beyond team's insights and contributions since 2020. That said, of course, the interpretation, framing, and synthesis of these ideas, and any associated mistakes, issues, or problems, belong to me.

Because the Bounce Beyond team itself has evolved since its inception, I also want to acknowledge insights generated from all members of the team during our many meetings, conversations, and initiatives over the years. At the time of writing, the team consisted of Steve Waddell, Ian Kendrick, Jonny Norton, and Lesley Southwick-Trask. Previous members other than me (hoping no one has been left out) include Indra Adnan, Karen Downes, Peter Jones, Zenda Ofir, and in the extended team, Stuart Cowan, Ned Daly, Tim Draimin, Ioan Fazey, Meenakshi Gupta, Jasper Kenter, Jean-Louis Robadey, and Coro Strandberg. To this list I add key members of the former SDG Transformations Forum, who contributed in so many ways, especially Tony Cooke, Bruce Evan Goldstein, Glenn Page, and Chris Riedy.

Also, I particularly thank Patricia Kambitsch of PlayThink (https://playthink.com/) for the terrific artwork that accompanies this book. Patricia really opened my eyes to the true power of art to reveal the core of what is really important in processes like the ones described in this book. She immediately "got" what was needed to explain the complicated path of system transformation in readily accessible ways. Thank you, Patricia!

Beyond Bounce Beyond, there are others whose insights, support, and good work needs to be acknowledged, including many who commented on earlier drafts of this book or whose ideas have influenced and informed my thinking over many years: Laura Albareda, Bobby Banerjee, Philip Clayton, Tony Cooke, Domenico Dentoni, Four Arrows (aka Donald Trent Jacobs), Ioan Fazey, Ed Freeman, Jody Fry, Irene Henriques, Andy Hoffman, Tony Hodgson, Chris Ives, David Korten, Petra Kuenkel, Chris Laszlo, Jegoo Lee, Ju Young Lee, Jeremy Lent, Daniel Hart London, Josep Lozano, Manuel Manga, Judi Neal, Isabel Neusse, Glenn Page, Michael Pirson, Edwina Pio, Kate Pitrew, Andreas Rasche, Kate Raworth, Chris Riedy, Andrew Schwartz, Robert Sroufe, Erica Steckler, Katherine Trebeck, David Wasieleski, Michael Weatherhead, and Maurizio Zollo, among many others. Importantly, I want to acknowledge the late Malcolm McIntosh whose passion for system transformation inspired me from the beginning. Though it was many years ago, I carry with me always the inspiration offered by my own mentors L. Dave Brown, Stan Davis, Jerry Leader, and (most centrally) Jim Post, my former dissertation chair so many years ago and friend to this day, plus all of the intellectual shamans in the book by that name so many others who could not be included there.

There are so many others whose work was inspirational from my intellectual past to name (or even remember!), so please forgive me if I have omitted you. I have been inspired by the commitment, insights, and work of the folks associated with SIM (the Social Issues in Management Division of the Academy of Management), IABS (The International Association of Business in Society), the Humanistic Management Association and Network, the Transformation Conferences, and more recently the IPBES assessment on transformation, particularly Chapter 2. Then, there's always my support network, which includes Judy Clair, Dawn Elm, Marta Geletkanycz, Jeanne Liedtka, Priscilla Osborne, Tish Miller, and the entire SAMW (Summer Acoustic Music Week) community and beyond. Also, the Jamaica Pond bluegrass jammers, and all the rest of my musician friends, who keep me sane when things get crazy. And of course, I don't want to forget the two people who light up my life: my life partner, Alan Rubin, and my son, Benjamin Wiegner. You all contributed significantly to this journey in your own ways. Any good ideas or thinking in this book can be attributed to your good influences. The bad ones I'll keep for myself.

We are truly all in this work and this world together!

# CHAPTER 1

# A New Social Imaginary

Imagine a world where everyone has a place to belong, where they can contribute as their talents allow, where they have voice in decisions that affect them. A world where people of every status, race, and ethnicity have what they need to live a decent life. Imagine a world governed from the bottom up, where everyone's voice is heard and where they have input into decisions that affect them. Imagine a world where nature flourishes and people live in harmony, where exploitation of both people and nature is a thing of the past. Where businesses have stopped exploiting people and nature and treat all beings with the dignity they deserve. Where production and provisioning practices are regenerative and restorative to both the human spirit and nature. Imagine peace, collaboration, and cooperation.

Imagine that everyone has enough. That creative, entrepreneurial, civic, homemaking, and care arts flourish. Imagine a world without war, scarcity, and greed, a world powered by values of stewardship, care for each other, nature, and the common good. A world where collaboration and cooperation rather than competition is emphasized, where symbiosis is recognized as the building block of life. A world where, as John Lennon wrote in his beautiful song "Imagine," there is "nothing to kill or die for," where people can actually live in peace. Where, in fact, there is no more need for greed and hunger, where relationships and connection are at the center of living rather than accumulation of, as Lennon said, possessions.[1]

We can all potentially imagine such a world. It would stem from a new social imaginary.[2] That is, a new, or maybe, more accurately, a very ancient yet modernized social imaginary, a set of shared values, along with the symbols, institutions, and the rules and laws that support them. Such a world can potentially be built from reimagined economies and the societies that support them. Economies drive so much these days. But economies in this new social imaginary emphasize equity, social justice, inclusive participation, and well-being in a flourishing natural world—contrary to today's financial wealth-driven orientation. I believe such social imaginaries are needed in multiple contexts—organized, as discussed later, around core values of stewardship, justice, equity, inclusiveness, and flourishing for all, including other-than-humans. I believe it is possible to get to those visions though it will not be easy.

Achieving that new social imaginary will take imagination and inspirational aspirations, new visioning, to *envision* new ways of being and acting in the world, particularly in light of the many obstacles in the world today. Furthermore, getting there also requires knowledge, insights, awareness, skills, and tools for effecting system transformation that are still emerging and that will be developed in this book, along with the hard work and new ways of understanding systemic change needed to bring about the whole system transformation. Change makers need to do that in the context of numerous ongoing, difficult crises, an entrenched system that wants to hold business as usual in place. Guided by a new social imaginary of well-being and flourishing for all, including other-than-humans, and by taking power into our own hands using the ideas and processes put forward in this book, we can each play a part in building such a world.

So ..., are we, as Lennon also said, dreamers? Or is such a world built on new social imaginaries[3] that honor all of life even possible? What would it take to get there, especially in the face of today's numerous—and existentially threatening—crises?

*Catalyzing Transformation* offers, I hope, a set of approaches and pathways to help bring about the world envisioned by this new social imaginary. Yes, it will be hard work. Yes, it requires thinking and acting systemically, and maybe quite differently from what is typical. Yes, it demands new capacities, skills, and insights, not to mention the willingness to work with others in new ways. And, yes, no one individual (or even group) has all the needed answers. Collectively, together, I believe we do have the answers if only we can find ways to tap into the knowledge, insights, and dreams that are already present. If we can connect, cohere, and amplify the changes toward a regenerative, inclusive, equitable, and flourishing world that might be called an *ecological civilization* that is collectively desired by many (perhaps not all) in the world. *Catalyzing Transformation* offers pathways for how to get to that world, relying on the insights, knowledge, and wisdom of change makers brought together in new ways.

## From a World of Woes …

There is no doubt that the world faces numerous crises, what some today are calling *polycrisis*, interacting, entangled, and often global crises that diminish future human (and natural) prospects. Indeed, the current system sometimes seems so strong and seemingly immovable and is causing so many issues that the condition of humanity on our beautiful blue planet feels stuck in endless crises. The unabating and potentially disastrous climate emergency continues despite increasingly desperate studies and global meetings arguing for the need for transformative change.[4] Millions of refugees, migrants, and internally displaced people flee each year from wars, economic hardships, discrimination and violence, human rights violations, climate change, political instability, famine, and other humanitarian hardships, often with nowhere safe to go.[5] Wealth inequality continues to increase globally, with the ultrarich capturing ever more and the less well-off left struggling.[6]

There is more. Biodiversity loss[7] threatens more than a million species and, because of integral links between people and other beings, has the potential to cripple human civilizations' capacity to thrive. While the devastating COVID-19 pandemic galvanized world resources, and incidentally highlighted how quickly things can change when the public will is there, insufficient attention is still paid to the ecological sustainability and climate change issues that threaten the future of humanity.[8] Too often these crises center around the apparently insatiable appetite that people have for oil and accumulating other resources, which seems to be both at the center of many conflicts and present a real obstacle to the needed change.

There are many other looming issues and unknowns, including political divisiveness, potential for ecosystem collapses resulting from overfishing, overuse of agricultural pesticides and human-made fertilizers, topsoil loss, deforestation, desertification, and both food and energy scarcity in some places. Social unrest about injustices bubbles beneath calm-appearing surfaces in a wide range of societies. War and conflict disrupt too many societies. Melting glaciers and sea rise threaten coastal communities, where about half the world's human population lives. And the litany could continue—from the dangers some thought leaders expect from artificial intelligence, loss of privacy, to the potential for famine, overgrazing of pastures, and overfertilization of farmlands. Today's approaches to economics, economies, and general provisioning,[9] that is, providing needed goods, services, and foodstuffs, need renewal and regeneration. In short, they need to be transformed.

There are too many other crises to note and detail them all, humanitarian, racial, and ethnic injustices, and ecological, economic, social, and political problems. It can all seem hopeless and overwhelming. Instead of succumbing to despair, however, I want to move toward thinking about what can actually be *done* to transform our communities, institutions, and societies. How can systemic change toward a desired set of futures be brought about? *Catalyzing Transformation* argues that together we can begin to explore what change makers can actually begin to do to deal more effectively with these problems rather than dwell on identifying them.

That is hard because the foreseeable future has characteristics that have been synthesized as VUCA (volatility, uncertainty, complexity, and ambiguity) (and too often desired futures remain undefined, or unagreed). Volatility means that the world is perceived as subject to constant and significant change. Uncertainty argues that events and their outcomes are unpredictable.[10] Complexity, as discussed in detail elsewhere, means that there is intricate interconnectedness of multiple difficult issues evolving unpredictably. Ambiguity signifies lack of clarity and difficulty of understanding situations.*

This world generates reactions among observers. Psychological reactions to a VUCA world generate what is synthesized as BANI.

---

* Though the origin of this term is not settled, it seems to have originated in Army War College documents in the late 1980s during the Cold War as a way of describing the difficult world future leaders would face, drawing on the leadership ideas of W. Bennis and B. Nanus in their book *Leaders: Strategies for Taking Charge.*

BANI means brittle, anxious, nonlinear, and incomprehensible.[11]† Brittle means that the world is perceived as susceptible to catastrophe at any time. The brittleness encompasses the realization that today's businesses and institutions are built on fragile foundations that can fall apart overnight. Anxious describes one of the most prevalent psychological symptoms in the world today, not just in people's personal lives and activities, but in work, economies, societies, and living situations. Increasing anxiety means that many are living on the edge. They are worried about the present and future and hold a sense of urgency that guides decision making. Nonlinear, which builds on the idea of complexity, means that the world's events seem disconnected and disproportionate, making it difficult to shape standardized structures and responses. That nonlinearity also makes long-term planning no longer feasible. Finally, incomprehensible means that the experienced world is very difficult to understand, and even when answers are generated, they do not seem to make sense.

Many entangled crises, the polycrisis, that we humans collectively face only add to the difficulty of coping in that world. It can make transforming the world for the better, for all, including the beings that philosopher ecologist David Abram calls the "more-than-human world"[12] seem impossible. But the presence of multiple crises does not mean that nothing can be done or that transformative change toward a world of equitable economies fostering human well-being and a flourishing natural environment is not possible. Such change is possible. It will, however, take considerable public will and purposeful, engaged, and effective efforts by many—activists, change makers, systems changers, nongovernmental organizations (NGOs), governments, businesses and multilateral organizations, to name a few. It will take new forms of know-how, new ways of organizing and thinking about how transformative change can come about. That is what this book explores and develops, how to bring people together in new, creative ways that are oriented toward creating a world that works for all.

---

† The creator of this new concept is J. Cascio, American anthropologist, author, and futurist. See also *From a VUCA World to a BANI One: How Uncertainty Has Changed and How Your Company Can Prepare*, www.mjvinnovation.com/blog/from-a-vuca-world-to-a-bani-one (accessed August 12, 2022).

Diverse actors, initiatives, NGOs, governments, businesses, institutions, and citizen groups need to learn how to catalyze transformation—and, in doing so, work together in new ways. All these parties and many more will need to engage far more deeply in the real systemic transformation efforts that even crises like the COVID-19 pandemic, the Global Financial Crisis of 2007–2008, dire reports about climate change, biodiversity loss, and unprovoked war, have yet to engage. It will take knowledge about pathways to system transformation, some willingness to give up one's self-interest in the interest of the whole, and an understanding of the context in which such change takes place to begin to make *purposeful* system change work. It will take new ways of organizing for transformation, catalyzing it, and new ways of engaging with others. That is what *catalyzing transformation* is all about.

## A New Social Imaginary: Socially Just, Inclusive Well-Being Socioeconomies in a Flourishing Natural World, or the Case for Ecological Civilizations

*Catalyzing Transformation* focuses on transforming economics and economies as well as social systems that interact with natural systems. Broadly, the focus is on facilitating socially just, inclusive, well-being socioeconomies in a flourishing natural world to evolve and take center stage, supplanting today's flawed economic and societal approaches that have resulted in the many crises of the world. These systems can be labeled social–political–economic–ecological systems, with all the above-mentioned descriptors, but for shorthand David Korten's (and EcoCiv's, i.e., Institute for Ecological Civilization's) term "ecological civilization"[13] makes the most sense to use.

It is important to recognize that ecological civilizations reflect social, political, economic, and natural systems that encompass a broad array of human endeavors. Each context will have its own definition of what an ecological civilization means there. Importantly, because shared values, as discussed later, are centrally important to systemic change toward what is often called *sustainability*[14], here flourishing, these expressions will most likely share ideas around social justice, equity, inclusiveness, and ecological flourishing that broadly define ecological civilization. At least that is my core belief! Economic, societal, and political linkages to nature are broadly conceived in the context of system transformation. So, the ideas here about how to organize to get to such outcomes have wide applicability to transformative efforts in many contexts.

Economy here means the systems of production, servicing, and provisioning (providing food and agricultural products) that serve humanity. Economy encompasses issues that affect socioecologies and bioregions, biodiversity, and other systems that rely on a healthy natural world. Many types of socioecological systems will fit this category. For example, systems that might be changed include political entities at multiple levels—local to global, bioregional, nations, and even planetary. Other change efforts might be organized around sectors or issues, recognizing that these broad categories intersect in any given set of activities and initiatives.

As the opening imaginary illustrates, there are many facets to the needed new social imaginary, framed as an influential narrative that helps shape peoples' worldviews and mindsets—paradigms. There are also many facets of the transformations needed. Generally, this idea of the new social imaginary builds a new narrative or vision that has the potential, as discussed later, to become a new cultural mythology.

One cultural framing, that is a potential new mythology, that has emerged in recent years is that of the well-being economy in a flourishing natural world. Forwarded by WEAll, the Wellbeing Economy Alliance,[15] the idea of well-being economy incorporates the elements of ecological civilization just discussed and attempts to create a new narrative around what the focus and purpose of economies really are. Core narratives, as discussed in depth later, provide vision and guidance for people collaborating to bring change about, though different groups and initiatives may approach that vision differently. WEAll's emerging narrative is potentially instructive in this regard.

WEAll's numerous partners or collaborators expressed four distinct future-oriented imaginaries in their membership applications. One was a serious critique of the current economic system and discussion of the urgent need for whole system transformation, along with a general critique of today's mostly neoliberal economics. What underlies this critique of conventional economics is elaborated more fully in Chapter 4. Fundamentally, this critique recognizes the need for a system transformation narrative and a dramatic shift of business-as-usual economics, with an emphasis on shifting away from destructive practices toward one that fosters well-being and ecological flourishing. But it does not really offer a new vision of what well-being economies might be.

A second narrative expressed by WEAll members focused on keeping human economic and other activities within the constraints of what the Stockholm Resilience Centre terms planetary boundaries. These boundaries are the nine geophysical limits that human activities should not transgress to maintain Earth's capacity to support human civilization.[16] Called the *planetary boundaries* narrative, it is generally ecologically oriented and argues for generating resilience, regeneration, balance, and localized decision making on a healthy, "alive" planet.

Another narrative from WEAll members with a different emphasis is the "good life" narrative. While it emphasizes sustainability, too, it is particularly oriented toward ensuring that all people get their needs met and are able to build and sustain a decent life. It is more people oriented than the planet-oriented planetary boundaries narrative. In the "good life" narrative, the emphasis is on economic well-being, ensuring that care is embedded, along with reduced inequality, poverty reduction, and providing necessary resources to assure healthy living standards. One person provided a phrase that neatly captures this orientation: "Enough, for everyone, forever."

The fourth narrative, and the one this book offers as ecological civilization, integrates the planetary boundaries and good life narratives as what I have outlined as an integrated ecological civilization perspective. This social imaginary narrative imagines life-centered, holistic, and integrated sets of economic activities and economies that recognize and support the value of all beings, human and more-than-human. It points to the interconnected web of life, as physicist Fritjof Capra called it,[17] and the connections that exist among social, economic, and ecological systems and issues. The orientation is toward fostering the well-being of both humans and nature through caring for all of nature, which includes humans and planet. Figure 1.1 and Table 1.1 illustrate these different ways of conceiving a future social imaginary.

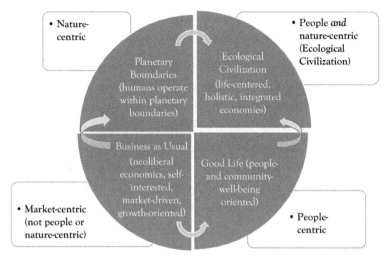

*Figure 1.1  Four narratives: new social imaginaries toward ecological civilization*

*Source*: Adapted from Waddock (2021).[18]

*Table 1.1  Narratives synthesized from WEAll (Well-being Economy Alliance) members toward ecological civilization as expressed through well-being economies*

| Four Narratives: Status Quo and Three Visions of Well-Being Economies as Ecological Civilizations |
| --- |
| **Business as Usual:** Conventional economic thinking, market-centric, laissez-faire government, self-interested profit maximization, and endless growth (not represented in WEAll member stories). |
| **Planetary Boundaries:** An ecological economics where humans operate within planetary boundaries, generating resilience, regeneration, balance, and localized decision making for all people on a thriving, living, and healthy planet. |
| **Good Life:** People-oriented economics emphasizing sustainability where basic needs are met and a good life for all people is possible through economic well-being, care, reduced inequalities, poverty reduction, and healthy lives sustainably—enough, for everyone, forever. |
| **Integrated (Ecological Civilization):** A life-centered, holistic, and integrated economics emphasizing the value of all beings, as well as the web of life or interconnectedness of social, economic, and ecological issues. This integrated approach fosters the well-being of both humans and nature, care for people and nature, human and planet. |

*Source:* Adapted from Waddock (2021).[19]

## Transforming to Just, Inclusive, Equitable Societies in a Flourishing Natural World—Ecological Civilizations

System transformation to achieve any of these social imaginaries and particularly the ecological civilization is difficult for many reasons. Partly, it is hard because there is still too little understanding of the realities of such change in complex systems where there are many wicked problems. Partly, because such change is so fundamental that is, because so much has to change and there are likely to be many perspectives on what is needed and how to get to that end. Systemic change, after all, means fundamental changes in the purposes, paradigms, and performance metrics that guide human (socioecological) systems—and the practices (policies, procedures, and processes) and power relations that structure them.[20] Partly, transformation is hard because it is difficult to envision both the *need* for and *possibilities* that transformative change might bring.

It is hard, that is, to create new social imaginaries and pathways to them that can inspire more of us to action that works in practice. Transformation is also hard because there are many obstacles to change, including strong institutions and powerful forces (and people) focused on sustaining business as usual, and because there is still too little knowledge about *how* to bring transformative change about and make it stick.

*Catalyzing Transformation* certainly does not have all the answers. But it does outline some pathways for new ways of organizing that can build needed skills, expertise, and transformative efforts. That said, it is important to recognize that transformative change requires many experiments and entails numerous failures, fits and starts, and renewals. *Catalyzing Transformation* argues that transformative system change can be catalyzed in purposeful directions. Using these ideas, and recognizing the need for new ways of organizing and acting toward transformation, I believe that collectively we can move our human—socioecological—systems toward just, equitable, inclusive human societies in a flourishing natural world—toward ecological civilizations.[21]

### Who Is Catalyzing Transformation *for?*

This book is intended for a variety of readers interested in transformative change. Of course, it could productively be read by *insiders looking out*: anyone who is already working toward such change from inside existing organizations and institutions who wants to improve effectiveness. For that matter, it is written for concerned citizens who think such change might be necessary in their communities and want to see what might be done to make it happen. More specifically, it is geared to change agents, activists, and thought leaders, particularly ones in boundary-spanning roles in business, governmental, multilateral, and nongovernmental organizations, who are attempting to bring about change from within their organizations. That category includes sustainability and corporate (social) responsibility/citizenship officers, public affairs and media relations professionals, organization development specialists, and anyone else in organizations who works to bridge multiple worlds, including sectors, disciplines, business activities, strategies, including top-level executives.

*Catalyzing Transformation* could also productively be used by outsiders looking in at problematic systems, that is activists and critics in communities, organizations, sectors, and issues, who see the need for and want to bring change about. Whole communities of people working at various transformation communities and coalitions that already exist to bring change about in their particular context could benefit from using the approaches outlined here. For example, the many people involved in transforming cities, regenerative agricultural, creating systems that include marginalized peoples, build in dignity for all, and attempt to shift human relations to/perspectives about nature, or dealing with the multitude of other issues facing our world. It could be adopted by organizational development specialists inside existing organizations and institutions—and out there in the society. Activists and thought leaders seeking to drum up support for their efforts—and to really make their desired changes effective—might well find it helpful. It could be used by social change agents, including artists, storytellers, reporters, and media-savvy activists, who want to bring ideas about what I broadly describe in the following as ecological civilization, that is, just and equitable human societies in a flourishing natural world, into more effective initiatives.

Then, of course, there are scholars and students of all types of system-oriented change. They can be found in numerous disciplines, for example, management, political science, sociology, social work, law, city/urban planning, regenerative agriculture and seafood, geography, journalism, international and development studies, ecology, and transition and transformation studies, to name some of the more obvious fields.

Beyond students, people in leadership positions in major sectors who clearly need to be transformed might find this book useful—fields such as seafood, agriculture, health care, social services, and rural, urban, and global development. The approaches outlined here could be adopted (and adapted) by scholars and researchers of transformation, transition, and social and organizational change who want to work with new theories of change that can be operationalized in numerous different contexts. Of course, *Catalyzing Transformation* could be used by students at all levels—doctoral, master's, and even advanced undergraduates.

As I have learned in recent years, people meeting these descriptions exist in just about any discipline or walk of life that can be imagined. They can be found managing and leading organizations in just about any sector, naturally. They are artists, community activists and leaders, actors, public and local intellectuals, citizen activists, teachers, biologists and ecologists, and government officials at all levels who want to bring ecological regenerativity, inclusiveness, equity, and justice into their contexts. These folks are found in multiple (and sometimes unexpected) disciplines—across the board. Just about anyone who wants to begin to understand at least one potentially potent approach to the *how* of systemic change might find this book useful.

### Organizing for Transformation

To get to what can broadly be called *ecological civilizations*, *Catalyzing Transformation* outlines a set of emerging ideas and *organizing* frames for an innovative approach to *how* the purposeful system transformation can be catalyzed. This catalysis begins with shaping stories and cultural myths to inspire new social imaginaries related to ecological civilization (Chapter 3). It continues with articulating a core set of values shared by people around the world who desire ecological civilizations, defined as just, equitable, inclusive societies in a flourishing natural world (Chapter 4), and identifying *what* needs to change (Chapter 5). These new ways of organizing are focused around developing new entities called *transformation catalysts* (Chapter 6) that work to steward (Chapter 9) the connection, coherence, and amplification of the efforts of numerous actors in purposeful transformation systems (Chapter 7), along with core design and stewardship principles for acting in these contexts (Chapter 9).[‡] The nature of transformative change is that it is unique to each context. As I will show, however, these core approaches and design principles (Chapter 8), geared to specific contexts, can provide viable pathways forward that offer the potential for real transformative change. That said, system transformation is not easy—and it takes many people getting deeply engaged, along with catalytic actions, to make it happen.

The general process, that is, the theory of change, to be explained in detail throughout this book, can be seen in the image *Catalyzing Transformation* (Figure 1.2). *Catalyzing Transformation* outlines an iterative set of processes of connecting cohering, and amplifying undertaken by transformation catalysts in the effort to organize purposeful, self-aware transformation systems. These transformation systems, comprised of all the actors attempting change in shared directions, can amplify their impacts by working both independently and collectively to achieve their shared aspirations.

In that process, many experiments—and likely lots of failures—will be needed. Transformative change takes guts and imagination because each context is unique. Yet the principles identified here apply. The imagination and will to even begin this catalytic process leave the specifics of *what* changes in the hands of actors who come together to connect, cohere, and align their efforts in purposeful *transformation (T-) systems*. Transformation catalysts spark but do not direct actions. In other words, catalyzing purposeful transformative change means quite deliberately setting *processes* and organizing efforts in motion and then being willing to let go to let others do their thing in their own ways. Thus, stewardship rather than leadership is required—and core design principles apply to ensure that everyone who wants a voice has one.

As discussed more later, catalytic change is not "planned change" in any real sense. That is because the nature of the issues and problems prevents real planning. There is little predictability that planning implies involved in transformative processes taking place in what we will explain

---

[‡] These ideas were cocreated in the context of the Bounce Beyond initiative, as well as from many other sources, and I wish to acknowledge the contributions of the whole team over its first three years.

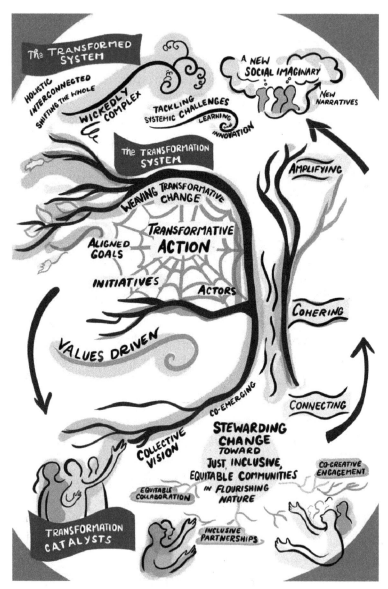

*Figure 1.2  Catalyzing Transformation*

*Image:* Patricia Kambitsch, https://playthink.com.

*Catalyzing Transformation* outlines an iterative set of processes of connecting cohering, and amplifying undertaken by transformation catalysts in the effort to organize purposeful, self-aware transformation systems. These transformation systems, comprised of all the actors attempting change in shared directions, can amplify their impacts by working both independently and collectively to achieve their shared aspirations.

as complexly wicked systems. Achieving transformation does, however, mean moving initiatives, efforts, and activities forward with clear directionality and purpose. Then being willing to "allow" different initiatives and the people in them to take actions from wherever they are in the system in the hoped-for direction. In short, the approach described here provides ways for initiatives and the people who head them to codesign, codevelop, and coemerge the future that they collectively desire. It does so without impeding the ability of any particular actors or initiatives to do what they desire. That is a tough process to develop but it is potentially the most powerful way to actually bring system change about. *Catalyzing Transformation* taps the expertise, approaches, and methods around systemic change that have already been developed, while providing a kind of roadmap that anyone can follow and apply to their own circumstances if they wish.

While there are in fact many, many change efforts already underway, with perhaps millions of people engaged in them, somehow their efforts are not yet being truly transformative. Indeed, in a 2007 book, ecologist Paul Hawken identified between one and two million such efforts—and that number has likely multiplied several times over since then. Today these efforts still suffer from much the same problem that Hawken identified then, what he called "blessed unrest."[22] Blessed unrest is the phenomenon that Hawken called the world's largest movement that no one saw coming. It is a movement of people who generally orient toward bringing a socially just and ecologically flourishing world for all into being. The problem, as Hawken saw it, is that these efforts tend to be small, fragmented, and, while generally having the same aspirations, unaligned, and therefore not effective enough in terms of their transformative actions.

Catalyzing transformational system change is fundamentally about working collectively, cogeneratively, as well as independently in aligned ways to overcome the fragmentation of blessed unrest, so that together we can build the world so many of us really want. That world is one that is socially just, equitable, inclusive, and ecologically flourishing. It is one where economies orient toward the well-being of all humans and more-than-humans. It is a world where nature thrives so that she can continue to support the human project.

*Catalyzing Transformation* offers hope and inspiration that fundamental change is not only desirable but possible through innovative ways of organizing transformation efforts. With the right kinds of tools (and there are many) and knowledge, and some degree of willingness to let go of control, everyone can be part of catalyzing transformation. That is because so many people already recognize the need to transform today's economic and social systems so that together we can build the better world that most of us want for our grandchildren. One key, a real core, is to get the shared vision and the values right and also to figure out who is doing what, where, and why. Then the key is helping all of those efforts to better align actions for effectiveness. Sounds simple, right? Of course, it's not nearly as simple as it sounds, but there are pathways to get there—and those pathways are the subject of this book.

## The Transformation Journey Ahead

In the rest of this book, I develop a theory of whole system change, emerging from many years of work and particularly from the work of the Bounce Beyond initiative, summarizing it in the final chapter. Chapter 1 has already introduced the importance of narrative and developing a new vision—a new social imaginary for the system undergoing transformation. Chapter 2 defines core ideas used in this book and illustrates the context in which transformative change of socioecological systems takes place. Chapter 3 discusses the broad context in which system transformation is needed, focusing, in particular, on the core cultural myths that hold the current system in place. Chapter 4 outlines the importance of articulating core values that uphold and support needed changes in what we call the values proposition, and brings forward values and principles that affirm life, particularly oriented toward a life-centered economic system that can play a key role in shifting cultural mythologies that hold the current system in place. Chapter 5 presents a framework for understanding *what* changes in a context of system change through a framework that discusses five "Ps" of systems: purpose, paradigms, performance metrics, power relations, and practices.

Chapter 6 explores the numerous roles and activities of a still-emerging entity that fosters catalytic change, the transformation catalysts, which connect, cohere, and amplify the work of numerous actors working toward transformational change so that they can become a transformation (T-) system. Chapter 7 develops insight into how transformation (T-) systems, that is, the set of initiatives, change agents, and other actors that are oriented toward systemic change, work when they are connected and cohered so that their work, particularly around important systemic challenges, is amplified and effective.

Because system transformation is difficult, involving numerous stakeholders with varying perspectives, approaches, and ideas, Chapter 8 develops a core set of design principles that can be used to support catalytic change efforts. Chapter 9 explores the very different stewardship roles, which require innovative approaches to leading, that individuals attempting to foster change need to assume in connecting, cohering, and amplifying the work of Transformation System participants. Finally, Chapter 10 synthesizes the whole theory of change developed, providing guidance through key activities and questions to change makers.

## Takeaways From Chapter 1

- The world needs new social imaginaries organized around values of stewardship, justice, equity, inclusiveness, and flourishing for all, including other-than-humans. Implementing new social imaginaries requires fundamental system change or system transformation of multiple human systems.
- Catalyzing system transformation is oriented toward purposefully bringing about these new social imaginaries to emerge a flourishing world out of today's polycrisis. Polycrisis, combined with complexity, create a VUCA, that is, a volatile, uncertain, complex, and ambiguous world. Reactions perceive that world in BANI ways, that is, as brittle, generating anxiety, nonlinear, and incomprehensible.
- System transformation involves fundamental and purposeful systemic change or transformation toward ecological civilizations, that is, just and equitable human societies in a flourishing natural world.

- The "how" of purposeful system transformation involves establishing a clear set of values and narratives to guide change along with new organizing approaches: transformation catalysts and transformation systems. Transformation catalysts catalyze change by connecting, cohering, and amplifying the work of existing and emerging initiatives in purposeful transformation systems, concepts fully developed in later chapters.
- Ecological civilization represents an integrated approach that incorporates attention to humans living within planetary geophysical boundaries and a people-oriented economics that envisions a good life or well-being for all people. This integrated or life-centered, holistic socioecological approach values all beings, the interconnected web of life, with care for both humans and nature at its core.

# CHAPTER 2

# Core Concepts for Transforming System Transformation

Over the years, many groups and people have tried to achieve system change. Indeed, sometimes systemic change actually happens without a deliberate strategy. In these instances, change can be seen as an emergent process in which many actors try new things and ultimately the whole system changes. Early in human history, the shift from nomadic foraging or hunter-gathering tribes to villagers farming and domesticating animals was one such shift, although it may have taken place over a much longer time period than generally thought.[1] While no one can know what actually happened, change likely resulted as the confluence of numerous activities and events. Hypotheses about its rationale range from farming's presumed capability to produce more wealth and economic growth than foraging, to the extinction of large herding animals, to environmental shifts, among others.[2] Whatever the reasons for the shift, and it is likely there is more than one, the transformation happened over many years, in multiple places, and in different ways depending on the context.[3] Nor were these shifts necessarily the *purposeful* whole system change envisioned by change agents catalyzing transformation today.

For a more deliberately organized or purposeful shift, consider how the U.S. Supreme Court's 2015 decision legalizing same-sex marriages in the United States came about. That decision was the culmination of many different types of change strategies employed over a long period of time.[4] For example, this transformation of how people and the law in the United States viewed marriage equity for gays and lesbians involved combinations of shifting language (or narrative) as a way of shifting mindsets, norms, and culture. It included numerous incidences of activism and protests by people demanding change from "outside" institutions and to bring attention to the issue and shift public opinion. Others worked from inside existing institutions to shift legislative and regulatory policies. Still others created innovations in language that changed understandings away from rights and pride in being who is toward recognition that love and commitment are at the heart of marriage.

A similarly long-term transformation has taken place in how smoking is viewed, where it is allowed, and how its health harms are understood. That transformation was away from most people smoking just about anywhere to today's far more restrictive norms (and far fewer people smoking). The shift was (and still is) mightily resisted by the tobacco industry, and, not incidentally, by many smokers, who, after all, are typically addicted to the product. The transformation involved shifting social norms, changing the narrative about smoking (i.e., from being sophisticated toward being damaging and unhealthful in multiple ways), and disseminating information about innovations in medical information about the health consequences of smoking. It also meant deploying that knowledge through many types of media, along with strategies involving regulatory moves to reduce smoking in public places, and many other activities.

Sometimes system changes seem to happen because some innovation or new technology shifts how things work—often without a whole lot of planning or purposefulness in advance. Think, for example, about the major impacts that computer, digital, and cell phone technologies have had on how modern life is lived, the ways people communicate, and the development of social media, just to name a few impacts. The advent of the digital era has transformed how work is done, how people relate to each other, and, more recently, how and where many meetings are held. Just think of how cell phones have made our lives different. While, for example, cell phones have vastly improved global communication, they have also created a 24/7 demand to be "connected" for some people. Then there is the addiction that some have developed around needing to be constantly online, constantly checking their texts and media feeds, and the like. Such transformations clearly have both positive and sometimes unintended negative impacts.

Humans' uses of other technologies have transformed landscapes and whole ecologies—often with considerably detrimental impacts on the animals, plants, and other beings that once lived there. Industrial agriculture, for instance, has transformed what farming means in many places. It has moved agriculture away from small family farms toward huge businesses that tend to focus on one or two crops. This transformation has shifted diverse ecosystems, such as meadows, fields, and even forests, into vast expanses of monoculture crops that have deleterious effects on both plant and animal diversity. As ever more human-made fertilizers and pesticides are applied, the result is erosion of topsoil and pollution of local waters, with crops and animals subject to risk because they lack sufficient diversity to be resilient in the face of new pests or adverse weather events.

Indeed, climate change, a globally transformative, relatively slow-moving (in human terms anyway) catastrophe, can be considered one of the more transformative impacts in human history. It is unlikely that anyone would deliberately have brought climate change about. Instead, climate change is the result of many millions of decisions, particularly over the past 150 years or so since the dawn of the industrial era. Climate change is often associated with the use of fossil fuels and their negative ecological impacts. Collectively, these decisions, any one of which seems innocent enough, have brought about this transformation of the earth's capacity to support human and other living beings. Industrialization similarly changed humans' relationship to work and how work is done, away from a craft orientation toward mass production. There are many other such transformations that have taken place over time, some more quickly than others, and most not purposeful in a design sense.

Sometimes, however, even deliberate or purposeful efforts to change systems have little impact and the systems retain their powerful business-as-usual stance. Human systems, whether social, political, economic, cultural, or institutional, have huge complexity and a great deal of inertia. Despite this resistance, it is also true that in living systems, which human socioecological systems certainly are, changes are constantly occurring. Cumulatively, even small changes can have major impacts over time. Thus, while many established institutions, cultural norms, power structures, and deeply engrained practices can keep systems from experiencing the foundational changes that system transformation represents, other incremental changes can cumulate to big impact over time. One clear example of resistance to transformation was the failure of most governments to reform major financial institutions significantly following the Global Financial Crisis of 2007–2008, despite these institutions having been clearly implicated in the crisis.

The point here is that few people, if any, would actually want the problematic outcomes associated with some of these shifts. Yet they take place because new norms, technologies, and practices are introduced without sufficient understanding of their long-term impacts. They also occur because most people in local contexts and beings in the natural environment have had little input into what is introduced and how it is used. That is because no one can know in advance what those impacts are likely to be or, necessarily, control outcomes.

All of this resistance, incrementalism, and potential negative by-products of change, though, is not to say that transformational efforts should not be undertaken. In fact, no one will *ever* fully understand the long-term implications of any given change. There are always likely to be some negative consequences of any transformation effort. Indeed, most of the technologies or changes that have proved problematic had good intentions at their initiation. That said, when core values are kept firmly in mind, and transformation is purposefully oriented toward shared goals by implementers, these negative outcomes can arguably be greatly reduced and desired visions achieved. In fact, that is the whole point of *Catalyzing Transformation*.

That transformative innovations can turn problematic over time speaks of the need to think about and design *purposeful* transformation, based on clear, positive visions and aspirations and shared values. Purposeful transformation efforts need to be fully informed by agreed values and long-term visions, and codeveloped by the people who will be affected by the changes made if they are to succeed in the long term. Further, change efforts need to be continually evaluated or assessed holistically against those visions and values, paying attention to shifts in power, how relationships are structured, and practices affecting resource flows.[5] That way change agents and implementers can ensure that they are achieving the desired ends, rather than perpetuating problematic practices, norms, technologies, and behaviors. Including these aspects in purposeful change efforts certainly will not completely eliminate negative by-products of change. That said, carefully attending to them can provide significant protection against the worst abuses and problematic outcomes.

The point of catalyzing transformation is that *purposeful* system transformation, organized through the work of transformation catalysts guiding the emergence of purposeful transformation systems, guided by shared aspirations and values, can be done more rapidly and effectively than evidenced by many past efforts at system change. That possibility is especially important, given the many crises that need to be dealt with in the world today. By drawing from the lessons of more successful efforts and applying understanding of how change happens in complex systems, we can learn what does and does not work. By understanding what transformation means, who and what are affected, and what is desired from it, it can be framed in inspiring and hopeful ways. By defining the core values that guide specific transformations, their purposes and potential impacts can be better taken into account. By consolidating and using emerging understanding about *how* purposeful transformation toward equitable well-being in a flourishing natural environment can best be catalyzed, collectively change makers can develop helpful and constructive pathways forward. What is needed are new approaches to system transformation: a *transformation of system transformation based on understanding catalytic processes of connecting, cohering, and amplifying the work of numerous actors in purposeful transformation systems.*

To be clear, this book explicitly focuses on transformative approaches to system transformation toward *equitable, socially just, inclusive well-being-oriented societies and economies in a flourishing natural environment,* summarized as *ecological civilizations.*[6] Of course, different change makers will orient toward other labels. Further, they will work to shift different types of systems, including geographically defined regions or bioregions, industry and social sectors, or issues-based systems. The point to understand is that incorporating aspirational visions and clearly articulated values that are shared by members and participants in the system remains critical, no matter what system is under consideration. And, as we will explore later, there are emerging new understandings of how such change can effectively be accomplished.*

---

* Here I want to explicitly acknowledge the ideas that have emerged from the Bounce Beyond initiative over time, and particularly from Steve Waddell, with whom I have written about them extensively.

## Understanding and Defining Transformative Change

Many transformation efforts do not succeed, in part because the approaches used are insufficiently purposeful. Alternatively, they fail because they are mostly geared to incremental change or reforms, rather than actual system change. Or they succumb to lack of the clout to overcome entrenched interests because of fragmentation of the efforts of change makers. Other transformations are only partly successful, because change approaches tend to use only a single strategy—when more holistic systems-based, yet contextually appropriate approaches are needed.

There is a clear difference between incremental, reformative, and transformative change, which Waddell has clearly differentiated.[7] Incremental change is oriented toward improving the current system through stepwise changes. It focuses on becoming more efficient at doing what is already being done and is generally oriented toward performance improvement. In taking that improvement-oriented stance, incremental change largely accepts the existing order, rules of the game, structures, and business as usual. It generally preserves the current power relationships, information flows, and sets of activities while accepting business as usual mostly without question. This approach to change can be compared to what Lindblom called *muddling through*, making changes without a whole lot of effort and without really expecting significant changes.

In some contrast to incrementalism, Waddell notes that reformative change asks new questions about what should be created and how it should be done. It focuses on deeper shifts to understand and change what the goals and purposes of the system are, opening the "rules of the game" or how things get done to revision. Some core aspects of identity, processes, and goals can change during reform processes during the improvement efforts associated with reform, existing power, information, and goal structures that tend to remain in place.

Transformative change, in contrast, is more fundamental. It shifts purposes and goals, power relations and structures, the way things are measured. Generally, as discussed in the following and in more depth in the next chapter, transformative change brings about wholesale shifts in how the organization, system, or entity is understood and operates. The classic transformation of the caterpillar to butterfly is frequently used to signify this type of change, as the end state can be quite unrecognizable from the beginning state. Transformation then is about changing fundamental things about the given entity or system: purposes or goals, the paradigms or mindsets by which it is understood, the ways in which performance is measured or its performance metrics, the core structures, power relations, informational flows, and other systems, and how business is done or the practices, processes, policies, and procedures by which the system's work gets done. The next chapter deals with all these aspects of system transformation in depth and the next section further defines system transformation as used here.

### Defining Transformation

The focus of *Catalyzing Transformation* is in the fundamental shifts embodied in transformative change. Since no one controls transformation, bringing about that much change requires the concerted efforts of numerous actors cohered and aligned, who are taking a catalytic approach at the whole system level. Thus, it is important to provide here some core definitions, including looking more deeply at what is meant by whole system transformation.

Transformative system change is fundamental reorientation and reorganization of a given system. It has breadth, depth, and scale, changing the most important aspects of the system, and takes place at multiple levels. Two fundamental changes associated with transformation are how the purpose or goal of the system is defined and how relationships among actors are structured, that is, the system's power structures.[8] For example, solar power has the potential to bring about significant transformative change in the energy/power industry. Currently, much energy production relies on fossil fuels typically distributed through huge and highly centralized oil companies. They have networks of extraction and production facilities, refineries, mass distribution systems, and retail outlets still largely controlled by the big companies. In contrast, solar energy can be produced in highly distributed (and far more democratic) ways, for example, by rooftop solar panels on people's homes and by larger solar power arrays established in local settings, that then feed back into more centralized energy companies. This redistribution of the source of energy puts a good deal more control in the hands of consumers or customers, who become what has come to be known as prosumers—both producers and consumers of energy, when excess energy produced at the single house level is returned to the energy company.

Put simply, transformation means a radical change or fundamental reorientation of the system, not just tweaks around the edge. As discussed in depth later, this shift affects the paradigm or mindset, that is, the understanding of the system by its key actors and stakeholders, the purpose(s) intended, and how performance is assessed. In turn, those shifts affect power structures and the operating practices of the system.[9] This type of system transformation takes place in the context of social, economic, political, cultural, and ecological (socioecological for short) systems. The next section defines what is meant by the term *system* and how systemic change can be catalyzed.

## A Catalytic Approach to Transforming Systems Transformation

Traditional approaches to system change have not been particularly effective; hence this book argues that transforming systems transformation is required. Transforming system transformation is grounded in taking *catalytic* approach to transformational change in socioecological systems, recognizing that no one actor can bring about the desired change. It takes the coalescing of purpose and energy from numerous actors and system participants to make change effective. That coalescing, here called *connecting, cohering,* and *amplifying,* requires novel approaches to *organizing* transformative efforts. In the following, I briefly introduce two important ideas that provide a foundation for organizing and catalyzing such purposeful system transformation that can guide such processes of transformation: *transformation catalysts* and *transformation (T-) systems.*

### Transformation Catalysts

In physical science, catalysts are substances that increase the rate of chemical reactions usually without changing themselves. In other words, in the physical sense, catalysts cause reactions among other substances to occur.

There is another sense of the word *catalyst* that is associated with social change: a social catalyst is a person or thing that precipitates an event or a change in a human (socioecological) system. Here the work of a relatively new type of entity, the transformation catalyst, becomes vital to purposeful systemic change. *Transformation catalysts are entities, that is, people, groups of people, organizations, and initiatives, that work to bring about systemic transformation by cocreatively connecting, cohering, and amplifying the change efforts and activities of multiple transformational change agents working toward similar aspirations in a given context.*

Transformation change agents work to produce purposeful transformation (T-) systems, discussed next. Unlike catalysts in physical contexts, however, transformation catalysts are actually a part of the socioecological systems they are attempting to change. Thus, during processes of change, they can and do change, too, sometimes subtly and sometimes more so, coevolutionarily, as the systemic changes occur. Such changes occur as a result of learning, evolution, and developmental processes, and receiving new ideas and inputs from the system itself (and, of course, from internal shifts that take place as well).[10]

### Transformation (T-) Systems

Just whose efforts are transformation catalysts working to connect, cohere, and amplify? Well, in any given social context, there are very likely already numerous initiatives working toward change. We can call those initiatives a *collective*, that especially when organized and self-aware, becomes a transformation (T-) system. *Transformation systems are the collection of actors, initiatives, and efforts working to bring about systemic change in a given context. Purposeful transformation (T-) systems emerge when actors and initiatives align to connect, cohere, and amplify their efforts toward achieving collective aspirations.*

Most of the time, existing initiatives' tend to work independently of each other; that is, they are fragmented and separate. That is why the organizing efforts of transformation catalysts are needed: to bring such initiatives and actors together in new ways, through connecting and cohering their efforts, so that they can amplify their collective and independent work. While they may be doing great work independently, such efforts tend to be relatively focused and too small in scale to achieve the desired transformative impact.[11] They are, as noted in the first chapter, part of what Paul Hawken called *blessed unrest*, that is, the many fragmented initiatives working toward social justice and flourishing nature but without connecting to each other.[12]

Collectively, if they are organized to align (connect, cohere, and amplify) their efforts, the initiatives in a given context that are working toward change emerge into a purposeful transformation system. Collectively, if organized in new ways *as purposeful transformation systems*, they can potentially achieve far greater impact than any one of them can do on its own. Thus, all of the initiatives working toward the accomplishment of similar agendas can be considered part of a transformation system. That is, the T-system is an *ecosystem* of change agents aligned and acting in connected and cohered ways that enable their collective impact around systemic change.

Bringing actors in a potential transformation system into such alignment is the work of *transformation catalysts*, which are relatively recent entities working in innovative ways to bring disparate change agents together. As we will explore later, connecting involves "seeing" and sensemaking processes. All of those so that transformation systems, aware of themselves as such, can begin acting purposefully toward transformation in cohered ways to amplify their impact by contending more effectively than in the past with the many polycrises and systemic challenges many socioecological systems are facing today.

## What Is a System?

Before we go much further, it is important to understand what a system is. Socioecological systems of interest here, which are inherently living systems, are interconnected, integrated wholes, with permeable yet reasonably defined boundaries. The basic boundaries of a given system are determined by its aspirational purposes or goals. A system comprises all those elements required to achieve a particular goal or set of goals, and its boundaries are determined by how its definition is framed and how participants in, or observing, the system understand it. One formal definition of a system is that it is "a functioning whole that cannot be divided into independent parts."[13] In a system, different aspects or components are interconnected and interdependent, so that what happens to one part affects the rest of the system, and these elements cannot be teased apart without destroying the integrity or wholeness, that is, the living quality, of the system.

Systems usually have multiple subsystems, each of which can be thought of as what has been called a *holon*.[14] Holons are nested whole systems that exist within other systems. For example, an individual person can be considered whole, and also part of another "whole"—the family. Families in turn can be part of communities—villages, towns, cities, which themselves are part of larger political entities like states or provinces, themselves part of countries. And so on, right up to the universe level.

Holling calls this hierarchically nested system *panarchy*, noting that this understanding helps explain and describe how such systems evolve in adaptive cycles of growth, accumulation, restructuring, and renewal.[15] In other words, living, socioecological systems are in constant and somewhat cyclical change, which can be tapped for transformation purposes. Such systems adapt and renew themselves, Holling indicates, as a consequence of three properties: the system's inherent potential for change (or, loosely, what he calls its *wealth*); its internal controllability, that is, connectedness (or relationality), which reflects the system's flexibility or rigidity; and its adaptive capacity or resilience.[16] *Catalyzing Transformation* explores the potential of creating connections among change agents to bring about purposeful systemic change in these types of contexts.

Living systems, including social, economic, cultural, political, and ecological systems, can be classified by their purposes and the choices made to accomplish those purposes. That is true whether those systems are human social systems where people make explicit choices or natural systems comprised of purposeful elements that may "want" only to live and reproduce in some way.[17] The component "parts" or holons in a living system are interdependent and dynamically interactive—and how well it is performing is a product of those interactions.[18] Hence the *relationships* among different elements in a living system are very important, particularly because as discussed next, such systems are characterized by complex wickedness.

### Complex Wickedness

In the socioecological systems, fundamental purpose change, system reorientation, or transformation takes place in a context of "complex wickedness." Complex wickedness (or wicked complexity) is a combination of the characteristics of complex adaptive systems and wicked problems.[19] Most, if not all, socioecological systems can be characterized as complex, in the complexity science sense of that word. What that means is that they are dynamic; elements are interconnected, interrelated, and characterized by interdependence. Further, they are open systems, which means that their boundaries, while definable, tend to be permeable. They admit in new energy (people, initiatives, and actions), while eliminating elements that are no longer useful or fit for the purpose (i.e., they get rid of waste, excess, or unneeded aspects).[20]

Similarly, issues and problems in complexly wicked systems, that is, most human problems set in an organizational or ecological context, are what is known as wicked. Wicked problems have similar equally difficult characteristics as complex adaptive systems. For example, each problem or system can be considered a symptom of others. Issues are interrelated, interactive, and dynamic, with unclear boundaries. No definitive resolutions of such problems are feasible and there are no root causes, since there is no clear beginning or ending. Further, different stakeholders likely have different perspectives on the definition, nature, and potential resolution of the problem.[21] In other words, issues, problems, and dynamics in a given living system are linked across specific contexts that are at different levels and within them, and cannot really be teased apart if the system is to be kept intact.[22]

As can be seen, wicked problems and complex systems share many characteristics. In addition, such systems and their issues cannot be understood or dealt with by fragmenting issues or components into their parts. They need to be considered holistically because in a real way they are living entities. Relationships and dynamics resulting from actions and changes tend to be central to understanding systems. At the same time, these connections and their dynamics are nonlinear, emergent, and adaptive (or not), with coevolutionary processes at their core. Fractal or self-similar elements are frequently present at different levels or scales in living systems.

(Think of how the shape of a whole tree often resembles the shape of its leaves, as an example.) In such contexts, when initiatives are taken or shifts are started, their outcome is inherently unpredictable because wickedness and complexity intersect. Further, once a change is initiated, it is really not possible to return the system to its original state because changes are irreversible, a characteristic known as path dependence. Further, there are no clear "right" or "wrong" solutions or pathways forward, and sometimes small-seeming changes potentially have large impacts or outcomes—a phenomenon known as *leverage*[23] or the *butterfly effect*.[24]

Understanding the nature of complex wickedness, as well as the need for holistic approaches, means that change agents may need to be adept at "letting go" of control to allow for emergent processes and activities engaged by a variety of participants to do their work. Recognizing that transformation at the system level requires that relatively long time horizons is frequently combined with a sense of urgency to make change. Transformation in these contexts may also necessitate trying multiple experiments to see what works, while allowing for and learning from failure. Because change is unpredictable and uncontrollable in such systems, some way of organizing to provide guidance to change makers in the system is needed.

In conditions of complex wickedness, system transformation can only be guided, not planned or controlled. As discussed later, that guidance process is why developing powerful, inspirational, and aspirational new narratives in the form of visions, aspirations, and shared agendas is so important. Narratives provide the necessary guidance to change makers, allowing them to compare what they are doing to the vision to see if their effort is, in a sense, "fit for purpose." Thus, most of the important guidance happens through coemerging shared aspirations and common agendas. That is why transformation catalysts focus on helping system participants identify shared narratives, for example, visions, principles, and values, and common aspirations to envision and cohere their aspirations. They also need to recognize that different actors will, as the saying goes, do their own thing. By developing coherence, that is, the shared narratives and common aspirations, connected actors can cocreate generative and feasible change plans that simultaneously allow for individual and collective actions. Shared agendas and aspirations provide potentiality for amplifying individual initiatives' work through the collective impact of multiple aligned initiatives working together.

Holling, who has developed the idea of "panarchy" as a means of understanding complex systems, set forth several criteria that need to be satisfied to understand these complexities. His pieces of advice: "Be as simple as possible but no simpler than is required" …; "Be dynamic and prescriptive, not static and descriptive" …; and "Embrace uncertainty and unpredictability."[25] This book adopts those principles to the extent possible in presenting this theory of how whole systems can purposefully be changed.

The rest of *Catalyzing Transformation* explores how these ideas can be put to use to bring about system transformation toward an equitable, socially just, and flourishing world, that is, a set of ecological civilizations that work for all. The next chapter explores, in some depth, the foundational and important role that cultural mythologies play in shaping the paradigms, the worldviews or mindsets, that people hold, which in turn shape their attitudes, behaviors, and actions.

## Takeaways From Chapter 2

- System transformations have always taken place; however, most have not been purposeful, and often they have possibly unavoidable unintended consequences in part because of the complexity of human systems.
- Agreed values and long-term visions and aspirations codeveloped by system participants can inform purposeful system transformation that produces ecological civilizations that are equitable, socially just, inclusive societies in a flourishing natural environment.
- It is important to differentiate incremental change (improvements to the current system), reformative change (working with the system's operating norms and practices to improve it), and transformational change, which emphasizes fundamental, even radical, shifts in a system's purposes or goals, the paradigms or mindsets that describe it, its performance metrics, as well as the practices that operationalize its work and the power relations that structure it.

- Transformation catalysts are entities, including people, groups of people, organizations, and initiatives, that work to bring about systemic transformation by cocreatively connecting, cohering, and amplifying the change efforts and activities of multiple transformational change agents working toward similar aspirations in a given context.
- Transformation systems, or T-systems, consist of the many initiatives that are working toward a common vision or shared set of aspirations, who are willing to work to connect, cohere, and amplify their collective and individual efforts for greater transformative impacts.
- Socioecological systems are living systems that are complexly wicked, interconnected, integrated wholes, with permeable yet reasonably defined boundaries and often multiple subsystems.

# CHAPTER 3

# A Context of Cultural Myths

One of the things that becomes evident when thinking about system transformation is the importance of guiding narratives, visions, and aspirations. Such aspirations (or narratives for short) help shape the paradigms, worldviews, and mindsets of anyone who is trying to bring about change, as well as anyone involved in the relevant system. That is because, as noted, transformational change takes place in conditions of complex wickedness. That means it can at best be *guided*, not planned. Importantly, it is the narratives provided by shared visions, values, principles, aspirations, and other communal understandings that create potentialities and pathways forward. Shared narratives or aspirations and the memes of which they are built provide the coherence that is the basis for further action. They are the grounding for amplification processes needed for system transformation to actually happen.

The paradigms or belief systems that people in a context hold are core to emerging guiding narratives, effectively shaping attitudes and behaviors. If mindsets remain stuck in old paradigms or stories about "how things are here" that are no longer fit for purpose, people will likely continue to act the way that they always have. Only when the ideas and values that shape their thinking shift is it likely that their behaviors will shift accordingly. Similarly, the narratives or stories that we tell ourselves about what is important and what is not in a given context, what we want to happen, or how possibilities are envisioned, really matter. That is because, in complexly wicked socioecological systems, the activities of change agents are guided by shared and emotionally powerful narratives and by the values and principles that are embedded in them.

Given the lack of control in complexly wicked contexts, paying attention to core narratives, values, principles, and aspirations is very important to bringing about the desired system, since actors will likely "do their thing" in any case. In fact, to bring about significant transformative change likely means it is important to shift and redefine key narratives toward new ones that articulate different worldviews, visions, or aspirations. These narratives, when shared, provide a kind of "glue" around aspirations, visions, and practices that helps cohere transformative actions. New worldviews, in turn, shape correspondingly different ways for people to understand themselves in the world, the world around them, and how they relate to other people and beings.

This chapter explores the role of cultural mythology, values, and principles in shaping current thinking. Ultimately, I argue for new narratives or stories (aspirations, shared values, visions, and the like), that is, new core myths that articulate and support what gives life to socioecological systems. This life-giving frame is needed to bring about transformation toward equitable and flourishing socioecological systems throughout the world. Life-affirming values and principles have the potential to bring the idea of wealth back to its original meaning of prosperity, well-being, and health, in contrast to today's more common understanding of wealth as purely monetary or material goods. Life-affirming values align with different paradigms than are present in several of today's dominant cultural mythologies, as discussed next.

## Cultural Myths as Narratives Shaping Mindsets

Cultural myths are the important stories and narratives that shape how people view the world around them, hence their attitudes, beliefs, and actions.[1] They are vitally important because they provide key information about how the world *is* from that cultural perspective and what people's position in that world and relationship to it is. That is, cultural myths inform people's worldviews or their core paradigms, that is, their belief systems.

In the following, I discuss three prominent cultural myths that inform a lot of ways in which the world currently works. These myths are particularly relevant to the understandings of societies and the economics/economies that supply them with needed goods, services, and provisions. Further, they inform many different aspects of modern life. Each of these myths is important and has elements that are both true and helpful.

Yet when they are deployed in their more extreme forms, or misunderstood, as happens quite a bit, they become problematic. They need to be supplemented or supplanted by different ways of understanding, new narratives in essence, that are more based in the experienced (and yes, scientifically understood) world.

The three myths discussed in the following are scientism (as opposed to science), human distinctiveness from and dominance over nature (as opposed to humans as part of nature), and neoliberal economics (as opposed to alternatives that emphasize regenerativity, well-being, and flourishing). Each of these ways of viewing the world represents a story or narrative that we tell ourselves about how the world works that would benefit from a broader expression that encompasses different ways of knowing and a broader, more life-affirming set of values.

### Scientism (versus Science)

One of today's dominant mythologies that influence much current thought and behavior is that of science, particularly in its extreme form scientism. Although some are skeptical about science today, most people understand the importance of science and adherence to the scientific method as a way of systematically studying how the physical and natural world and the components of which it is made works. Good science is observational and experimental, drawing out conclusions and insights that lend new understanding, hopefully truth, about the world. Obviously, scientific advances and understandings have resulted in many of the amazing technological, social, and political advances that have been experienced during the past couple hundred years. We all rely on these advances for our health and well-being. Just think of how quickly vaccines were produced during the COVID-19 pandemic, for one thing. They also provide understanding of how the world works.

Scientism, in contrast, is the belief that *only* science provides useful and truthful knowledge and understanding. This perspective discounts other ways of knowing and understanding the world, for example, philosophical, experiential, sense perceptions, reasoning, memories, spiritual, creative, authority, intuitive, holistic, artistic, and systemic, to mention some alternatives. The scientism view is limiting in the extreme. It is a form of reductionism that author Jeremy Lent calls *ontological reductionism*,[2] which suggests that things, including living things, can be reduced to their parts rather than being perceived as systems or wholes. Despite advances by systems dynamics and systems thinking,[3] most scientific approaches today are reductionist in how they are operationalized. That is, they break what is being studied down into its component parts, atomizing it, and fragmenting it. Yet, as systems theory tells us, some things, particularly living things such as socioeconomic human systems and ecological systems, and even links between science and spirituality,[4] need to be considered in their whole.

Importantly, breaking living systems into their parts quite literally destroys them. If we are aiming for *systemic* transformation, then it becomes clear that we must treat the systems we are working in and with as wholes. They cannot be treated as just atomized or fragmented pieces of the whole. When organic or living things are taken apart, they can never be put back together quite the same way again and their integrity might be destroyed in that process. In these holistic contexts, we need to think about relationality, connectedness, the dynamics of interdependencies, and the patterns produced to begin to understand and change the *system*, not just its component parts. Melanie Goodchild characterizes this relational approach, which is deeply rooted in many Indigenous traditions, as relational systems thinking.[5] These relational perspectives highlight the interconnected reality in which we live. This orientation toward the importance of relationship and connectedness can enable change agents to recognize the complex wickedness as the reality that systems science, modern physics, ecology, botany, biology, and other sciences tell us is how the world actually works, which is in nonlinear, constantly dynamic and evolving, and interactive/interdependent ways.

The reality is that understanding generated through science is both helpful and necessary. And yet there are other ways of knowing, including relational, intuitive, instinctive, spiritual, creative, systems oriented, and holistic, that are also important. For instance, knowledge based in Indigenous wisdom and ways of thinking, which are rooted in holistic perspectives, can enhance thinking about what it means to be human in this world. Indigenous wisdom about relationality and connectedness[6] is particularly vital for understanding humans as part of rather than separate from nature, which is the next cultural myth to be discussed. These other ways of knowing are key to system transformation, which requires a holistic, systems-based understanding of the world as well as of change processes and dynamics. That is because they are more holistic, more "right brained," creative, intuitive, holistic ways of thinking, as Iain McGilchrist describes them in his pathbreaking books differentiating right- and left-brained ways of knowing.[7] As McGilchrist describes it, too often today left-brained or analytical, linear, static, fragmenting ways of thinking dominate more holistic right-brained understandings and thus tend to dominate in today's "developed," industrialized cultures. That certainly seems to be the case with scientism.

### Human Separation From Nature

A second cultural myth, in many ways related to the scientific reductionism just discussed, is that of human exceptionalism. Human exceptionalism is the idea humans are somehow separate from, distinct from, and rightfully holding "dominion over" nature. Human exceptionalism, as summarized by McDonald and Patterson[8] from the work of Catton and Dunlap,[9] assumes four things. One assumption is that cultural heritage makes humans unique among animal species, hence the exceptionalism. A second argues that sociocultural and technological factors are far more varied than are biological traits. A third is that the sociocultural environment is significantly more important for humans than the ecological context. Fourth is the idea that both social and technological progress can continue indefinitely and solve all social problems,[10] despite the reality of planetary boundaries.[11]

These assumptions can limit humans' capacity for self-awareness and reflection, as well as their ability to develop needed technological, social, ecological, and interpersonal innovations that allow for living within planetary constraints. All of those innovation capacities do exist and have been vitally important in human development over many thousands of years through processes of both cultural and technological evolution.[12] Carried to extremes, however, these ideas have the effect of separating humans from nature and somehow posing us as superior beings to other more-than-human creatures and entities. They posit that we humans can survive without relying on nature and by fully "exploiting" nature solely for human benefit without much regard for other beings. In this perspective, humans are seen as having dominion over nature, rather than being stewards of nature's bounty. Sometimes, this perspective means that people may not be willing (or able) to acknowledge human interdependency with and integral dependency on nature's abundance for thriving and, indeed, for basic survival.

One outcome of this myth of human exceptionalism is that humanity is, as UN Secretary General António Guterres put it in 2022, "sleepwalking to climate catastrophe."[13] He called it a form of *collective suicide*.[14] Guterres's fundamental argument here is that people need to shift their collective mindset away from one that ignores the climate and other ecological crises because they will purportedly be technologically resolved. Guterres argues for recognition of humans' integral interdependence with and dependency on nature's capacity to support human civilization.

It is true that unlike many other beings on Earth, humans do have the capacity for self-awareness and reflection and that is a distinctive quality.[15] That capacity also provides the opportunity to design human systems so that they are either in line with nature's ways, or working counter to them. It enables us to recognize the reality of our dependence on and interdependency with nature—as science, ecology, and quantum physics now acknowledge. It could incorporate Indigenous thinking[16] that highlights the ways in which people are connected to, part of, and interdependent with more-than-human beings and the rest of nature. It means recognizing, as the Lakota saying goes, *Mitákuye Oyás'iŋ*, "We are all related."

In contrast, Western thought and core mythology tend to place humans above or separate from nature, and therefore in control of natural forces over which we actually have little control. Thus, human exceptionalism makes exploiting nature's resources possible without guilt. But the reality is one of devastating ecological consequences, as seen in the many crises facing the world, not least of which are civilization-threatening climate change,[17] species loss,[18] and massive, destructive exploitation of natural resources. As with Indigenous wisdom, a life-centered systems perspective instead places humans in, as part of, and interdependent with nature and other beings—stewarding or taking care of her resources and abundance. As thought leader David Korten is fond of saying, "We are living beings born of a living planet. We forget that at our peril." The cultural myth of human separation from nature allows us to effectively forget that reality.

### Neoliberalism and Its Flawed Assumptions

The third myth is about today's conventional economics, known as *neoliberalism*, which is today's dominant economic belief or philosophy. It identifies free markets, individual self-interested responsibility, free trade and consequent globalization, and laissez-faire or minimalist government as the best way to produce needed goods, services, and provisions.[19] While there have been many attempts to offer heterodox alternatives to this orthodox economics,[20] neoliberal tenets remain dominant forces in the world. That dominance is particularly important in the minds of key influencers in business, governmental leaders, and mainstream media.

Neoliberalism's dominance remains true despite the fact that its core values and assumptions have proven highly problematic. For example, neoliberalism argues that humans are always self-interested profit maximizers (and hence so should their businesses be). It maintains, as Margaret Thatcher famously stated, that "There is no such thing as society." It further postulates that governments and regulations are invariably problematic and that endless economic growth is always desirable and possible. These assumptions, particularly the growth one, flawed as they are, dominate economic discourse, not to mention the daily news cycle. Note the emphasis on how or whether the economy grew, whether company profits grew, and what future growth expectations are in the nightly news, for example. The growth orientation is so prevalent that it goes largely unquestioned and leaves little room for thinking about the negative consequences of growth on whether ecosystems or other-than-human beings flourish or not. The constant attention to growth is highly problematic because the Earth is a finite planet. Planetary resources are already being strained beyond their regenerative capacities, putting humans' future at the considerable risk of the "collective suicide" UN Secretary General Guterres introduced.

This core mythology promotes competition over cooperation and self-interest over the common good (which is claimed, along with society, not to even exist). It argues for endless growth, and market dominance over other possible ways of dealing with social and ecological problems. The Club of Rome has argued convincingly that this approach, that is, this mythology, is ecologically unsustainable and socially problematic.[21] The core problematic issue is that its belief system has become deeply embedded in many people's minds. That especially includes people in leadership positions in businesses and governments. That is because, as former UK Prime Minister Margaret Thatcher also argued, it fosters the belief in TINA, that is, "There is no alternative" to doing economics in this way.

In a very real way, neoliberalism builds on and is consistent with the other two dominant mythologies discussed. It values monetary and financial wealth over what gives life to systems. It fails to take what are known as *externalities* or negative by-products of economic activities into account, foisting them outside the economic process. Ultimately, it pushes those negative by-products into the human and natural ecosystem as a whole. There the costs are held, and the price is paid. Through its most dominant metric of GDP (gross domestic product), and obsessive attention to company profitability and share price, neoliberalism values endless growth on a finite planet. It implicitly endorses whatever it takes to bring that growth about. That includes layoffs of workers to save costs, externalizing as many costs of production as possible, and private ownership over the common good. Indeed, neoliberalism basically ignores or argues that the common good does not exist, since "there is no such thing as society." And it focuses only on what gets measured as economic activity, while ignoring unpaid care and volunteer work.[22] It also conveniently ignores environmental impacts of economic activities, since the environment also does not exist within its parameters.

In contrast, well-being or life-affirming economics and economies would recognize the ecological realities facing productive and provisioning activities associated with economies.[23] They would value the dignity and worth of all people and, indeed, of all beings, and focus businesses on cocreating collective value, that is, value from which everyone benefits. Life-affirming values, discussed in more depth later, would emphasize stewardship of the whole, collective value, the embeddedness of economies in the natural environment and the need for local-to-global interactions. Production approaches would be regenerative, reciprocal, and circular, emphasizing relationship and connectedness among all humans—and with other beings. The result of these core values would be equitable markets and trade.[24] Chapter 4 explores these values and their implications in considerably more detail.

## Why Cultural Myths Matter

Cultural myths like the three described earlier matter a lot. They shape perspectives, that is, worldviews and mindsets, which are central to how people ultimately act. Such narratives, stories, or mythologies are constructed out of what are known as *memes* or core units of culture as Susan Blackmore describes them.[25] Memes, a term invented by biologist Richard Dawkins as a cultural analog to the idea of the gene in biology,[26] are the core elements of what we know as culture. They can be ideas, phrases, words even, sometimes images or artistic expressions. When they are successful or resonant, they get "replicated" from one person's mind to another's (i.e., repeated in pretty much the same form).[27] Importantly, memes are what the stories and narratives that shape thinking, that is, our cultural myths, are made up of. In his book *The Web of Meaning*, author Jeremy Lent offers a similar concept that he calls *cultural attractors*, things like shared ideas, visions, aspirations, values, and behavioral norms, of what I earlier described as narratives. As Lent points out, with powerful elements like cultural myth or resonant memes, such ideas can last over decades, drawing people to them because of their power of attraction.[28] Resonant memes, for instance, get repeated a lot or replicated, for example, in the nightly news! They thus become core elements in our understanding of the world as it gets expressed in the cultural myths that shape our paradigms, worldviews, and ultimately behaviors and practices.

Thus, in conventional economics, core memes (or cultural attractors) are the ones we all know and recognize. They frame how we think about what economics is, how economies are supposed to operate, along with why they operate in those ways. In the dominant understanding conventional economics still shapes business decisions and governmental policies today. Markets are supposed to be primary problem solvers in shaping social good. They are supposed to be "free" along with global trade. People (and the companies they build) are self-interested profit maximizers in the conventional economics narrative. The purpose of firms, in this narrative or myth, is to maximize profits or, alternatively, maximize shareholder wealth. That narrow definition of purpose, of course, ignores both other stakeholders and their interests. It also discounts other possible purposes that might better benefit the whole of society, not to mention completely ignoring nature. Yet that story from economics is a powerful cultural mythology, because it has been widely and consistently disseminated over many years, is pervasive and widely believed, is internally (if not externally) consistent, and is in many ways emotionally compelling. It is powerful because its memes or core ideas are commonly repeated or replicated in ways that have been deliberately promulgated by its proponents,[29] and because those memes can be used in different ways by different actors to construct their own versions of the narrative.

Systems theorist Donella Meadows called these types of narratives and stories (and cultural myths) *paradigms* or mental models (also known as worldviews), because they shape mindsets. Paradigms are mental frameworks for understanding the world, how it works, and what our relationships to it are. Meadows claimed that shifting paradigms or changing mindsets was (and still is) the most powerful lever of systemic change. She amended that thought to argue that mindset shift is second only to the capacity to transcend mindsets and begin thinking differently.[30]

Think about the impact of the memes or core ideas embedded in the three cultural myths discussed earlier, what can be called core memes, for example, that humans are distinct from and dominant over nature; that the purpose of economies is to build ever-growing wealth (mostly for the already well-off); that the only knowledge that matters is empirical knowledge. It is easy, in reflection, to recognize the potential for problems to arise from those ideas and the belief systems they engender. The paradigms they inform do not accord with the complexity of reality (or even, for that matter the latest scientific understandings). Further, these memes have serious implications for how humans behave with respect to how we treat each other, nature, and other species.

Belief systems founded on these cultural mythologies and their core memes have impacts. For example, these beliefs allow for human domination over nature and other beings, permitting exploitation not just of nature and more-than-human beings. They emphasize dominance over others, competition at all costs, and disregard for the sacred or sacrosanct, for example, the inherent beauty, worth, and dignity of nature and her beings. They ignore human needs for connection with and care for other people, other beings, and the natural world around us. They allow for human and company exploitation of nature and natural resources. After all, they argue that humans should have "dominion" over nature, rather than us seeing ourselves in relationship to and dependent on nature and her beings. These myths also place human needs and interests above others and posit that selfish instincts aimed at personal (and company) gain are always appropriate.

Ultimately, the core stories, narratives, and cultural myths/attractors and the memes from which they are shaped matter. They shape belief systems, attitudes, behaviors, and practices at individual, community, organizational/institutional, and societal levels.[31] People construct paradigms for living, for understanding what is important and what is not, for relationships with others and nature, that is, the individuals, family, community, organizational, and national cultures and practices, out of these paradigms. The more firmly embedded the stories we tell ourselves are, the more difficult they are to change.

These three cultural myths shape a view of life that is based on accumulating wealth by the few (economics), separating and giving humans dominance over other living beings. They foster beliefs that the only thing that matters is what can be measured. These myths embody an approach that allows values-associated exploitation, greed, and dominance. Collectively, they auger very poorly for what actually brings life to the living systems in which we humans actually operate.

We need new cultural mythologies, ones that affirm life in all respects and in all its aspects, including in economics, science, and relationships to other beings. Other perspectives, other paradigms, and other memes that foster what gives life to systems are not only possible but also desperately needed given the many crises and issues facing the world. The next chapter explores a very different set of values, that is, potential memes, that could orient cultural myths and norms toward honoring what gives life to our systems.

The world desperately needs such a new set of memes that support a transformed, life-affirming set of social, political, economic, and cultural systems. That is what catalyzing transformation is about. New memes need to orient toward *life* in all its wondrous manifestations rather than just accumulation of monetary wealth and power. Memes that foster social justice and equity for all people. Memes that support the flourishing of all life, both human and more-than-human.

Cultural myths and the memes, including principles and values, that support them are powerful because they are deeply engrained in people's worldviews. Yet there are many cases where people's worldviews, that is, the paradigms that guide them, have shifted dramatically. That shift is what is needed in the context of system transformation. We need new or actually quite ancient cultural myths, stories, and narratives that provide both more realistic and grounded in the realities of complexity and wicked problems and humane ways of conceiving the world. To get there, we need to create and promulgate life-affirming values, narratives, and stories, based on very different memes and cultural attractors from the ones currently dominant. For example, building on and understanding the importance of relationality and connectedness, we can begin to rethink core myths and resulting paradigms, building economics, relationships, and systems understanding around what gives life, not just monetary wealth and power over others and nature. Ultimately, with new stories and narratives, we can begin to reshape our attitudes, behaviors, and practices based on life-affirming values and beliefs.

In the next chapters we will explore a set of principles and values drawn from a wide array of disciplines and literatures. The values and principles to be discussed suggest that there are, indeed, alternatives to the values embedded in today's dominant cultural myths, and, particularly, in economics, which drives so much of today's thinking. They can become the new and resonant memes needed to support transformative action, building new cultural myths. We need, and there are, in fact, other possible mythologies, based on values that affirm life, that we can and need to adopt in culturally and contextually appropriate ways. Shaping such life-affirming cultural myths is a core aspect of catalyzing transformation toward ecological civilizations, as defined earlier, just, inclusive, equitable societies in a flourishing natural world.

## Takeaways From Chapter 3

- Shared narratives in the form of visions, values, paradigms, principles, aspirations, and agendas are vital guides and the basis for action for transformative change agents.
- New narratives in the form of cultural mythologies, that is, core cultural myths, need to focus around principles and values that give *life* to socioecological systems.
- Three core cultural mythologies inform problematic worldviews that can get in the way of systemic change toward ecological civilizations and need to be shifted toward more realistic and life-affirming mythologies.
- Scientism is the problematic belief that the only knowledge or insight that matters is empirically based and generally reductionist. In contrast, understanding the world as an interconnected web of relationships that constitute systems, linking in many different ways of knowing, from intuitive and spiritual to systems thinking, is needed in the transformative change context.
- Human exceptionalism is the belief that humans are separate from and should dominate over, exploit, and control nature. In reality, human beings are part of nature and need to recognize our integral relationships and interdependence with other-than-human beings and the natural world as a whole.
- Conventional economics today, sometimes called neoliberalism, relies on beliefs in self-interested actors (people and the companies they create), free markets, and minimalist government to solve society's problems, while ignoring both the social and ecological consequences of productive activity.

The world needs life-affirming economics based on values that support life in all respects, including stewardship, collective value, local-to-global governance, regenerativity, and relationality resulting in equitable markets and trade.

- Cultural myths matter because they shape worldviews or paradigms that in turn shape beliefs, attitudes, and ultimately behaviors and practices, by individuals and human organizations, businesses, and institutions. The world needs a new set of cultural mythologies, memes, and attractors that foster and respect all of life.

# CHAPTER 4

# The Values Proposition

This chapter discusses the reality that, contrary to Margaret Thatcher's much-repeated statement that "There is no alternative" (TINA) to today's economics—or systems—there *are* in fact alternatives and some of them are coming into being. The core mythologies discussed in the last chapter are just that—myths, narratives, or stories, and stories can be changed. When important narratives are no longer fit for purpose, in fact, they *need* to change and changing stories changes actions and behaviors. Here I argue that we need new stories and myths framed on values and principles that give *life* to systems[1] to achieve desired ecological civilizations, that is, just, equitable, inclusive societies in a flourishing natural world that transformation agents generally seek.

More accurately perhaps, sometimes we need to revive and refresh ancient stories that already have these values deeply embedded in them, particularly ones derived from numerous Indigenous traditions, and weave them into dominant new narratives and stories. This chapter focuses on a set of life-affirming values and principles that can be used to inform such mythologies. The reason to focus on values and principles here is that they represent, along with shared visions and aspirations, a form of "glue" that helps to guide transformative actors and their actions.

Taking an explicitly life-affirming values stance is counter to today's dominant (economic in particular) values, which emphasize financial control and centrality, power over others and nature, continual growth, and self-interested actions over caring communities. This life-focused perspective weaves together ideas drawn from a wide range of sources that include Indigenous, Eastern, and Western traditions, social sciences, economics, physics, and many other sources, allowing the strands of these ideas to retain their integrity while still shifting dominant narratives or myths.

Toward that end, this chapter discusses, first, a set of principles that give life to human or socioecological systems in general. Then it focuses on a related set of values, core memes or foundational ideas, that can support a range of socioeconomic approaches and transformation initiatives affirming life. That discussion is followed by a discussion of core principles drawn from the "heterodox" (or alternative to neoliberal) economics literature by a global team. In short, the chapter illustrates that there *are* alternatives to current ways of thinking, particularly about economics. It sheds light on how we can develop new core myths that support life-affirming attitudes, behaviors, values, and practices! Importantly, this chapter argues that such values and whatever other ones are relevant and important in particular contexts need to be explicitly articulated for a given context and built into efforts for catalyzing transformation.

Somewhat ironically, societies and transformed systems with socioeconomies and ecologies that support life-affirming values foster greater wealth. Though here "wealth" does not mean the conventional financial understanding of that word. A life-affirming framing of economics, societies, economies, and ecologies brings the idea of "wealth" back to its original meaning of *well-being, welfare, health, and prosperity*. Extended to nature, "wealth" taps and augments or even regenerates the abundance and diversity that healthy natural systems exhibit. Life-affirming stories and narratives, that is, new mythologies and relevant, resonant, and repeatable memes that can be used in a variety of ways and contexts, can potentially help with some of the major crises the world is facing. They can begin to reshape attitudes, beliefs, and behaviors toward practices that are regenerative and lead to flourishing rather than depletion. That reshaping of attitudes is the first and vitally important step in shifting the paradigms and mythologies that currently shape our world (as Meadows pointed out[2]). Shifting these paradigms can help us all transform our systems, particularly the economies that drive so many crises, including climate change, growing inequality, ecological challenges, biodiversity loss, political divisiveness, and many others, into ecological civilizations in a flourishing world so many desire.

# Principles Affirming Life[*]

Many disciplines, including architecture,[3] urban studies,[4] physics and systems thinking,[5] cognitive theory,[6] enlivenment[7] and living systems theories,[8] regenerative capitalism,[9] ecology,[10] along with Indigenous wisdom,[11] and others, have discussed principles that give life to systems in various ways. Following is a synthesis of six core principles that give life to complex systems and to transformative change. These ideas are drawn from this vast literature as framed by Petra Kuenkel and Sandra Waddock in two papers.[12] Petra and I argued that such values and principles, defined as fundamental truths, are the foundation of paradigms. Paradigms, in turn, are belief systems that influence how people think, behave, and act in the world.

These six core principles can potentially be used in different settings to construct new life-affirming narratives, serving in a sense as "memes" or core units of culture[13] that can be woven into many different contexts and stories supporting all of life. New narratives shape resonant life-affirming cultural mythologies and ultimately new belief systems or paradigms that influence behaviors, attitudes, and practices that value all of life. Doing that is core to catalyzing purposeful systemic change, because of the importance of guiding narratives. It also matters because of the important role that shared values and principles play in helping actors and initiatives come together to form shared aspirations, which is core to catalyzing change. The core idea of the life-giving principles discussed in the following is that having them present in a system fosters what architect Christopher Alexander called *the quality without a name* or *aliveness*.[14] That quality is the same thing that German biologist Andreas Weber calls *enlivenment*, the invigoration or animation of systems.[15] It is the central

---

[*] This section and the principles/values articulated, as further noted in the text, draws from collaborative work with Petra Kuenkel, published in two papers: P. Kuenkel and S. Waddock. 2019. "Stewarding Aliveness in a Troubled Earth System," *Cadmus* 4, no. 1, pp. 14–38; S. Waddock and P. Kuenkel. 2020. "What Gives Life to Large System Change?," *Organization & Environment* 33, no. 3, pp. 342–358.

quality that, in my view, change agents need to be instilling into their transformation efforts if humanity is to thrive in the future.

## Purpose

The first principle of systemic aliveness is *purpose* or intentional generativity. The principle of purposefulness recognizes that all living systems orient toward survival or continuity into the future. They all have purpose. As Andreas Weber indicated in his book *Enlivenment*, this sense of purpose or intentionality involves renewal, restoration, and replenishment of existing systems through what ecologists call the *waste equals food* principle.[16] "Waste equals food" means that what is waste to one part of the system becomes food for other parts. Purpose is the same quality that architect Christopher Alexander called the *quality without a name*,[17] that is, what it is that makes a system come alive, that is, aliveness. According to this principle of purposefulness, all living systems, including socioecological systems, have purpose, even if it is only to survive (and procreate).

Purpose and the desire or drive for continuity, however, do not necessarily manifest in endless growth in size or numbers, as neoliberal economics would have it with respect to economies. Living beings achieve optimal growth for their species rather than going for endless growth as part of the processes associated with life (and death). Who among us want to keep growing in size endlessly? That said, people might in fact be interested in ongoing intellectual/cognitive, emotional, and moral *development*, which tends (as nature does) rather toward complexity and abundance than mere size. Thus, desired "growth" is better conceived as development in the sense of evolving greater awareness, understanding, breadth, and even diversity. Development as used here can thus be defined as an evolution toward more complexity in conceptual ability and understanding in humans, and greater abundance and diversity in social and ecological systems. In other words, it is not that "bigger is better," but rather that movement toward complexity, diversity, and abundance signifies health, well-being, and the potential for abundance or life-giving qualities.

### Connectedness and Diversity

A second principle fostering life is *connectedness* combined with *diversity*, as may be obvious from the earlier discussion. This principle contrasts with the view that humans are separate from nature and from each other, as cultural myths discussed in the last chapter argue. Instead, the idea of connectedness, which is related to interdependence, stems from recognition coming from ecology, physics, Indigenous wisdom, and many other fields and disciplines, that everything is intricately connected with everything else. That means that humans are connected to each other and the natural world, as *part* and of nature, not separate (or having dominion over her). From this perspective, as the great spiritual traditions and modern physics universally declare, in a very real sense, all is one, an integrated whole. That wholeness manifests itself in natural systems as ever-greater diversity[18] or abundance, which is what sustains aliveness and creates systemic resilience, that is, the quality without a name, in natural systems. Arguably, the same principle of diversely connected beings applies to human institutions (including, as urban scholar Jane Jacobs articulated, what gives life to cities[19]).

The core insight here is that everything is connected and that diversity really matters in healthy systems. Thus, when something happens in one part of an interconnected system, there are ripple effects, some noticeable and others less so, throughout the system. Because healthy living systems tend toward greater diversity, towards abundance and complexity rather than simplicity, it is that diversity that in fact enhances the aliveness, the quality of "life" within them. Humans depend on nature for everything and therefore cannot fully separate themselves from other beings. We are fundamentally communal beings (babies are born helpless, for one thing, and cannot survive on their own). We humans cannot truly separate ourselves from nature, because we are intimately dependent on nature for everything we have, do, eat, live in, and wear. Technological progress, which many seem to rely on to save humanity from itself, also depends integrally on natural resources.

Further, biology and cultural evolution theory now tells us that symbiosis and collaboration are the basis of healthy life and living systems, not competition.[20, 21] As noted earlier, healthy living systems do "grow," but unlike what the economic theory suggests, they actually *develop* in complexity, that is, diversity, connectedness, and abundance, not size, or what Andreas Weber characterizes as abundance in healthy natural systems. In human development, as noted, growth is toward greater cognitive, emotional, spiritual, and moral development complexity,[22] as few people want to continually increase in size!

### Boundedness

A third principle associated with systemic aliveness is *boundedness* or permeable boundedness. By definition, systems have to have boundaries. Boundaries help define the parameters and character of a given system, depending on what lens is used to view them and what level of scale is under consideration. Defining boundaries suggests a particular filter or lens being applied to a given context (e.g., social, ecological, geographical, economic, sector, issue, and the like), which is a human-defined definition of a given "system." But for transformational change purposes, such definitions are needed so that the context into which change strategies are woven can be understood by participants. At the same time, living systems are open systems, including socioecological systems. Their boundaries are and have to be somewhat open or permeable. That means, however the system is defined, that the system's boundaries need to allow for new inputs (see the next principle) when needed to reenergize and "feed" them, and allow for innovation. Permeable boundaries also need to allow for eliminating waste, excess, harmful elements, or what is no longer needed or fit for purpose.

Living systems are dynamic and in constant change. Permeable boundedness recognizes that reality. They are in a process of emergence and coevolution among the interdependent parts[23] rather than static. The principles of connectedness and diversity, along with boundedness, recognize the inherent relationality and complex wickedness of living systems. They provide helpful insights into understanding socioecological systems that need to undergo transformation as living entities that are never static. Change is always happening at some level. It can be accelerated or decelerated by different processes and approaches and, as argued here, catalyzed and transformed toward new purposes that shift the definition of that system. New inputs can provide motivation and incentives for change. Eliminating no longer fit-for-purpose elements can get rid of obstacles to desired change.

### Novelty

Living systems are in a constant state of flux, which means they also constantly evolve and change, and hence seek *novelty*, that is, new inputs and innovations, through their emergence process. Novelty implies a capacity to change as needed in a given context and dynamics. In socioecological systems, novelty provides the potential for inspirational and aspirational changes, for example, new ideas, insights, and memes that foster generative practices and activities that bring people together in new ways. Human systems, too, continually go through a process of cultural evolution[24] and change (sometimes not always for the better) and are never stagnant.

The inherent dynamism of living systems is reminiscent of the saying by Heraclitus that "you can never walk in the same river twice." This dynamism recognizes the centrality of processes of emergence in living systems, where different parts of or actors in the system come together in new ways that allow something novel and perhaps unexpected to emerge. Emergence, in this sense, is a cocreative evolutionary process that can result in ever-increasing diversity that, is, greater abundance, when the system is healthy (a deterrent to the entropy that is inherent in nonliving systems at least for periods of time).[25] Once two (or more) things interact in conditions of complexity, the system is changed, and generally cannot be brought back to its original state. Healthy systems adapt to their context and internal dynamics in an ongoing way. This adaptiveness,[26] creativity,[27] and orientation toward novelty are part of the unpredictability of living systems and of complexly wicked systems in general. But here again, note that the "growth" implicit here is a developmental process oriented toward greater complexity, not just material (or financial) growth. It is a growth around interconnectedness, symbiosis, and abundance.

### Wholeness

A fifth principle, already discussed in defining systems, is that living systems must be considered as integrated (interconnected) wholes, which

is the idea of *wholeness*. Living systems cannot be atomized or fragmented into their component parts without destroying their integrity.
Living systems thus are integrated wholes, though they may well have
subparts and subsystems, some of which constitute their own wholes.
Such "whole" subsystems themselves can be considered holons,[28] as discussed earlier with respect to systems more generally, and can be nested
within the larger system.

It is key to recognize that taking living systems apart destroys their
integrity, their oneness. Fragmenting or taking apart systems too much
destroys systems' (living beings') capacity to survive. For example, though
the circulatory system in a living being is itself a holon, no one can take
the circulatory system out of it and expect that being to survive. Though
it is itself a holon, that is, a whole that is part of another whole, the circulatory system cannot function apart from the bigger system.

Though less obvious, when species go extinct in an ecosystem, that
loss also affects the whole in damaging and often unseen or unrecog-
nized ways. That species might be food for or predators of another species, for example, which is also affected with knock-on ripple effects that
cannot be predicted. Indeed, physicist David Bohm called this idea of
"wholeness" the *implicate order*.[29] Like architect Christopher Alexander,
he argued it was an essential quality of aliveness.[30] The combination of
wholeness and connectedness stands in distinct contrast to the cultural
myth that separates humans from nature. It also contrasts with scientific
reductionism (scientism) and neoliberalism's deliberate ignoring of both
society and nature. All these systems are interconnected and depend on
each other. Thus, the principle of wholeness argues for a very different
perspective that recognizes the inseparability and wholeness of living
systems.

### Awareness (Reflective Consciousness)

The last principle associated with life-affirming systems is a specifically
human one. It is called *proprioceptive consciousness* or, more simply,
*reflective consciousness or self-awareness*.[31] This principle is based on the
reality that humans have self-awareness or consciousness that allows
them to make decisions to consciously design socioeconomic systems,

as discussed throughout this book. That design process includes human ways of building community and organizing. Human consciousness is more complex (as far as we know) than that of other living beings. This principle builds on Maturana and Varela's idea that living systems are cognitive systems by definition and therefore that life is about a continual process of learning.[32]

In other words, people can and do make choices about how they want to live in the world, what their communities look like, how they interact, and so on. Indeed, that is what system transformation is about: making a different set of choices than the ones that have gotten us into so many potentially existential and intersecting crises that is today's polycrisis. Because of the importance of economics and economies in today's world, we also need to look closely at the values underlying today's economics, which dominates many societies and which is driving many of these crises.[33] In part, we need to do that because economies are actually *part* of societies, which in turn are part of natural ecologies (because of the wholeness principle, just discussed).

Catalyzing system transformation is inherently about the human capacity to be reflective, to make conscious decisions and choices. Choosing to go along with the status quo, particularly a problematic one, is a choice, too. Choosing to construct a set of values and dynamics that foster life rather than wealth and power is another choice, one that might better serve all humanity and other-than-human beings, too. Awareness or reflective consciousness gives humans that capacity and makes forward-looking choices possible.

## The Economics Values Proposition: Supporting What Gives Life

Values, along with visions, are the guiding stars for system transformation, particularly in economies and economics of interest here. Remember the importance of narratives and myths discussed earlier. In conditions of complex wickedness with little predictability or control, visions and values provide the basis for new, inspirational and aspirational narratives. They are, in a sense, the glue that can potentially bind otherwise fairly independent, sometimes fragmented actors and change agents into transformation catalysts and systems who might collectively achieve transformation. Values, principles, and visions can help actors and change agents cohere and align their activities to begin to amplify impact.

But values and visions only work in this way when broadly shared. That is, values need to become core aspects of dialogues, shared understandings, and conversation shaping transformative actions. Only then can broadly shared narratives that ultimately reshape cultural mythologies and inform emerging paradigms and behaviors evolve. Long-term, life-affirming values provide the basis for shaping contextually appropriate cultural mythologies that provide a framework for acting to "give life" to systems.

Problematically, today's economies and societies are largely dominated by the values embedded in the three cultural myths of scientism, human separation from nature, and neoliberal economic ideology, introduced earlier. These myths emphasize selfishness over care, acquisition over sharing, separation over connectedness, growth over stability, competitiveness over collaboration, individual over community, humans over other beings, money and power over relationship, and markets over societies. When stated so bluntly, it becomes clearer why understanding what is valued and what core values are underpins the need for change.

The powerful memes embedded in today's dominant forms of economic thinking have been particularly successfully deployed over many decades.[34] When we look at the disarray and divisiveness of today's world, we see a constant striving for "more." More stuff, more money, more power, and, unfortunately, more social and ecological damage as wrought by today's money, growth, and profit-at-all-costs orientation.

The need for dramatic change in these values has never been clearer. A shift of memes, a shift of values founded on life-giving principles, is arguably desperately needed. We can each recognize that the memes that are the building blocks of the cultural myths or narratives that inform our lives can help change makers consciously make a different set of values-based choices.

In the following, I introduce five core values—potential new memes—drawn, like the principles that give life to systems, again from a wide array of literatures. These values can inform—potentially be memes for—a reconceived economics as well as providing a broad life-affirming values base for the societies in which economies exist. The shorthand versions of these values are stewardship, collective value, cosmopolitan-localist governance, regenerativity, and relationality. Together, these values can be used to construct equitable markets and trade, which in a sense represents a sixth economically-oriented value. Ultimately, they inform cooperative, life-affirming different ways for us humans to live in vibrant communities in the context of a living Earth.

These values come from thinking that includes care economics,[35] planetary boundaries,[36] ecological and well-being economics,[37] quantum physics,[38] Indigenous wisdom,[39] cultural evolution,[40] humanistic management,[41] political economy,[42] and many other sources.[43] They are highly consonant with the life-affirming principles just described. They also make clear the reality that societies themselves are embedded in and deeply dependent on the natural environment for their own well-being.

### Stewardship of the Whole

*Stewardship of the whole* means taking shared responsibility for whole systems, whether they are communities, societies, organizations, institutions, or even the whole world. This value relates to the principle of wholeness discussed earlier. Stewards are caretakers, often so that others can benefit. Stewardship is fundamental to developing an ethic of care, whether for others, for more-than-humans, for the planet itself, or for marginalized peoples and future generations.

The idea stewardship of the whole can be contrasted to today's ethic of exploitation of both people and nature. Exploiters take advantage of others' or planetary resources in ways that are ultimately unfair and even cruel for their own gain. Stewards take care of others and of what belongs to others. The value of stewardship suggests that we all have some responsibility for ensuring the health, that is, the well-being, of other people and beings, and of Earth itself. Earth in a very real way is a global commons; it is a world that all beings, including future beings, share. Through the lens of stewardship, change agents might view the world, communities, the enterprises that provide the food, services, and other goods that are needed, as shared commons.[44] Stewardship of the whole thus argues for a care-based approach to ensure the long-term viability of all. At its most basic, stewardship means that human activity should operate within planetary boundaries for the good of all people and more-than-humans.[45]

## Cocreating Collective Value

*Cocreating collective value* emphasizes that businesses and other enterprises and people who create things need to go beyond simply creating private (financial) wealth. Actually, they need to cocreatively evolve collective value, otherwise known as the public or common good. That can be interpreted as a life-affirming ecosystem that enables all stakeholders, including the natural environment, to flourish. The phrase "collective value" comes from the work of Thomas Donaldson and James Walsh, who argued that creating such value is the real purpose of businesses. They further indicated that such value creation should take place without violating the dignity of people.[46]

Indeed, supporting human dignity means meeting a broad array of real human needs, including for relationship, inclusion, voice, freedom, and other needs.[47] It also means allowing for dignity for all[48] as central to cocreating collective value. Further, given humans' integral interconnectedness with each other and the natural world, I would add that nature itself should not be violated beyond her regenerative capacities in the process of creating value. Nature and all nature's beings have integrity and dignity of their own, that is, worth, which needs to be valued just because they exist, without reference to their economic worth. Such integral value needs to be cogenerated (cocreated) by relevant stakeholders, not just private interests, or imposed by governments and broadly shared. While we humans clearly need to draw from nature's resources to survive, how we do so and what we do with what is withdrawn is central to the cocreation of collective value, that is, value for all, where "all" goes well beyond human needs to bring about new balance.

## Subsidiarity or Cosmopolitan-Localist Governance

*Subsidiarity, framed as cosmopolitan-localist (cosmo-local) governance,* as explained by Gideon Kossoff, argues for globally linked local networks at different scales, where decisions are placed at the most local possible level to ensure participation and voice.[49] It is more bottom-up in decision making than many of today's centralized, top-down approaches. In other words, it pushes decision making to the most local possible level, where the people affected by decisions are the ones who get to make them for given types of decisions and contexts. It argues for a more networked, participative structure of mutually supportive communities that value ecological flourishing, where ideas and resources are exchanged and shared, including knowledge, culture, skills, and technologies.[50] The argument in favor of localism in part is that such approaches are more ecologically and human-friendly because of their localist-grounded-in-practice orientation. That orientation fosters the stewarding of resources, and recognition that local decision making better honors local knowledge of what is best for a given community. At the same time, the cosmopolitan element recognizes that communities and human civilization, in fact, exist and are dependent on shared planetary resources, connectivity, and networks.

### Relationality and Connectedness

We have already noted the importance of *relationality and connectedness* from the systems perspective, acknowledging that everything in a very real way is linked.[51] The disconnections inherent in the three problematic cultural myths discussed earlier are not in accord with reality as understood by physicists,[52] ecologists and planetary scientists,[53] biologists and botanists,[54] cultural evolutionists,[55] care economists,[56] among others. Core among human needs and wants are relationship and connection with others, a sense of belonging, and of course, the ability to satisfy basic needs.[57] Relationality and connectedness are succinctly expressed in the African word *Ubuntu*, which means "I am because we are,"[58] meaning that humans only exist in the context of community and that community is both human and more-than-human.

### Regenerativity, Reciprocity, and Circularity

*Regenerativity, reciprocity, and circularity* define that approaches to productive activities dramatically alter today's take-make-waste approaches to provisioning (broadly defined as providing needed foodstuffs, goods, and services).[59] The combination of regenerativity, reciprocity, and circularity argues for a very different provisioning approach that recognizes nature's limits and human beings' place within the context of the natural environment. Drawing on the ideas of relationality and connectedness, this value emphasizes that Earthly resources should only be used insofar as nature's capacity (and time frame) to regenerate these resources permit,[60] core aspects of what was earlier called *ecological civilizations*. Further, this value argues for reciprocity or mutually beneficial relationships among humans and between humans and the Earth. This approach explicitly recognizes the principle of *Mitákuye Oyás'iŋ*, as the Lakota put it, the idea that "all are my relations."[61] It is expressed in approaches like regenerative agriculture, biomimicry,[62] and similar nature-based practices that respect and enhance nature's bounty and that tap human creativity and propensity for innovation.[63] The idea of circularity embodies the principle that "waste equals food."[64] Production processes should be circular in their design, because, after all, there is really no such thing as an externality. That is because from a systems perspective, whatever is produced in one system ends up in another, so it needs to be beneficial, bringing in the idea of reciprocity.

### Equitable Markets and Trade

These five values converge, in a sense, to create the foundation for *equitable markets and trade*, which are based on equity, social justice, and ecological principles that are fundamentally regenerative and cocreative when fully implemented. In conventional economic thought, the centerpiece is "free markets and free trade." In theory, free markets will resolve societies' problems through the mechanism of what Adam Smith called the *invisible hand*. Of course, the reality is that markets today are not really free because they are dominated by monopolistic and oligarchic mega-corporations (despite some evidence that their dominance is waning[65]). Further, many socioecological problems do not lend themselves to resolution by market dynamics, because the incentives are misaligned or there simply is no "market" for some public goods.

To build caring, connected, regenerative societies, therefore, means rethinking markets so that they are not just "free" in the conventional sense.

They actually need to be fair and equitable for all participants and, by extension, for nature. Fairness and equity ensure access to markets by all without excessive exploitation or destructive practices. Fairness and equity mean that products, services, and provisions are fully costed; that is, they are the very real costs of "externalities" associated with their production, manufacture, and distribution in their costing and pricing. That means taking the restorative, regenerative, socially just and equitable approaches implied by the five values discussed earlier. Companies would have to incorporate these costs into their business operations. Of course, it is likely that customers would have to pay such costs. They would be doing so, however, for products and provision that are created in ways consistent with the Earth's regenerative capacities. In turn, that pricing would put pressure on companies to produce not just mass quantities of (sometimes unneeded) goods and services, but rather high-quality, durable, recyclable, reusable ones.

## Principles for a New Economics[†]

Lest you think the values just articulated are unrealistic, I would like to provide a set of core foundational (first) principles derived from a global initiative that has drawn them out from a broad swath of economics literature that advances beyond mainstream thinking. Tapping into 37 different published approaches to economics, labeled "new economics," GANE, the Global Assessment for a New Economics, synthesized 10 "first principles" that underpin a well-being or life-affirming economics. The principles, which are straightforward and do not seem to require further explanation, are listed in Table 4.1 and were presented at a conference in 2021 though are yet to be formally published at this writing.

The six core values discussed in the previous section clearly link to and reflect these principles, with multiple principles needing to be in place and fully implemented to support them. Given its holistic

---

[†] Here I quote directly from the 10 first principles developed by GANE out of numerous "heterodox" economics sources, to provide a key set of alternatives to neoliberalism. All descriptions of the principles are direct quotes. In the interest of full disclosure, note that I was and am part of the GANE team. Note that the formal paper is still under review at this writing and the framing of these principles may change.

**Table 4.1  First principles for a new economics (from GANE: The Global Assessment for a New Economics 2021 presentation)**

| |
|---|
| Holistic principles: <ul><li>*Social–ecological embeddedness and holistic well-being*: Recognize that the economies are embedded within societies and ecosystems, and that the basic purpose of economics is to support human and planetary well-being.</li><li>*Interdisciplinarity and complexity thinking*: Acknowledge complexity and the need for interdisciplinarity in addressing economic problems.</li></ul> |
| Ecological principles: <ul><li>*Limits to growth*: Acknowledge that economies have fundamental biophysical and biochemical limits to growth.</li><li>*Limited substitutability of natural capital*: Recognize that human-derived capital fundamentally depends on nature.</li><li>*Regenerative design*: Design economics systems to be circular and regenerative.</li></ul> |
| Social principles: <ul><li>*Holistic perspectives of people and values*: Embed pluralistic models of values and human behavior, based on well-being, dignity, sufficiency, and holistic freedom, in all economic thinking, decisions, and actions.</li><li>*Equity, equality, and justice*: Consider equity, equality, and justice as central questions of economic inquiry.</li></ul> |
| Political economy principles: <ul><li>*Relationality and social enfranchisement*: Embrace pluralistic social and relational approaches that support social enfranchisement, social needs, and the common good.</li><li>*Participation, deliberation, and cooperation*: Embed participation, deliberation, and cooperation, and core to economic thinking and policy.</li><li>*Postcapitalism and decolonization*: Take postcapitalist, decolonized, and postdevelopment economic perspectives.</li></ul> |

*Source:* Kenter et al. Global Assessment for a New Economics (GANE) 2021.

orientation, all 10 of the first principles, for example, are needed to truly build a system that supports stewardship of the whole. Designing a system for collective (rather than individual) value and implementing cosmopolitan localist governance means emphasizing and building in the social and political economy principles. Those principles can help provide a basis for rethinking how societies are designed, governed, and developed over time.

Regenerativity, reciprocity, and circularity relate most specifically to production processes within economies, which means that the ecological principles and the holistic principle of embeddedness will need to be addressed. Relationality and connectedness are most associated with both the ecological principles and the social principles, since there are significant implications for both humans and nature reflected in this value set. Finally, achieving equitable markets and trade as, in a sense, the outcome of economies means ensuring that all 10 of the first principles are implemented across the board.

## Shifting Cultural Myths toward What Gives Life

Values and associated principles, as discussed, along with aspirations and visions, are essential guides to system transformation. They are the memes that make up the stories and narratives that form cultural mythologies. They necessarily do so because the wicked complexity of systemic change means that unless these guides are present, initiatives and change activities can be rather directionless, all over the map, so to speak. Having clear visions, already discussed, and clearly identified values and principles that guide change makers is essential to achieving the type of transformative changes that is desired. The paradigm, worldview, or perspective (sometimes called *mindset*) of change agents is made up of those visions and values and they also need to be built into the systems being transformed to affirm life in all its aspects. How such values and principles define the desired system and the purposive attempts at transformative change play a big role in defining the particular system of interest and how it will operate when transformed.[66]

Understanding that values and principles provide key guidance for catalyzing transformation, and adopting ones that affirm the real wealth of life to systems (versus merely producing monetary wealth, typically for the few), is core to catalyzing transformation. The next three chapters will introduce, effectively, a theory of change, to introduce two key concepts: the transformation catalyst and the transformation system, which are essential to achieving whole system change.

## Takeaways From Chapter 4

- Values and principles that affirm life are central to transforming toward ecological civilizations, that is, just, equitable, inclusive, and regenerative societies and economies in a flourishing natural world.

- "Wealth" needs to return to its original meaning of well-being, welfare, health, and prosperity for all.
- Build principles that give life to transformative change actions and desired outcomes:
  - Purpose: Be clear about the system's (aspirational) purpose.
  - Connectedness and Diversity: Acknowledge and foster connectedness and diversity's importance for a healthy living system.
  - Open Boundaries: Recognize the need for definition of living systems' permeable boundaries, which allow for new energic inputs and elimination of waste/no long fit-for-purpose elements.
  - Emergence and Novelty: Know that living systems evolve, emerge, and constantly seek novelty, new inputs and innovations, and adaptation to their context to maintain their vitality.
  - Whole System Perspective: View living systems as wholes with their own integrity as a whole that needs to be maintained as such.
  - Human Self-Awareness: Acknowledge the importance of self-awareness or consciousness, learning, and experimentation in humans to be able to design and implement better systems going forward.
- Shared values, principles, and visions provide a form of "glue" that helps hold systems and transformation initiatives together. Life-affirming values can constructively inform socioeconomies and their relationships to ecological ecosystems:
  - Stewardship of the whole involves taking responsibility for *whole* systems (not just their parts) and approaching transformation holistically, with care for all beings in a context and viewing the Earth as a global commons that all share.
  - Cocreating collective value means that productive and societal processes need to value the common or collective good, including the flourishing of nature and the inherent dignity and worth of all beings.

o  Subsidiarity, or cosmopolitan-localist governance, drives decisions to the localist possible place, shifts power to the ones who are affected by decisions, and favors creation of structures and technologies that connect people everywhere, while stewarding resources carefully.

o  Relationality and connectedness acknowledge the essential importance of perspectives like *Ubuntu*, "I am because we are," that humans exist and thrive only in the context of community.

o  Regenerativity, reciprocity, and circularity define ecologically and human-sensitive approaches to production, services, and provisioning that are needed for long-term human well-being and ecological civilizations, recognizing the Lakota principle of *Mitákuye Oyás'iŋ*, that "all are my relations."

o  Equitable markets and trade incorporate these five values to identify new approaches to production, servicing, and provisioning based on fairness, equity, social justice, and ecological principles with the intent of serving human needs while restoring and regenerating the natural world.

• Incorporate new principles into economic thinking that are fundamentally life-affirming, including socioecological embeddedness, complexity-based thinking, limits to growth, regenerative design, holistic perspectives, equity, relationality, and decolonization.

# CHAPTER 5

# *What* Needs to Change in System Transformation

To get a handle on *what* needs to change during system transformation, this chapter addresses and defines five core dimensions of systemic change, the *what* of system change, before we delve into the *how to* of whole system transformation in the next two chapters. Coming to a common understanding of what is meant by a particular system is important to bringing transformational initiatives into alignment, while recognizing that different lenses exist and are all valid is also important.

## Five Core System Dimensions That Focus Change Efforts

This chapter outlines five core dimensions of "what" needs to change in a system as a result of transformative actions, in as simple terms as feasible. Although complex to accomplish in practice, this "what" can be synthesized into five core dimensions of a given system, or five Ps or dimensions of socioecological system transformation,* which are best aligned with approaches that work in nature. Because humans can consciously design systems in ways that nature does not (that we know of anyway), it makes sense to think of human systems as operating in the context of and affecting or being affected by the natural environment.

---

* Some of the material in this section is drawn from S. Waddock. 2020. "Achieving Sustainability Requires Systemic Business Transformation," *Global Sustainability* 3, no. 312, pp. 1–12. https://doi.org/10.1017/sus.2020.9; S. Waddock and S. Waddell. 2021. "Five Core Dimensions of Purposeful System Transformation," *Journal of Management for Global Sustainability* 9, no. 2, p. 1–41. https://doi.org/10.13185/JM2021.09203.

The first three Ps are overarching (and interactive), because they influence how the other two shape up. Purpose(s) determine and set the standard for what the system is, how it defines itself, and when implemented properly what it actually does. Paradigms, that is, the perspectives, worldviews, or mindsets of key actors, determine what these actors believe about the system and their relationship to it. Performance metrics or assessment approaches determine how well the system is doing whatever it does. These three overarching and interconnected aspects of any human system, in turn, drive the other two: practices and power relations. Practices includes operating practices that determine how a given system does its work, and also the policies, procedures, and processes that support those practices. Power relations or structural characteristics structure where resources are and how they flow.[1] Each of these dimensions, which represent *what* has to change to bring transformation about, is explained in somewhat more detail here.

### Purpose

*Purpose* is the core reason for the existence of a given entity or system, and it is directly related to how the system's boundaries are defined. Trying to get a handle on a system of interest as a subject of transformational actions means determining what its boundaries are, which in turn means figuring out what its purposes are.[2] Purposes, in fact, are part of how systems can be defined. Purposes can be stated as goals, aspirations, visions, missions, or by other labels. As noted in the previous chapter, purposes are supported by core values and principles that help provide definition that distinguishes one system from another.

Socioecological systems are by their nature complex and open to inputs, outputs (and outcomes), and waste elimination. Drawing the boundaries and thereby establishing the relevant purpose of a system in many respects depends on the lens used—which level of analysis is most relevant, which subsystems and stakeholders are to be included, what focus should be taken and why, are among the relevant questions. Particular designations of a system are context-, stakeholder-, and phenomenon-specific, and depend on what is of most interest to the persons defining a given boundary or set of purposes.[3]

Systems can be defined in numerous ways, for example, by their function (e.g., supply chains in business, green energy), spatially or geographically (e.g., community, urban, national), or through a cultural lens (industrial, agricultural).[4] Even with these lenses, however, to determine where a given system starts and ends, that is, what its boundaries are, is difficult because of the inherent openness, complexity, and intertwining of subsystems, issues, and other aspects of complex wickedness already discussed. For example, WEAll, the Wellbeing Economy Alliance, has focused its purpose around defining and forwarding "well-being economies," stating on its website that it is "a collaboration of organizations, alliances, movements, and individuals working toward a well-being economy, delivering human and ecological well-being." Statements of purpose like this one delimit the focus and activities that will be relevant in a given system. In WEAll's case that definition emphasizes well-being for people and planet through economic activity.

Systemic complexity and the different possible lenses appropriate for defining a system's boundaries and hence purposes mean that how the system is defined and why those choices were made needs to be transparent, consistent, and clear to participants in transformational change efforts. How boundaries are defined influences how purpose is defined in multiple ways, because different definitions produce very different analytical approaches and metrics, with consequent very different potential results deriving from transformation efforts.[5] One clear implication is that a straightforward conversation about what the system of transformative interest is, how its boundaries are defined, and, as discussed next, what its aspirational or intended purpose is seen to be is important at the initiation of any transformation effort. Agreed values and principles, along with shared visions, can help with the (sometimes politically charged) determination of system boundaries and definition of relevant purposes.

Purpose and related concepts help guide the work that is done in human (socioecological) systems. Purposes are also helpful in delineating and identifying nonhuman systems. For example, we can readily conceive of economic systems as having the core purpose of producing goods, services, and provisions needed within a given context with a goal of maximizing business productivity and shareholder wealth (as with neoliberalism) or, as in the case of WEAll, as generating human and eco-logical well-being, quite a different framing of purpose.

In nature, oceans have boundaries associated with sea water and cer-tain geographies. In the case of oceans or trees and related plants, they are related to land ecosystems, for example, for a specific forest. The purposes of such ecological systems are less obvious than are the ones in socio-ecological systems. Yet one could say that the core purpose of an ocean system is to provide a home and substance for its particular species of marine life. Similarly with forests, purposes could be stated for whatever species of trees and other beings that are supported there. Subsystems that are holons, wholes within other wholes as discussed earlier, have their own purposes. For example, the circulatory system in mammals has the core purpose of circulating blood to sustain life and the digestive system of providing sufficient nutrients to do the same, taking in new sources of energy and eliminating ones that are no longer useful.

Of particular interest as subjects of transformation efforts are socio-ecological systems, human systems. They could be sectors such as the economic, social, or political system, or whole societies (or communities within them), which encompass multiple subsystems. As noted earlier, some systems may be issues-based, for example, poverty or economic, while others are sector-based, as with, for instance, agricultural or sea-food systems. The self-awareness and consciousness of human beings, discussed in the last chapter, means that people have the capacity to define and redefine the nature of purpose in social, political, economic, and ecological systems, communities, sectors, and issues. In contrast, the "purpose" of natural ecosystems has to be deduced or imputed. It is, however, frequently assumed that continuation of life or the intention-ality that is *an impulse towards survival' as Enlivenment* author Andreas Weber terms it.[6]

Socioecological systems defined by humans are frequently (at least in theory) guided by purpose or vision statements, core sets of values, and principles by which they (supposedly) live and operate. The core purpose of a given system as defined (and redefined) by system participants in socioecological systems is thus an important guide for system changers. Using a set of resonant memes to define systemic purposes provides a way for different subgroups to reinterpret their system as changes occur. Yet using similar memes allows differently articulated narratives to still be

I am here calling new approaches to organizing transformative change. Somewhere in the midst of all these different types of change actions, there needs to be an integrator, or in a sense a healer of the system (that some might call a shaman) to bring the collective wisdom of many different types of actors together. That healing, integrative role is exactly the work of the TC.

## Transforming System Transformation

As outlined earlier, the world faces multiple crises today, including growing inequality, climate change, biodiversity loss, deforestation, desertification, threats to privacy, regressive policies, and political divisiveness. As noted earlier, such crises are now being called *polycrisis* because they are deeply entangled and cannot be dealt with particularly well in fragments. Some of these crises pose real civilizational threats that argue for the need for the type of system transformation that is core to catalyzing transformation. Tinkering around the edges of change will not do. Traditional approaches to change, discussed briefly earlier, have proved insufficient and inadequate to bring about the purposeful system change, that is, transformative or fundamental system change, which is needed. None of these approaches seems to be actually transformative over the long term.

For lasting and transformative change to occur in ways that bring about equitable, inclusive well-being for people in a flourishing natural world, transformation processes themselves need to be transformed. For one thing, it is typically insufficient to use just one of the strategies just discussed. Further, it is insufficient to tackle only one of the core dimensions of systems that can be changed (purposes, paradigms, performance metrics, practices, power structures). Put another way, as Geels points out, transformation (or what he calls sustainability transitions) require changes in multiple dimensions and levels of a system. That includes technological change, public and political shifts, major changes in economics, including how businesses and markets operate, and more normative changes that influence culture, narratives, and public opinion.[5] Transformation implies all of these shifts and more.

More particularly, there is a need for a different understanding of *what* needs to change, as discussed in Chapter 5, and how that change can happen, and what values underlie the desired changes. Approaches to system transformation require transformation themselves. That is where TCs that work to organize transformation systems come in.

Given the complexly wicked context in which it occurs, system transformation needs to be conceptualized as a process of *catalysis*, enacted in ways that suit different contexts and involving the people who will be affected by and have to carry out the transformation. The system needs to be approached as a whole, not in its pieces. But since no one actor can tackle all the different elements that need to be changed, numerous actors need to align, to connect and cohere, their efforts in new ways to make change actually happen in ways consistent with their collective aspirations. Thus, transformational change efforts need to be considered as experiments, yet they are experiments in which actors understand the context, understand what needs to change, and bring together actors who can bring those changes about.

Change agents with system awareness and an understanding of how change happens in complex wickedness can greatly accelerate transformation, recognizing that different context may require different approaches. But there needs to be a certain level of readiness for change. Holling has argued that systems go through phases of conservation, release, exploitation, and reorganization over time in what he calls a nested set of adaptive cycles of "panarchy."[6] Viewing the system as in constant flux (or adaptation) enables change makers to determine the readiness of a given system or context for transformative change to work. Like Geels, who points to the multiple levels at which change happens, from niches, to regimes, to landscapes in his terminology,[7] Holling argues that systems are constantly reinventing and renewing themselves, albeit at different paces, with faster, smaller levels (niches) able to adapt more quickly than larger, slower-moving (regime and landscape) levels.[8] For example, if a system has gone through a disruptive phase and is in the process of restabilizing or reorganizing, change efforts may be welcome if they help with the reorganization that needs to occur. In contrast, if the system is in what Hollings calls the conservation phase, where things are reasonably stable, then disruption may be needed for transformation efforts to become effective.

Change agents need to acknowledge the need for whole system transformation, yet also recognize that transformation cannot be "scaled" because systems are invariably context specific, that is, with their own stakeholders, resources, dynamics, phase state, and other considerations. Rather, because each society, community, culture, and ecosystem has its own unique properties and context, it is best to consider that transformational efforts can be "propagated" rather than scaled, which is a more organic way of viewing the situation. Just as seeds grow uniquely, according to the environment in which they are planted, yet belong to families and species that are similar, so too transformational seeds need to fit appropriately into different places, contexts, cultures, and dynamics. We can learn from successful (and failed) efforts, but will be unlikely to "replicate" or "scale" them in the traditional understanding of those words.

Thus, there is no "one size fits all" when it comes to transformation. Rather, as discussed throughout this book, changes need to and can emerge as an approach, a set of principles, and values-based processes and understandings. The right principles and processes can help change agents in different contexts bring people in that setting *together* to figure out what is needed *for them and their place or situation to catalyze purposeful transformation*, and how to go about making it happen. In short, there is a need for a *catalytic* approach to developing systemic change. Catalyzing transformation recognizes the core imperative of somehow linking the many ongoing and emerging change activities into impactful and purposeful transformation (T-) systems that can cope resiliently with the complex wickedness of socioecological systems.

Because of that complex wickedness, transformational and purposeful whole system change cannot be planned, predicted, or controlled in the ways that many people would like it to be. If effective transformation systems are to evolve, there needs to be an effort to *catalyze* the change— and then allow what is going to happen, to happen. Catalyzing change is the work of TCs, who connect, cohere, and amplify work already being done by initiatives, or could evolve in a context. The rest of this chapter develops these ideas.

## Transformation Catalysts

Relatively new as ways of organizing systemic change, TCs* generally orient toward helping to connect, cohere, and amplify the work of initiatives and efforts aiming to bring about socially just and ecologically flourishing communities, sectors, bioregions, and other systems. Generally focused on complexly wicked problems, issues, bioregions, and sectors, that is, socioecological systems, TCs explicitly work to deal with the fragmentation of blessed unrest that frequently exists in such systems.[9]

TCs arise out of a premise: system transformation, which inherently exists in complex wickedness, is notoriously difficult to achieve successfully. But there are many initiatives, efforts, and activities that *already* exist and are oriented toward achieving transformative change. As noted several times, their problem is one of fragmentation, small scale, and relatively low impact. TCs work to bring these initiatives into alignment for impact. That is, TCs connect, cohere, and amplify the effectiveness of these actors in specific transformation (T-) systems to help develop a shared and agreed agenda.

TCs help actors coevolve action plans, some parts of which will be implemented jointly and others independently. They develop and leave in place a transformations infrastructure that enables the work to continue over time. This work is that of the catalyst, the one who integrates existing initiatives in new ways, rather than necessarily being the "doer" of transformation. The TC connects otherwise largely independent actors

---

* Ideas in this chapter are integrated from multiple writings, including S. Waddock and S. Waddell. 2021. "Transformation Catalysts: Weaving Transformational Change for a Flourishing World," *Cadmus* 4, no. 4, pp. 165–181; J.Y. Lee and S. Waddock. 2021. "How Transformation Catalysts Take Catalytic Action," *Sustainability* 13, p. 9813. http://doi.org/10.3390/su13179813; S. Waddock. 2020. "Thinking Transformational System Change," *Journal of Change Management* 20, no. 3, pp. 189–201; S. Waddock, S. Waddell, P. Jones, and I. Kendrick. 2022. "Convening Transformation Systems to Achieve System Transformation," *Journal of Awareness-Based System Change*; and S. Waddock. 2021. *Bouncing Beyond to Next Economies*, e-book. www.bouncebeyond .global/book-bounce-beyond-ebook; as well as documents internal to the Bounce Beyond initiative, in which I was an active participant and which Steve Waddell founded, https://www.bouncebeyond.global/. They also emerged from Bounce Beyond's work with Seafood 2030.

to bring them into interaction in new ways to see what they can coemerge together. TCs recognize that participants in the T-system need to "own" their interactions, plans, and ultimate actions, not have them imposed by others.

It is important to recognize that evolutionary and developmental processes in complex systems are interactive and emergent. Further, unlike chemical catalysts, TCs are an integral *part* of the emergence processes themselves, changing and evolving as the transformation (T-) system becomes a more effective *ecosystem* for transformation, as discussed in the next chapter (and their presence changes the system itself). Learning how to foster this catalytic interaction is potentially a breakthrough in how whole system transformation is approached, going well beyond any one of the strategies discussed at the opening of this chapter. But doing so is hard, complicated, time-consuming work that requires breakthroughs in many domains. To make those breakthroughs possible, the next sections discuss in detail the type of work that TCs actually can *do* to connect, cohere, and amplify T-system efforts.

## Contexts for Catalyzing Transformative Whole System Change

No two systems, particularly socioecological systems, are alike. The unique attributes of each require attention to the specifics in a given context. Yet as argued here, approaches, patterns, and processes can be devised that apply in many different circumstances to enable transformation. Here is how TCs have been defined:

> Transformation catalysts (TCs) are promising organizing innovations specifically designed to address complexly wicked societal problems and opportunities and bring about purposeful system transformation. ... Specifically, they connect, cohere, and amplify efforts of other initiatives in cocreative and emergent efforts to overcome the fragmentation and lack of impact. ... They help coalitions of actors emerge shared visions, goals, aspirations, or other narratives that enable them to align their efforts, even while they pursue their individual agendas.[10]

TCs work catalytically with actors in a transformation system (T-system) to enhance their collective speed and ability to address the complexity and scale associated with transformation. ... As catalysts, TCs attempt to bring other actors synergistically together toward greater needed *system* innovation, alignment of efforts, and transformation into powerful transformation (T-) systems. That is, TCs cohere collections of actors oriented toward systemic change in a given arena without necessarily "making" the change themselves,[11] enabling them to cocreatively innovate and implement action plans, amplifying their collective impact.

Some TCs can take typical organizational forms, like a nonprofit or coalition. Others are self-organized, self-governing entities in which their participants are loosely coupled, as are the transformation (T-) systems they organize. Some may be individuals or small groups that are not formally organized. As discussed further in the next chapter, in transformation systems, different entities, efforts, and initiatives likely already have their own identity (and organizational form). Still, though they may not (yet) be aware of it, they generally share or emerge a common agenda or set of aspirations around improving and transforming a particular system. That system could be a sector (such as fisheries, health care), an issue (such as how landscapes are treated or narratives shift), or a bioregion or other place-based region.

What is shared across TCs is their emphasis on systemic transformation, or the type of fundamental change introduced at the outset of this book. TCs focus on *catalytically* (rather than directly) tapping existing resources, initiatives, and institutions or actions connecting and cohering them into effective transformative action. In doing so, they work to emerge or organize effective T-systems as more *self-aware* and organized transformation ecosystem capable of bringing desired change into being. TCs generally operate from an understanding of the complexly wicked nature of socioecological systems. They work to support holistic system change through a variety of other initiatives and activities, rather than "doing" the change themselves.[12] In work Ju Young Lee and I undertook to assess how TCs view their actions, we found that they emphasized multiple things: cognitive transformation or mindset/paradigm shift, as well as whole systems change using integrative approaches, shifting

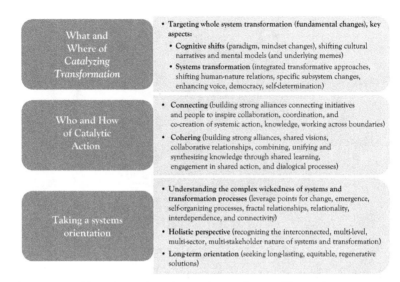

*Figure 6.2 Identifying the what, when, who, and how of system transformation*

*Source*: Adapted from Lee and Waddock (2021).[13]

human-nature relations, and working on specific systems. Key is that this approach is a whole systems approach, as detailed in the following synthesis table (Figure 6.2).

Because they attempt to catalyze and amplify efforts by working with others already attempting change, TCs have a clear transformation agenda. Taking a systems perspective, they engage the actions of connecting, cohering, and amplifying to coemerge shared agendas among actors that might not be feasible were they acting individually. Operating from an understanding of complex wickedness, TCs recognize the difficulty and complexity of accomplishing system transformation, taking both holistic and long-term perspectives. They also articulate the systemic problems they focus on with a good deal of urgency in an effort to galvanize action by multiple parties.[14]

TC's main activities are summarized in Figure 6.3, then elaborated in the sections that follow. In the process called *connecting*, TCs bring actors in a given T-system together, help them figure out who is in the system, what the system dynamics and needs are, and what they are doing with respect to systemic change. This connecting process helps system participants develop self-awareness *as* a system and make sense of what could

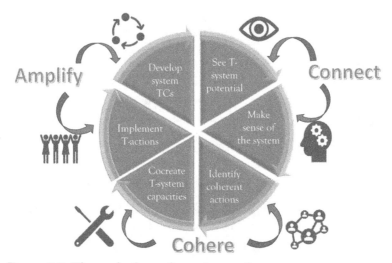

**Figure 6.3** *The work of transformation catalysts*

be their collective or shared actions through processes of "seeing" and "sensemaking." In the process of *cohering*, TCs enable T-system actors to create coherent action plans and cocreate their transformational capacities. In doing so, they focus on a number of deep system challenges to be discussed in the next chapter, and others as appropriate to the specific context.

Finally, TCs help actors in T-systems work catalytically to *amplify* their impact through implementing their shared and individual action plans, by actually working to establish and maintain effective transformation systems. Amplification involves implementing action plans, learning from experience and experimentation, and changing and adapting as needed, and build similar transformation infrastructure in the multilevel, multispatial context of the system, where needed, to sustain transformative impact over time. In that process, actors learn from their experiments and experiences, and change and adapt as needed. T-systems operate best under a broad umbrella of a shared set of aspirations, and focus on amplifying impact, as discussed in depth in the next chapter.

## Connecting

Connecting means bringing actors in a system together to define common and individual strategies and act both together and independently in new ways to achieve generally shared aspirations. Two activities are central to the connecting function: seeing and sensemaking. Seeing means figuring out who is in the system and what they are doing. Seeing helps define the relevant system, scoping out its boundaries, stakeholders, and dynamics. Sensemaking helps participants codevelop understanding of the system and their broadly shared aspirations and agendas.

## Seeing

TCs frequently undertake activities that can help actors better "see," that is, comprehend and understand their system. Seeing the system means learning about who is doing what in the system, understanding key issues and dynamics, including opportunities for and obstacles to change. Seeing can involve stakeholder identification and mapping process that outline what is going on in the system, where is doing what, where, how, and why. It can be done more or less formally and in a wide range of levels of detail, depending on the needs and interests of participants. Mapping processes of various kinds can be useful tools for helping participants see and understand. Mapping also helps determine where gaps in needed activities and actions are, where duplications are happening, and where possibilities for change exist. Seeing is often a first step in connecting. In a very real sense, seeing means connecting the dots for participants in a context, because it is important to know who key actors are, what they are doing, and where possibilities for greater alignment of efforts exist.

Mapping strategies, of which there are many,[15] include developing stakeholder maps that identify who the key stakeholders are and where in the system they are placed. Some maps show networks and linkages among actors and initiatives, that is, webcrawl and 7Vortex maps. Other maps help identify patterns, relationships, and subsystems in the whole context, like synthesis maps.[16] Influence maps and others like them can help illuminate system dynamics and highlight patterns of behaviors, interactions, and obstacles to change. All these types of maps work best when actually generated *by* system members themselves (versus, e.g., a consulting group preparing and disseminating them).

Understanding the patterns in a system can be very helpful to "seeing" or understanding how the system actually works and also simplifying, or at least making understandable, the inherent complexity. Patterns are recurrent configurations in a given context that help determine its unique identity.[17] Understanding patterns helps participants gain perspective about where leverage points for systemic change, as Meadows termed them,[18] may exist. Leverage points are the areas of change that provide the most potential for significant change in the desired direction. Most powerful, according to Meadows, are shifting paradigms, redefining purposes and goals, and power relations, as discussed earlier in defining the key aspects of what changes in systems.

This type of seeing enables actors in a system to gain awareness of the existence of an ecosystem of change agents and efforts that can potentially be evolved into an effective T-system, as discussed in the next chapter. Seeing serves as a potentially effective way to co-generate initiatives change processes. New meanings, understandings, analysis of gaps, and aligned ways of acting can be generated that help with the next process of sensemaking that co-develops shared aspirations, that is, or new narratives.

### Sensemaking

*Sensemaking* is a term originated by scholar Karl Weick, which builds on the seeing processes just discussed. It is the process that gives meaning to (shared) experiences.[19] Sensemaking helps groups come into alignment around narratives, visions, values, and shared aspirations during transformational change efforts. Sensemaking processes in the context of system change help participants coemerge shared visions (aspirations) and the types of powerful, inspiring, and emotionally engaging narratives with supporting memes that are needed to guide successful transformations. Common agendas, including shared visions, articulation of values and principles as discussed in Chapter 5, and other ways of representing common goals and aspirations, are all types of narrative development associated with sensemaking. To be effective, these efforts need to be readily communicable and reasonably broadly agreed by participants. They are frequently articulated in documents like vision and mission statements, statements of operating or underlying principles, core values, and other shared aspirational statements. Sometimes images can help, too, along with statements of goals, aspirations, and statements of "what we are about."

Memes, that is, core units of culture like words, phrases, images, symbols, and ideas[20], make up these narratives. Memes are the most basic elements of culture (here, think ideas, phrases, even images) that can be woven together in different narratives depending on the need in different ways, but that carry shared meanings in powerful and, when resonant, emotionally engaging ways. The reason memes are important in this type of context is that the various actors being brought together by TCs are likely to have their own agendas and ways of stating them. They can construct their own narratives and stories yet still be consonant with others oriented toward the same aspirations. That is, memes provide a basis by which different actors can have their own narratives relevant to their initiative considered independently yet still cohere actions, agendas, and aspirations with others, too.

Ultimately, sensemaking in this context is a collective process that means emerging separate efforts into transformation ecosystem, which also means emerging a (set of) shared narrative(s) that participants can buy into. Then efforts of actors that have been connected can ultimately be aligned into transformation systems through the guidance provided by those narratives. Shared memes or core ideas allow participants, in a very real way, to get on the same page with each other while still retaining their individual purposes and operations. Powerful memes are broadly resonant, and therefore get repeated a lot, while still allowing that type of flexibility.

Sensemaking processes that TCs use can include visioning exercises that enable participants to codevelop a shared sense of the future. Tools like the ones developed in Three Horizons mapping,[21] Appreciative Inquiry,[22] and Theory U,[23] among numerous others, are all useful as ways of helping participants align with each other. Many such approaches and how to apply them are explained by Jones and Van Ael in a book entitled *Design Journeys through Complex Systems*.[24] Key steps for TCs here are having (or bringing in) the skills to help system participants establish coherent and aligned narratives, that is, visions, purposes, values, principles, agendas, and aspirations (whatever they might be called in a given context). These visions can enable participants to develop powerful and resonant expressions, for example, stories, videos, images, stories, and symbols, to ensure that these aspirations are deployed into the relevant parts of the system and, as necessary, beyond.

Sensemaking deals with the "why" and "how" and "when" of catalyzing change, according to work that Ju Young Lee and I undertook in exploring how TCs do their work.[25] This means that TCs need to clearly acknowledge why and when transformative change is needed in the relevant contexts. The issues embedded in that context require acknowledgment. Thus, a key role for TCs is articulating and disseminating the urgent need for transformative change, and how it will or could come about, including shifting key narratives, as summarized in Figure 6.4. That includes, for the initiatives we studied, problematizing, according to TCs, specific areas for change, including social and ecological systems, the economic system, taking an integrated socioeconomic–ecological approach, and reducing inequality and inequity. It also means recognizing the urgent need for timely action to address needed changes.

Through process of seeing and sensemaking, TCs use the connecting function to work with all three of the overarching core dimensions of system change: purpose, paradigms, and performance metrics that were introduced earlier. Connecting processes help participants consolidate and define purpose for a given system (e.g., through visioning and seeing what needs to happen to make the system more effective), thereby making sense of the system for themselves and others in new ways. Sensemaking

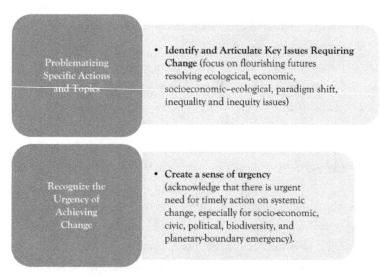

*Figure 6.4 Sensemaking processes for catalyzing transformation*

Source: Adapted from Lee and Waddock (2021).[26]

works to begin to shift mindsets of people working in and beyond the system, reshaping their perspectives and paradigms around those new visions, relationships, and understandings.

Finally, a key aspect of sensemaking is developing the kinds of performance metrics and evaluation tools that are needed to understand the system holistically, not just in terms of profitability of a given entity. Doing so is really important because performance metrics guide practices or the policies, procedures, processes, and operating practices that get the work of the system done. Metrics also allow for evaluation and assessment that informs learning what does and does not work as transformative efforts are implemented. One approach to such holistic evaluation has been developed by Michael Quinn Patton, who calls this principles-based approach *Blue Marble evaluation*.[27] This approach, discussed more in Chapter 7, is holistic, principles-based, systemically oriented, and geared toward the ongoing learning and improvement needed in long-term systems transformation.

## Cohering

Cohering is the process of bringing together actors so that they can do their own action planning by eventually forming into a transformation (T-) system capable of amplifying their impacts, discussed in the next chapter. Collectively, actors can develop needed transformation capacities and deploy them as appropriate. In one sense, cohering is an extension of the sensemaking process, in that it takes the shared ideas and narratives and puts them into aligned actions. That alignment, however, means action planning substantially different from the fragmented actions that typically exist in such systems before they recognize themselves as a T-system.

### Action Planning

The point of action planning is to have participants identified by TCs come together to jointly identify and begin to experiment with actions that could strengthen (amplify) their collective impact. Action planning involves developing ideas about what needs to change and how, and aligning the activities of various actors and initiatives to collectively achieve their desired impacts. Unaligned initiatives and efforts tend to be too fragmented and small scale to bring about the desired changes. Yet together and aligned, such initiatives have considerably more power to actually effect change. Many of the processes used for visioning and mapping can be extended into action planning, which is where the catalysis comes in, that is, bringing together initiatives and actors who might not otherwise connect that they can cohere their actions.

Cohering frequently involves convenings, which can be online as well as in person. Approaches like the ones discussed earlier can be useful in these processes, including various approaches to dialogue,[28] Appreciative Inquiry,[29] Three Horizons,[30] Theory U,[31] Future Search,[32] World Café,[33] Open Space,[34] and the like. It is important that the system is represented reasonably holistically and diversely in these processes, even though initially actors in different initiatives might not recognize themselves as part of a transformation system. The work of catalysis, in fact, is to help them evolve this collective recognition. Given the scope, breadth, and depth of most socioecological systems, getting "everyone" into the room is unlikely,[35] however, it is important to be as representative as feasible. Sometimes organizing subsystems that can better represent local, subsystem, or sector views is needed. That's why the mapping processes used to "see" and understand the system in the connecting processes are so important for beginning to evolve systemic coherence around shared aspirations. Seeing the system helps TCs figure out who needs to be invited to participate in convenings to help align the system toward whole system transformation to ensure the broadest possible representation of allies, not resistors, while still making organizing processes feasible.

Convenings of key system representatives and networks, whether in person or virtual, are opportunities for participants to share their own agendas and their ideas about future actions as well as to share and shape their common aspirations. In dialogical and future-oriented processes, they can begin to cohere synergies that enable them to work across boundaries collaboratively or in alignment, rather than as competitors. For example, convened participants might develop and agree on a common set of evaluative performance metrics rather than competing ones, agree to address redundancies, thereby reducing duplications of efforts. Alternatively, they might be able to identify gaps in the action plan that a particular actor might step in to fill. Convenings focused on such collaborative or aligned efforts can also help reduce potential conflicts. Or they can help resolve them when they inevitably do arise. That means recognizing the power of the shared agenda, that is, the good of the whole rather than simply the good of the individual initiative. Getting ego and personal or organizational agendas out the way to the extent possible, as discussed later, is important in such processes.

Sometimes actions that require more resources than one initiative has might be needed. That is, when achieving coherence across action strategies can help participants develop collaborative or coordinated actions that are considerably more effective than individual actions could be. As an example, a collection of initiatives might cohere around codeveloping not only common metrics but also a shared information system or a particular type of innovation. There are many other ways in which the dialogical processes involved in convenings can be helpful, including helping participants redefine priorities as the system itself evolves and changes, or, for example, if the original objective is met or the need for it dissipates or shifts.

### Cocreating Transformation Capacities

Cocreating transformation capacities means developing the ability of numerous actors in a context to undertake connecting and cohering processes themselves to establish a platform for ongoing systemic change. Cocreated transformation capacities are also needed to contend effectively with the deep system challenges discussed in Chapter 7. In addition to cohered actions, the actors that TCs bring together to catalyze change can implement new ways of dealing with the systemic and transformational challenges they are collectively facing, that is, emerging core transformation capacities. These capacities include developing and deploying new narratives and creating holistic measurement, evaluation, research, and learning systems that guide transformational efforts. Transformation capacities include emerging collective action structures that organize actors within the system for effective action, which is collective rather than individual action. In a sense, what this process means is building a cascading series of transformation catalytic capabilities throughout the system at multiple levels and in different spaces or contexts that matter to the system. All of that is part of establishing coherence.

The question of interest around cocreating transformation capacities is: what is needed for TCs to help enable actors to develop and emerge into a transformation system and to sustain that T-system over time? One answer, as just noted, is that there likely need to be numerous TCs in different places with the requisite skills to connect and cohere local actors and initiatives. Various perspectives on large system change help pinpoint some of the transformation capacities needed. In addition to seeing and making sense of the system, actors need to understand that complexly wicked systems have multiple levels and multiple possible pathways forward, which have been described as transformation, reconfiguration, technological substitution, and dealignment and realignment.[36] As introduced earlier, one framework, called the *multilevel perspective*, argues that there are three levels at which sociotechnological transitions or system changes can happen: niches or small networks of actors offering innovations, regimes or relatively stable configurations that represent a social or cultural order, and landscapes or whole systems.[37] TCs attempt to connect and cohere actors at all of these levels, recognizing that each level is important and offers potential ways for innovations and change strategies to happen.

Particular system capacities need to be embedded into the transformation systems that TCs are evolving. Among these are the capacities for seeing, including visioning and revisioning as necessary, coming into collaborative and collective action as necessary, and making sense of what has been learned when experiments and initiatives are tried. In other words, as TCs work with actors, they are undergoing a constant learning process at different levels and in different subsystems and contexts, so that capacities for connecting and cohering are constantly renewed and reinvigorated in different parts of the system.

What is needed in a given context is necessarily context specific, but when transformation systems begin to form, there are a number of critical or deep system challenges that they need to work with. Much of that work occurs through experimentation and learning from those experiments, since there is little chance that "planned change" in its traditional sense can work. So, the ability to experiment when needed, and to fail as experiments sometimes do, and to gain both experience, insight, and learning from those experiments is an important capability to evolve.

Recognize that the work of the initial convener as TC is only the beginning. New TCs need to emerge at different levels of the system and with respect to specific subsystems. These sub-TCs (if you will) help these subsystems connect and cohere their own transformational efforts. That is part of the capacity building that TCs need to engage. Capacities for adaptiveness, stewardship, and designing change strategies, need to be evolved as discussed in Chapter 9, and embedded in the system. By following the design principles articulated in Chapter 8, TCs can help actors to emerge the core capacities needed to bring about system transformation, not just the minor changes associated with reformative and incremental change. That means ensuring that there is a learning orientation that enables emerging new TCs and actors in the transformation (T-) system to evolve as necessary is vital. There will be much more to say about these ideas and the approaches that need to be taken in the next three chapters.

## Takeaways From Chapter 6

- New ways of organizing to transform system transformation are needed. Transformation catalysts work to create effective and purposeful transformation systems. Most conventional transformation efforts and strategies fall short because actors remain independent, separate, and do not act coherently or in aligned ways.
- Transformation cannot be "scaled" because each context is unique. Instead, think of propagating transformation by using a set of principles, values, approaches, and processes that can be adapted to the particular context in which change is desired.
- Transformation Catalysts (TCs) are entities that facilitate actors and initiatives in a given socioecological system or context to connect and cohere their efforts so that they can form into purposeful and effective transformation systems that collectively amplify their transformative impact.

- TCs target whole system transformation through paradigm or cognitive shifts and whole system transformative approaches (what and where), connect and cohere actors in transformation systems (who and how), taking a systems orientation that understands complex wickedness, is holistic, and is long-term oriented.
- Connecting involves bringing actors together to "see" and "sensemake" their system and transformative aspirations:
  o Seeing involves describing and understanding system, typically through various sorts of stakeholder and initiative identification and mapping processes, outlining who is doing what, where, and how, and sensemaking through visioning how the system might be and emerging shared aspirations, visions, values, and narratives of various sorts.
  o Sensemaking involves engaging in processes that emerge shared meanings, visions, values, and aspirations with respect to systemic change.
- Cohering involves enabling actors to come together to cocreate coherent action plans needed transformational capacities.
  o Action planning involves developing ideas about what needs to change and how, and aligning the activities of various actors and initiatives to collectively achieve their desired impacts.
  o Cocreating transformation capacities means developing the ability of numerous actors in a context to undertake connecting and cohering processes themselves to establish a platform for ongoing systemic change so that collectively and independently actors can deal with systemic challenges.
- Amplification involves implementing action plans, learning from experience and experimentation, and changing and adapting as needed. It involves building other TCs and related transformation infrastructure in subsystems in the multilevel, multispatial context of the system, where needed, to sustain transformative impact over time and to enable the emerging transformation system to cope with difficult and complex systemic challenges. (Discussed in detail in the next chapter.)

# CHAPTER 7

# Catalyzing Transformation (T-) Systems

What the TCs described in Chapter 6 are attempting to do is organize the many initiatives, actors, and efforts oriented toward similar aspirations in a given context into effective and impactful *transformation (T-) systems.** This chapter focuses on the development and emergence of powerful and effective transformation systems as a means of bringing about *whole system transformation* rather than the more piecemeal and fragmented (or focused) transformation efforts that are more typical. That said, it is important to recognize that the idea of the transformation system is still new and whole system change is complex. Therefore, the understanding of how to bring this approach into effectiveness is still emerging. There will be many stops and starts, new things to learn, experiments that fail. Yet the idea of organizing T-systems for whole system change offers promise for the *how to* of systemic change and that is the focus here. Figure 7.1 depicts the core elements of weaving together actors into purposeful and effective transformation systems.

## Defining Transformation (T-) Systems

Transformation (T-) systems are the collection of initiatives, actors, and efforts oriented toward achieving similar transformational aspirations. Purposeful transformation systems are connected and cohered to amplify

---

* The concept of transformation systems originated in the Bounce Beyond initiative (of which I was a member) with Steve Waddell, and has been more fully developed here: S. Waddock, S. Waddell, P. Jones, and I. Kendrick. 2022. "Convening Transformation Systems to Achieve System Transformation," *Journal of Awareness-Based System Change* 2, no. 1, pp. 77–100. Some of this chapter is based on that article.

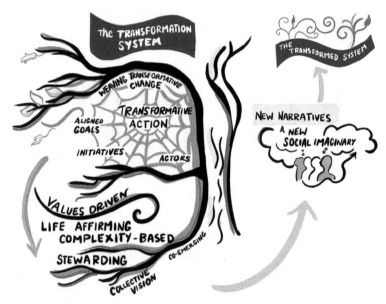

**Figure 7.1  Transformation (T-) systems**

*Image:* Patricia Kambitsch, https://playthink.com.

their transformative impact in a given context, and are organized around cocreated and collectively aligned strategies for achieving systemic change. In particular, transformation systems are comprised of those initiatives *willing* and able to work together to connect, cohere, and amplify their efforts[1] to realize their collective agendas and aspirations through both joint or shared and individual activities, efforts, and initiatives.

Since the goal of transformation efforts is to activate and transform *whole* systems, whether issues-based, bioregional, sector, or geographical, it is important to recognize the long-term nature and complexity of this task. Such whole system change is difficult to achieve in part because, as noted earlier, far too often initiatives that have similar goals are in the fragmented, disjointed, and separated state that ecologist Paul Hawken called *blessed unrest.* These initiatives experience fragmentation, small scale, and lack of sufficient power to bring about their desired ends. Building connected and cohered T-systems is explicitly meant to provide an antidote to this fragmentation.

By organizing previously disconnected efforts into connected and cohered transformation (T-) systems, TCs attempt to help them figure out how to better amplify their own and collective efforts. To accomplish that TCs bring groups of willing actors and initiatives with shared agendas together, using the connecting and cohering strategies discussed in the last chapter, to cocreate and coemerge ideas, initiatives, activities, and actions that they can take collectively or independently to achieve their common agendas and aspirations. Once they are connected, it is mainly up to actors within the emerging T-system to cocreatively (with the help of TCs, most likely) figure out ways to amplify their impact and put into place the necessary infrastructure to sustain transformative potential as needed. That is why capacities for systemic change, very likely additional TCs in different subsystems, and other capabilities, plus core transformation infrastructure, need to be developed to sustain change efforts over time.

In particular, TCs facilitate the emergence of the T-system's capacities to cope with multiple, common, and pervasive systemic challenges that face any transformational change efforts. In research with nearly 100 change agents, asking what their major challenges were, Steve Waddell identified six core challenges that face most transformation efforts in their efforts to amplify transformative impact. These challenges involve how to develop new narratives; how to cocreate needed collaboration capacities; how to develop necessary and holistic metrics that inform and enhance change; how to govern and organize the emerging new system; and how to transform financing mechanisms to support transformation.[2] Dealing with these challenges as well as others that may arise in context-specific ways is what it means to amplify impact.

In addition to these six challenges, of course, particular systems or contexts might have other broad-based systemic challenges. Such challenges could encompass knowledge and educational systems, health provision, agricultural provision, and other production systems. They might relate to ecosystem challenges related to sustainability, climate change, biodiversity or species loss, or ecosystem health. They might be more intangible challenges that involve changing cultural, identity, or values and belief systems (e.g., away from human separation from nature toward envisioning us humans as part of and interdependent with nature and other beings). Or they might have to do with shifting organizational and institutional arrangements and purposes. Or something else.

The catalytic actions of TCs come in the form of helping or enabling T-system participants amplify their impacts through well-formulated action plans with identified implementation processes. TCs also need to ensure that T-system itself survives by developing appropriate connective tissue—infrastructure—along with system capacities, to keep the system aware of itself as a T-system and effective over time.

## Amplifying Transformative Impact

Amplifying impact means developing processes to implement action plans for change, and ensuring that participants in a T-system are taking the types of actions that work on key leverage points for systemic change. Once T-system participants have figured out their common agenda, what the strengths and potentialities of various actors in the system are, they can formulate ways to act. In doing so, they need to recognize that such actions should be viewed as experiments or prototypes to learn from in an ongoing way rather than fully articulated processes, procedures, and practices.

Experiments are vital to achieving system change because of the uniqueness of each context in which initiatives are tried. That means there will be differences that matter and require unique solutions and approaches. Different people with different perspectives, different social and ecological environments offer considerably different potentials, opportunities, and, yes, challenges. Experiments are more like seeds that propagate and spread than items produced in an assembly line that are all alike. Seeds represent examples of their species, and still can grow in their own way in their unique settings. Actions, activities, plans, and processes in T-system implementation activities have similar characteristics: they will be unique to each setting. Still, as noted earlier, the catalytic processes of connecting and cohering, and the design guidelines and principles discussed in the next chapter, work in a wide variety of contexts because they are adaptable to particular circumstances. They explicitly allow for that uniqueness to develop, in a context of shared aspirations and agendas.

The rest of this section explores how TCs help participants in T-systems tackle (at least) the systemic challenges identified by Waddell, plus others that may arise in a given context.

### The Narrative Challenge: Developing Shared Aspirational New Narratives

The narrative challenge involves reframing visions and aspirations in ways that reframe paradigms (mental models, worldviews) toward aspirational goals like achieving ecological civilizations. Earlier, I explored the importance of narratives in shaping mindsets and the paradigms that shape peoples' belief systems, attitudes, and, ultimately, behaviors. Particularly powerful narratives become core cultural mythologies that have strong influences on culture, purposes, and practices in a system. Such narratives can be very "sticky," meaning that it is hard to dislodge them. But that is exactly what often has to happen for transformative change to take place. If people in a T-system remain stuck in old ways of thinking, that is, they retain old paradigms, worldviews, or mindsets, then it becomes difficult to change. Old ways hold the system in place through memes like "That's the way things work here" or "That's how we've always done things."

New visions or other types of narratives, when broadly shared, inspirational, emotionally engaging, and supported by resonant memes that can be repeated in a variety of ways are powerful guides to transformative change. Thus, in the context of systemic change, narratives (broadly defined to include visions, aspirations, agendas, and cultural myths) play a particularly important role. That is because whole system change can at best be guided, not "planned" in the traditional sense of planned change. There are too many different actors, moving parts, and independent initiatives all doing their things at the same time to think that it is possible to predict specific outcomes from activities that change.

Here is where narrative in the form of shared visions, goals, aspirations, agendas, values, and stories, however they manifest is central. Through the connecting and cohering processes described in the last chapter, TCs participants in transformation systems envision or re-vision collectively. Doing so they can cocreate shared aspirations and desired futures that can reshape and reconfigure how the world is understood and thereby begin the process of emerging new paradigms, which are the most powerful levers for transformational change.[3]

New narratives provide frameworks that help make sense of what is needed when systems are changing. They provide directionality for actions, even when they are not necessarily specific about which actions are to be taken. Indeed, that is their benefit: they point the way toward what needs to be done. At the same time, they allow the freedom for different change agents to pursue actions and create their own stories each in their own ways, while having a guiding star to keep them aligned.

Such narratives, jointly developed by members of a transformation system thus provide an important foundation for transformative change. That is where seeing, sensemaking, and action planning activities are really important. Narratives identify what it is that change makers collectively envision, what the key values that support those changes are, and point to a viable set of pathways that might be taken to realize those new narratives. They can clarify what needs to change and why. They can articulate pathways forward toward achieving the shared aspirations and desired changes. And that is important: this process of re-visioning or re-storying the world or at least a given system provides vital *guidance* that enables change makers to align their activities and initiatives.

### Developing Collaborative Capacities

Actors and initiatives in T-systems need to develop collaborative mindsets and the capacities to collaborate intensively while maintaining their own agendas and aspirations. Operating in the context of a transformation system is not the same as doing so in more hierarchically structured, or even networked, organizations. Actors and initiatives in a T-system are coequals, each with something to contribute. They do not report to each other in any hierarchical or authority-driven way. Even TCs who are trying to organize them into effective transformation systems have no real authority or power to ensure that participants in a T-system act or do things in specific ways or toward specific goals.

Instead of being built around power or formal authority structures as traditional organizations are, T-system and TC relationships are cocreative, collaborative, and for the most part completely voluntary. T-systems are not even "organizations" in the conventional understanding. They are collections of actors willing to engage with each other because they can amplify their collective impact by doing so. In a sense that is why coevolving shared aspirations and narratives is so important.

Those narratives, whether expressed as visions, values, or other aspirations, provide the foundational "glue" that holds the potential for keeping the T-system together.

The skills needed to operate effectively in such contexts are *collaborative* capacities. One such capacity is an orientation toward ongoing-learning, along with a willingness and ability to work in a context of great diversity. Others include willingness and ability to cocreate agendas without holding too tightly to one's own agenda. Another important collaborative capacity is skills in dealing with conflict and conflict resolution as the actors in a T-system will bring many different ideas, perspectives, and agendas into the system with them.

Listening well and truly hearing what others say is also vital, since many of the processes that help to evolve effective T-systems are dialogical in nature. Of course, actors also need to be able to clearly and effectively express their own positions, while retaining the ability to compromise when necessary. That is, visions and proposed actions are not ideas or agendas imposed on the system but rather whatever actors in a T-system decide to do that can be cogenerated with others. Using approaches such as dialogue,[4] action inquiry,[5] active or reflective practice,[6] presencing,[7] and similar approaches can be ways of moving shared purposes and agendas forward. At the same time, it is important to be able to remain true to one's own (or one's organization's/initiative's) agenda even while coemerging new ideas and plans with others, as happens in T-system evolution. Many of these capacities are explored in more depth in Chapter 9, which discusses the need for stewardship (versus conventional leadership) in transforming contexts.

### Holistic Assessment and Performance Metrics

Holistic approaches to evaluation of system performance are also needed to support the emergence of T-systems. Overly narrow performance metrics cannot really address systemic issues, so holistic approaches are needed. For example, as noted, most nations still rely on GDP, as noted earlier, a measure solely of economic (paid) activity to indicate the "health" of economies. Yet the flaws in that metric have been known since its introduction. Transformation efforts and T-systems require considerably more holistic metrics because they are generally not oriented just toward monetary or economic growth. Rather, the whole purpose of transformation is generally aligned with well-being for people in a flourishing natural world, which demands more qualitative and certainly broader metrics oriented toward what I earlier discussed as *collective value*. Indeed, holistic approaches to metrics development argue from the need to think about evaluation processes and metrics as ways not just to assess progress, but also to inform learning, continual improvements, and hence ongoing changes as needed, building in ethical considerations as part of the measurement and evaluative processes.

Approaches like Blue Marble evaluation,[8] alluded to earlier, can provide an overarching framework for measurement, evaluation, and learning systems that support transformative change. Measurement and learning provide an orientation toward a *practice* of assessment or evaluation that generates a holistic assessment of how well a given experiment or implementation strategy is working.

Blue Marble evaluation is a relatively new approach to holistic assessment and evaluation metrics is the principles-based approach (Table 7.1) developed by Michael Quinn Patton[9] (see also https://bluemarbleeval.org/principles). This evaluation approach argues that "we need principles to guide us, not a rule book to tie us down." Blue Marble thinking develops three holistic and overarching principles and a set of operating principles that are highly relevant both to catalyzing transformation and to thinking about how to emerge holistic ways of assessing those changes. While these principles are explicitly directed toward people developing metrics associated with catalyzing transformation, many of them are also clearly relevant as guides to thinking about that catalytic process itself. Hence transformative change agents would be wise to keep them well in mind.

In addition, ethical considerations are particularly relevant in approach systems change because of all the stakeholders, places, and other-than-humans generally involved. One recent approach argued that four important considerations should be considered in designing evaluation. The first ethical consideration is motivation, which includes purpose definition, considerations of who benefits, and what defines success. The second consideration is power, which involves who are (or should be) making decisions, what resources are (should be) needed and taken into account, and

*Table 7.1 Blue Marble evaluation principles*

| |
|---|
| Overarching Blue Marble Evaluation Principles:<br>• Apply global thinking: Apply whole Earth, big picture thinking to all aspects of systems change.<br>• Anthropocene as context: Know and face the realities of the Anthropocene and act accordingly.<br>• Transformative engagement: Engage consistent with the magnitude, direction, and speed of transformation needed and envisioned.<br>• Integration: Integrate the overarching and operating Blue Marble principles in the design, engagement with, and evaluation of systems change and transformation initiatives. |
| Operating Principles<br>• Transboundary engagement: Act at a global scale.<br>• Glocal: Integrate interconnections across levels.<br>• Cross-silos: Connect across sectors and issues<br>• Time being of the essence: Act with a sense of urgency short-term and support resilient sustainability for the long term.<br>• Yin-Yang: Harmonize conceptual opposites.<br>• Bricolage methods: Conduct utilization-focused evaluations incorporating Blue Marble principles to match methods to the evaluation situation.<br>• World savvy: Engage in ongoing learning relevant to Blue Marble principles and practice.<br>• Skin in the game: Acknowledge and act on your stake in how the Anthropocene unfolds.<br>• Theory of transformation: Design and evaluate transformation based on an evidence-supported theory of transformation.<br>• Transformation fidelity: Ensure that what is called *transformation* constitutes transformation.<br>• Transformation alignment: Transform evaluation to evaluate transformation.<br>• Evaluation as intervention: Integrate and network evaluations to inform and energize transformation. |

*Source*: Michael Quinn Patton, https://bluemarbleeval.org/principles, and *Blue Marble Evaluation: Premises and Principles* (Guilford Publications 2019).

how are decisions outside decision-makers' control being made. A third ethical consideration is that of knowledge: who is or needs to be included as experts and with what expertise, and how should they define and ensure success. The fourth consideration is that of legitimacy, which involves determining whose interests are affected and how should the interests of people not involved in the process be taken into account, how are affected parties interests enabled and ensured (including self-determination), and, finally, what different worldviews or paradigms do people affected by the transformation hold—and how can they be reconciled with the transformation.[10]

Whatever metrics are adopted in evaluating and assessing T-system performance clearly need to go well beyond narrow economics and monetary measurements and take many different interests into account. That includes the interests of marginalized people, future generations, and unvoiced other-than-human beings. Ways to incorporate understanding of what has changed in the system and how, and whether objectives of well-being and flourishing are being achieved are needed. That probably means that multiple, not just singular, measures will be appropriate in such situations. In addition, some measures will need to focus on how well collaborative processes are working, and where improvements might be needed. Holistic approaches to assessment metrics, that is, like system change itself need to reflect the very real complexities involved.

Taking these issues into consideration in the economics realm, for example, means moving well beyond using the conventional measure of GDP (gross domestic product) to assess societal well-being. Other indicators now emerging that are more holistic, include for example, the OECD's Better Life Index, the Genuine Progress Indicator, the Gross National Happiness Index, and the Human Development Index. While none of these assessment approaches have yet supplanted GDP, they each provide a considerably broader more holistic evaluative lens on economic well-being than is provided by GDP.

### Meeting the Governance and Organizing Challenges

The same characteristics that make collaborative capacities and holistic metrics important also necessarily influence how governance occurs in a T-system. Governance is the process of overseeing the system, setting directions, and making decisions in a given institution, context, or system. Because the whole point of organizing transformation systems is to generate collective action consistent with shared agendas, governance issues need careful consideration and development. The nature of T-systems, with actors who are fundamentally independent from each other, aligned in a common purpose yet with no formal authority structure, means that such systems cannot be governed in conventional ways. Conventional governance occurs through formal rules, regulations, and mandates issued by authorities. T-systems, especially at the outset, have no such formal authorities. While the TC may serve as the convener and facilitator of connecting, cohering, and amplification processes that catalyze transformation, it otherwise is coequal with any other participants.

One important aspect of transformative capacity has to do with the reality that bringing actors together to catalyze transformation means emerging shared resources or agendas in the T-system and the system undergoing transformation, in effect, a commons. Because of that reality, and because the participants coming together typically remain independent actors, despite that they are coemerging shared agendas, action plans, and aspirations, governance might be approached through a commons governance lens. Using the managing commons approach pioneered by Elinor Ostrom[11] may be one way to achieve T-system coherence, directionality, and decision making to ensure fairness, equity, and inclusiveness. Ostrom's ideas could well inform the ways TCs and system participants approach the organizing of T-systems and their activities. Ostrom argued that managing commons involves specific ways of interacting, assessing, and governing, which are worth a brief excursion as follows.

### Ostrom's Principles for Managing Commons and Shared Values

Ostrom's principles for managing commons address how shared interests, that is, a commons, can effectively be managed, an important element of cocreating transformation capacities and T-systems. Ostrom defined such problems as occurring in situations characterized by interdependence, which we have already seen, is a characteristic of living systems and the T-systems that TCs are evolving.[12] Problems such as climate change, inequality, and political instability make clear that we humans are interdependent with each other, wherever in the world we might live. From Indigenous thinking[13] as well as quantum physics,[14] we learn equally clearly that we humans are interdependent with more-than-human beings and the natural ecological contexts in which we live, as discussed in Chapter 4.

The world, as most wisdom traditions state (and as the famous "Blue Marble" picture of the whole Earth taken from space attests), is one big system. It is characterized by connectedness and interdependence, not fragmentation and separation; there are no national boundaries or other divisions on Earth viewed from space. Cohering work and efforts in a T-system, however, means overcoming the fragmentation and divisiveness that too often appears in human socioecological institutions like nation states. Ostrom's eight principles for managing common pool resources[15], in this case the global commons, are applicable in T-systems at different scales.

Ostrom's first "design principle" for managing the commons is that clear boundary rules must exist. These boundary rules determine who is in and who is out of the system, and who can use the system's resources. At the global level, of course, that is all of us as well as other beings and nature's ecosystems. At more specific system levels, defining boundaries becomes even more important, in part because the lens(es) through which a system is viewed determine what the designated boundaries are likely to be. That definition permits identification of key stakeholders or system participants and determination of their relationships to each other, which is another a rationale for "seeing," mapping, and understanding the T-system.

Ostrom's second design principle emphasizes the "rules-in-use" in a given context. These rules determine resource usage (including when and how much to harvest), as well as how benefits from that resource are to be allocated, all of which needs to be contextually appropriate and perceived as fair. In the context of a T-system, system participants can design their own principles for working together (see next chapter). Further, such rules-in-use articulate how people want to see the system working. They can also help participants allocate scarce and shared resources, determine who has the decision-making authority, and develop evaluative criteria that help the whole system continue to learn from its activities.

The third design principle for working effectively in a commons like a T-system or the system undergoing transformation ensures that individuals affected by decisions in a "resource regime" are part of the decision process. In this case, that regime is the relevant system. Participants need to have voice and capacity to participate in developing the rules that govern it. This principle thereby tailors those rules to take active roles in different contexts, which is needed given the uniqueness of each T-system. Involvement in rule-making or voice helps ensure that people in a context or T-system understand and abide by the rules. Since they created them, they presumably learn to see those rules as fair, as a consequence of that participation.

The fourth through sixth design principles for commons governance (and here T-systems) as articulated by Ostrom are interrelated. One ensures that the people who are in a system that is to be monitored and governed select their own monitors and ensure their accountability to participants in the relevant system. This means that T-system participants need to design their own evaluation processes (e.g., consistent with the Blue Marble principles and the ethical considerations discussed earlier, or similar ones), and determine who will hold them to account. That is part of the measurement and learning process, which involves assessment, evaluation, research, and learning.

Ostrom's fifth principle defines who has the rights to use system resources and provides for graduated sanctions for misuse of those resources, depending on how problematic the misuse is (and increasing the sanctions when misuse continues). The same principles apply in T-systems and the transforming context, where Ostrom's principle six, which argues for low-cost, quick conflict resolution mechanisms that are widely known is important. This principle is another aspect of cosmopolitan-localist governance, enhancing cocreative collective value.

The last two principles Ostrom identified are the emergence and development of more effective governance over time, and the need for governance activities at different nested layers in an evolving system. These principles recognize the complexity of systems (and system change) and the fractal-like quality of different systemic aspects, much as T-system participants need to do to begin to act effectively.

### Coping With the Financing Transformation Challenge

Financing system transformation is difficult, requiring whole systems, long-term, process-oriented approaches. And since the concept of transformation systems is quite new, many funders are not yet familiar with it. Most current funders, whether governments, granting agencies, charitable institutions, or even individual funders, want to see outputs or products relatively soon. But system transformation, as must be obvious by now, is not like that. Despite its urgency, it is a long-term, complexly interlinked proposition, process-oriented, and outcomes are not readily quantifiable. Financing transformation, like T-system development itself, requires a whole systems perspective rather than a more defined programmatic approach.

Still, financing is an imperative. Financing and resourcing transformation and T-systems means ensuring that adequate resources are present for people to do the work that needs to be done, wherever they might be in the T-system. There are funders who are attempting to shift their priorities to a more systems-based understanding of systemic change. One recent study of financing transformation undertaken by Catalyst 2030 and led by Steve Waddell argues for the development of "ecosystems for financing transformation."[16] As this study indicates, the logic or intent of financing transformation goes well beyond funding businesses or even nonprofits to thinking about flourishing futures for planet and people can come about.

While typical funding sources see themselves as funding the implementers of change directly, the study suggests that there is a far more complex ecosystem that needs to emerge for financing systems change. That is because the processes associated with transformational change are more complex than project management. Among the numerous roles that are needed to develop such approaches are a "core ecosystem for financing transformation" led by a change agent—a steward for financing ecosystems or TC. The steward holds "the system" in mind, bringing together systemic perspectives and making connections among the numerous players in the ecosystem so that appropriate financing mechanisms and approaches can be codeveloped. In a sense, emerging this EFT is the same process of connecting, cohering, and amplifying impact that all T-systems go through, although this particular one is needed to begin to help finance other transformation efforts.

Lest anyone think that such an approach is unrealistic, the report identifies multiple such EFTs in development. For example, Conscious Capital focuses on high net worth individuals seeking to integrate traditional and transformational investment. Climate-KIC, the European Union's main initiative aimed at climate innovation, is another such initiative. It uses a combination of public and private partners to create expertise networks to innovate products, services, and systems aimed at mitigating climate risk.

Despite such advances, clearly there is quite a distance to go to revolutionize the financing system to support systemic change. This means that TCs and T-system participants will need to work to creatively align existing financing to support their efforts. Additionally, they need to work with funders to help expand their perspectives to encompass systemic change, and understand the rationale for its being needed.

### Emerging Innovation Capacities

The final area that Waddell uncovered in his investigation of systemic challenges is that of creating innovations that develop the infrastructure needed to support the desired future. Innovation in the T-system context means the development of new systems, ideas, norms, aspirations, collaborative efforts, and processes, as well as products and services that meet the particular goals of shared agendas. Innovations can also include the new infrastructure that helps maintain the T-system over time. That includes the development of subsystem TCs in specific contexts where they are needed, for example. It can also mean creation of dialogues, networks, conversations, and meetings among T-system participants through in-person sessions, webinars, and other means of ensuing ongoing connections and further advances as needed.

Innovations could conceivably also be in the narratives and stories that inform peoples' paradigms and mental models, as well as how people think about their system, each other, and what needs to be done to make the needed changes. Innovations could be in defining the boundaries of the system or reframing its purposes. They can be at different scales, global, national, regional or bioregional, or local, or in different contexts like different sectors. Innovations will be specific to the context (though, as can be seen, some common forms may emerge). For example, innovations evident in what has been called the *sharing economy* have shifted the concept of ownership dramatically for some people. For example, car sharing services like Zipcar make owning a car less attractive in some circumstances, and shift the focus from car ownership to on-demand transportation.

In the area of well-being economics, a group of us have identified core innovations of a well-being economic operating infrastructure, many of which represent innovations. Arenas for this infrastructure include narrative, for example, ideas about well-being economies replacing conventional economics. New types of economic governance are needed, as with the suggestion to use principles for collaborating both in T-systems and possibly in communities, and new financing mechanisms like crowdfunding, which makes for more equitable forms of financing when designed properly. Other aspects of the economic infrastructure innovations include new or reinvented types of exchange mechanisms. That can include innovative markets such as direct exchanges among customers and producers or sharing innovations, new currencies, including cryptocurrencies like Seeds or local currencies that support local communities' economies and build in principles of equity and flourishing. Additionally, more holistic metrics have been evolving in recent years, including innovations like the Global Reporting Initiative's standards for nonfinancial reporting and the Value Reporting Foundation's integration of sustainability accounting and integrated reporting. Innovations in business structures like B Corporation provide opportunities for rethinking businesses and their contributions to society and how they deal with the natural environment. Finally, products, services, and provisions produced in circular or regenerative ways can represent other aspects of economic infrastructure innovation.[17]

## Developing Transformation Infrastructure to Sustain Momentum

Transformation infrastructure or the capacities for ensuring, maintaining, and forwarding systemic change need to be built to ensure ongoing processes of connecting, cohering, and amplification of transformative change where needed. Tackling the systemic challenges discussed earlier, as well as challenges that are particular to a given context, is what effective transformation systems have to do to amplify their impact. Transformation infrastructure comes together in new ways, typically in dialogical processes, to cocreate and coevolve new action strategies geared toward shared aspirations and greater transformative impact. It is not all physical—it partly comes in the capacities that people have to collaborate, to use skills associated with connecting—seeing and sensemaking, to help others cohere and to amplify their impacts. That is where experimentation, some failures, and many successes as things begin to shift, comes in.

Just as shifting, for example, to new forms of economics requires new economic operating infrastructure, just discussed, sustaining transformational momentum over time requires putting transformational infrastructure in place. Doing so means thinking about where in the system new TCs, focused on core aspects of the change processes, might be needed to bring additional system participants and actors together to form more localized transformation systems.

Developing transformation infrastructure like this means building and developing T-system participants' capacity to sustain and further weave the activities of connecting, cohering, and amplification into the system long term. That means recognizing that system transformation is an ongoing process rather than a once-and-done event. The transformation infrastructure consists generally of the connective mechanisms like dialogues, convening structures, networks that enable the emergence and ongoing development of shared visions, values, principles, and similar aspirations and agendas. In effect, it means developing system-based TCs where needed so that *they* can continue to iterate the rest of the steps in an ongoing way for that system. It can mean widely disseminating new narratives and ensuring that there are processes in place so that people understand them. Similarly, shared values and aspirations will do little good if only a few people know about or understand them. Shared values, visions, and aspirations need to be widely and publicly disseminated to change relevant cultural mythologies, hopefully toward futures in which people and nature can both flourish.

Accomplishing these long-term processes probably means engaging a system of educating people in understanding systems (systems thinking and dynamics), understanding change processes, and understanding and evolving the roles and function of TCs and T-systems suitably to a given system. It could mean instilling knowledge about different methods and tools for mapping, stakeholder analysis, visioning, and the like in a lot of people. Once that knowledge is gained, different people can then lead TC and T-system building efforts in specific contexts, once they know which kinds of tools, for example, mapping tools, futures-oriented tools, synthesizing tools, are useful in different types of situations and contexts and can gain skills in how and when to deploy those tools. The evaluation and performance metrics are important too, that is, the measurement, evaluation, research, and learning approaches that enable synthesize and dissemination of what has been learned so that others can learn from it as well, is also an important element of transformative infrastructure. As will be elaborated in the next chapter, there are certain design principles that underlie the success of TCs work to connect, cohere, and amplify efforts of a multiplicity of initiatives in a transformation system.

The next two chapters will drill down into design guidelines and principles that can greatly enhance catalyzing transformation and then focus on the stewardship skills needed to catalyze systemic transformation.

## Takeaways From Chapter 7

- Transformation (T-) systems are the collection of initiatives, actors, and efforts oriented toward achieving similar transformational aspirations. Purposeful transformation systems are connected and cohered to amplify their transformative impact, and are organized around cocreated and collectively aligned strategies for achieving systemic change.
- Amplifying impact means developing processes to implement action plans for change, and ensuring that participants in a T-system are taking the types of actions that work on key leverage points for core systemic challenges, including: how to develop new narratives; how to cocreate needed collaboration capacities; how to develop necessary and holistic metrics that inform and enhance change; how to govern and organize the emerging new system; and how to transform financing mechanisms to support transformation.
- Tackle core systemic challenges (present in most systems), including:
  o Narrative: The narrative challenge is to reframe paradigms toward aspirations (e.g., of ecological civilizations—socially just and equitable, inclusive societies in a flourishing natural world). New visions or other types of narratives, when broadly shared, inspirational, emotionally engaging, and supported by resonant memes that can be repeated

in a variety of ways are powerful guides to transformative change.

o Collaborative capacity: Actors and initiatives in T-systems need to develop collaborative mindset and the capacities to collaborate intensively while maintaining their own agendas and aspirations. Collaborative capacities include a learning orientation, working with diversity, dealing with conflict, listening, facilitating dialogue, steering and guiding while "allowing" emergence.

o Learning and Assessment: Holistic and principles-based approaches to evaluation of system performance are needed to support the emergence of T-systems, along with incorporation of ethical considerations that take into account the interests of voiced and unvoiced stakeholders in the system undergoing change. Ongoing learning from activities is vital.

o Govern as Commons: Governance or the process of overseeing the system, setting directions, and making decisions in a given institution, context, or system needs to incorporate principles for managing commons, including the transformation system and the system that is transforming.

o Financing: Financing system transformation is difficult, requiring whole systems, long-term, process-oriented approaches and creating an ecosystem of financial institutions and mechanisms specifically geared to financing systemic change.

o Transformative change infrastructure: The development of transformation system infrastructure requires long-term attention to innovations and innovation capacities that support and maintain transformative efforts, including new systems, ideas, norms, aspirations, collaborative efforts, and processes, as well as products and services that meet the particular goals of shared agendas. These capacities ensure, forward, and maintain systemic change and ongoing processes of transformative change, where needed.

# CHAPTER 8

# Design Guidelines and Principles for *Catalyzing Transformation*

Catalyzing purposeful system transformation toward ecological civilizations and related aspirations is demanding work, because each system is unique. Each context and change initiative has its own dynamics, personalities, stakeholders, institutions, culture, resources, and settings. And they are, as noted earlier, all complexly wicked. In such circumstances, working from a "plan" that is applied to "scale up" across contexts is not feasible. Rather, change makers need to use an adaptive set of strategies based on *core shared design guidelines and principles* that help them figure out how to design what is needed for their specific context.

Because of the uniqueness of each context, transformational change works differently from planned change or scaling up, which assumes that the same things can be done similarly in different settings. Thus, while similar ends may be desired in different transformation efforts, the actual context will dictate exactly how those efforts play out, who is involved, and what they look like. As with the values for the *content* of transformational change to get to ecological civilizations that are identified in Chapter 5, there are equally important guidelines and associated principles that are quite consistent across contexts for *designing processes used by TCs in emerging purposeful transformation systems*. These guidelines and principle are the focus of this chapter.

## Designing Transformation: Getting to How

Design *guidelines* are general rules or pieces of advice that (in the case of system change) represent the most important and effective considerations for designing and stewarding successful transformation efforts. *Design* guidelines are like advice that outlines how participants in a system can think about designing interventions and activities that will work. In particular, they inform how TCs and transformation system participants manage their relationships with each other and with community members. Importantly, the system's relationship to nature within the focal system also needs consideration. That relationship cannot safely be ignored in today's context of polycrisis where so many issues arise in and for nature as a consequence of today's economic and societal activities.

Design guidelines need to support and align with a core set of associated design *principles* agreed by system participants, possibilities for some of which are outlined in this chapter. Design *principles* are basic truths and beliefs about what works best (in this case) to help change agents implement change activities and support the guidelines so that systemic change can be achieved. In the case of system change, they also need to support emergence of the TCs that work to cohere, connect, and amplify the work being done in transformation systems. System change design guidelines and principles thus provide pathways toward *strategies* for the "how" of bringing about system transformation more effectively in complexly wicked contexts. Design principles provide insights, perspectives, and understandings to help TCs and participants in T-systems know how to best move their efforts and initiatives forward successfully.

The combination of design guidelines and principles provides a solid basis for emerging a general principles-based yet context-specific approach to system change. *Design* guidelines and principles, importantly, are closely associated with *how* the transformation work itself gets done most effectively. Although ideally design guidelines and principles will be aligned with the overall system's values and the values embedded in the aspirational processes associated with visioning, they really deal with the "*how to transform a system*" question rather than the qualities of the desired system itself, which are represented by the types of *values* discussed in Chapter 4.

Of course, TCs and transformation (T-) system participants need to develop and use core *design* guidelines and principles specific to their own contexts, potentially drawing from the general ones presented in this chapter and adding their own as needed. By doing so, they can approach their work together in ways that provide sufficient consistency across initiatives, while still allowing for the inherent differences in contexts. This chapter offers a potentially useful starting point for TCs: a set of design guidelines and principles to help align actors in numerous contexts.

### Design Guidelines as Guides to Action

Why are design guidelines and principles important? I have already argued for the important role that guidelines play in helping to envision the future we want to transform toward. In thinking about how that transformation work gets done, *design* guidelines and principles act as a compass on which system participants agree that helps guide actions. Guidelines and associated principles indicate desired behaviors, actions, and practices needed for many different actors in a given system to work together connecting, cohering, and amplifying transformative impacts.

Design guidelines help participants shape coherent narratives that articulate shared aspirations, while acknowledging the potential for conflict and providing standards for coping with it when it arises. In that guiding function, design guidelines and principles serve as a kind of template that enables TCs to figure out the best ways of interacting to most effectively move the system forward. Thus, they provide insight and shared understandings about how processes, relationships, interactions, and system dynamics ought to work—and a touchstone that can be referred to over and over again when needed.

### Design Principles Provide Coherence

Design *principles* are used in all sorts of fields. For example, artists and designers often agree on core principles, including things such as balance, scale, contrast, pattern, movement, rhythm, emphasis, white space, variety, and unity when working together so that they can provide an agreed or coherent approach to their work. Similarly, engineers may agree on a set of design principles like research and analysis to determine the state of the art, ergonomics, how to effectively use Occam's Razor (the idea that the simplest explanation is usually true), to recognize independent functioning of parts of a system, and the like, to ensure that their designs have the necessary functionality, usefulness, and safety.[1]

In the field of building design, architect Christopher Alexander developed a set of principles he called *patterns* that he argued are what gives what he called the "quality without a name" (i.e., a quality of aliveness) to buildings.[2] Following similar logic, urban designer Jane Jacobs uncovered similarly useful design principles for developing vibrant cities.[3] And, of course, organizational development specialists and other change agents understand the importance of including certain design principles—which are relevant in the system transformation context as well—in how interventions around change are designed, including factors such as participation, dialogical processes, and identification of core guidelines,[4] many of which are reflected in the guidelines shared in Figure 8.1.

## Design Guidelines for System Transformation

In Figure 8.1, I discuss four overarching design guidelines that change agents should take: (1) Life-affirming approaches, (2) values-driven change processes, (3) complexity/systems-based approaches, and (4) system

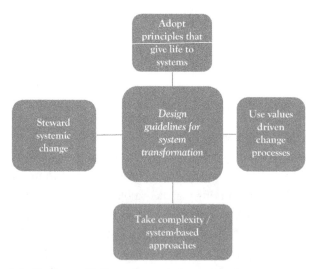

*Figure 8.1 Design guidelines for transformative change*

stewardship. The next section describes the underorganized context of systemic change, then I outline the overarching guidelines and unpack specific principles associated with each of them.

## Understanding the *Underorganized* Nature of Transformation Systems

Context matters. *Systemic* change and transformation (T-) systems emerge in *underorganized* contexts[5] and, as discussed earlier, complexly wicked socioecological contexts, where relationality and issues of process and resourcing cannot be handled sufficiently through conventional hierarchical management and leadership processes. TCs generally do not have any specific hierarchical power or particular authority, other than persuasion and shared visioning, combined with the processes of organizing, gaining commitment and buy-in, and otherwise bringing diverse actors together. This means that catalysts cannot mandate or require specific actions as a conventional "boss" or leader might do.

T-systems (and sometimes TCs as well) are actually not "organizations" in any traditional sense of the word. Instead, they are "loosely coupled"[6] sets of actors and initiatives, operating in what L. Dave Brown called *underorganized systems*.[7] In such situations, actors and initiatives retain their independence while agreeing to work collectively on a shared set of aspirations. That is the situation when TCs organize transformation (T-) systems.

T- systems resemble "collaborative interorganizational networks where three or more organizations are working together toward a common purpose."[8] Interorganizational networks, however, are characterized by "enduring *exchange* relations between organizations, individuals and groups"[9] (quoted in,[10] emphasis added), with a focus on interorganizational relations.[11] T-systems, however, are not focused on exchanges, but rather on coemerging collaborative and collective (and sometimes independent) visions, strategies, and, ultimately, *actions*. The role of the TC is to *guide* the emergence of these aspirations and actions—then, in a strange way let go of the need to control the outcome as will be discussed later.

Further, T-systems, in some contrast to interorganizational networks, are often comprised of many different types of actors, institutions, and initiatives. They work collectively *and* independently around aligned (cohered) purposes and aspirations, while continuing to engage in their regular work. The key in enhancing T-systems' ability to amplify the transformative impact of ongoing (and new) efforts is coming together around shared purposes, values, and aspirations. Finally, the T-system's transformative focus is on the *system* that is to be transformed rather than the interactions among T-system participants (although those interactions obviously cannot be ignored).

Transformational system change from this perspective is about seeing and understanding the system as a whole, not just the organizations and institutions that are in the system. In that sense, developing a self-aware and consciously acting T-system is about shifting the dynamics, interactions, and processes among system participants. When that is accomplished, T-system participants can collectively emerge a shared and coherent understanding of the system and of the need for change so that cocreated or otherwise aligned actions can be developed. The very nature of the connecting, cohering, and amplifying that TCs do with various initiatives to bring T-system participants together dictates the need for a shared set of operating principles, particularly given the generally underorganized context.

To get there, however, change agents need to use design guidelines that work in these types of underorganized contexts. Here four such guidelines are identified: adopting principles that give life to systems, using values-driven change processes, taking complexity/systems approaches, and stewarding (versus conventionally leading) systemic change.

## Adopt Principles That Support Life

Because socioecological systems undergoing transformation are living systems, it is vitally important to adopt principles that support life. In other words, supporting transformative change needs to be oriented toward principles that give life to and enhance the life-giving properties of systems,[12] as opposed to wealth-centered, materialistic, or other possible values. Toward that end, three of the core principles that "give life" to socioecological systems, discussed earlier, are emphasized here[13] (others are discussed under the taking complexity/systems approaches guideline): identifying clear and aspirational purposes or intentionality, recognizing permeable boundaries, and acknowledging systemic dynamism that gives rise to novelty.

*Design Clear, Life-Affirming Purposes and Intentions:* The first life-affirming principle is purpose or intentionality. Change makers need to recognize that all living (and some supposedly inorganic) systems have *intentionality or purpose*, even if that purpose is merely to stay alive or procreate. T-systems and TCs have to (co-)identify aspirations for a given context or system that help define or frame its purposes and give overall definition to the system, as they (and other stakeholders) see it. The understanding of a given system's purposes or intentions then guides the actions and focus of TCs. It provides a focus to help bring together actors in the transformation system around that purpose or shared aspirations with respect to how the system will change. As argued in Chapter 4, purposes in the latter context for many transformations focus around emerging socially just, equitable, inclusive ecological civilizations.

In a very real way, purpose is what is *done*, not just what is stated as a desired outcome.* So it is important to keep track of how the system is actually functioning—and whether it is achieving desired goals—and change course if necessary. As an example of the latter point, healthy natural systems renew, replenish, diversify, and restore themselves to stay resilient—in other words, they evolve. Similarly, transformational efforts need to understand and acknowledge explicitly the purpose(s) of the system to be transformed, framing those purposes in life-affirming ways, recognizing, acknowledging, and supporting core purposes—and change when necessary.

*Recognize the Permeability of System Boundaries:* Boundedness here means that like all living systems, socioeconomic systems undergoing change have *permeable or porous boundaries*. Boundaries, as discussed earlier, are important because they, first, help catalysts and participants define the system of interest. For example, a given system might be defined as economic, geographic, social, sector-based, or in other ways that give shape, meaning, and clarity to the *what* that is to be transformed. Second, permeability means that the boundaries of the system are open or porous.

---

* Thanks to Ian Kendrick formerly of the Bounce Beyond team for this insight.

Porosity allows the system to take in new energy and dispose of waste as necessary to survive and, ultimately, thrive. Some new actors and initiatives will enter into the system as it evolves—and others will exit. That is part of the cycle of living beings. Defining a system's boundaries thus is an important part of understanding and specifying the context of interest, including its purpose(s). Knowing the boundaries provides guidance for what needs to be done, who needs to be brought in at what time, and what needs to be let go when it is no longer fit for purpose. Obviously, figuring that out is a balancing act that will be context specific—and most likely a skill learned over time.

*Emerge Dynamism and Novelty as Needed*: Boundaries being porous means that living socioeconomic systems undergoing transformation are dynamic and in constant flux. Things never stay the same for very long, if at all. Even though living systems' boundaries are permeable or porous, however, they provide sufficient constraints that purposes or intentionality can be defined. For the system to evolve toward its transformational aspirations, new ideas, processes, policies, resources, and even changed purposes will need to be introduced. In the context of an emerging T-system, and in accord with any living system's need for *novelty* (something new at times to refresh the system), it means that some new actors, change agents, and initiatives will enter the system as new demands and activities develop. As with many living systems, this novelty introduces diversity—and most likely enhanced complexity if the system remains healthy. Also, over time, some ideas will be left behind, and some actors and initiatives will leave when their efforts are no longer needed or wanted. In the context of a transforming system, understanding and defining the boundaries, recognizing constant change dynamics, and introducing novelty that enhances systemic diversity (and hence resilience) a basis for emerging a healthy living system.

## Use Values-Driven Change Processes

The second design guideline is that transformation processes need to be *values-driven*. Values, particularly shared values, are important mostly because they define what is important or considered worthy of attention in a given context. Values, when jointly agreed, are one of the elements that help connect and cohere actors in a T-system. Like visions, values can provide a kind of "glue" that can integrate people coming from different perspectives into shared aspirations and actions. Aspirational values affect the content of the transformation process—the *what* of transformative change as discussed in Chapter 4. Here the focus is on *how* to use values-driven change processes to generate the relationality, engagement, and shared aspirations needed to connect and cohere diverse actors in a T-system.

Values-driven change processes explicitly articulate what is important as a way of engaging potential partners and participants. That is important because values are also linked to emotion or affect. Because of that link, values-driven change processes help to motivate action by articulating or referencing desired aspirations and outcomes, transcending the particular circumstances to something more generally shared. In addition, values serve as standards and criteria for evaluation of a situation or action, and can be ordered by their importance, which also guides action.[14] Further, values can be distinguished by their content, that is, the motivation or goal expressed.[15]

Chapter 4 discussed a key set of values associated with the *aspirations* for what the transformed system will look like as envisioned by many TCs and T-system participants. That orientation is what I earlier summarized as ecological civilization, or just, equitable, inclusive, and flourishing societies in a flourishing natural world. The rest of this section focuses on the principles associated with *how TCs and transformation (T-) systems can be designed to operate most effectively.* An integrated set of *values-driven change processes* for designing effective transformation interventions is needed in a system. Three principles summarize a rather vast set of these processes: (1) inclusive participation, (2) equitable collaboration, and (3) cocreative engagement.

### Create Conditions of Inclusive Participation

Most strategies and approaches for working toward large system change, for example, Appreciative Inquiry,[16] Theory U,[17] or Future Search,[18] emphasize the importance of *inclusive participation* and equitable collaboration (see next) in designing the T-system and implementing its activities. Creating conditions for inclusive participation means that active participants are broadly representative of what the whole system looks like. It also means they are enabled to actively participate in planning for changes within their own context. In other words, participants are assumed to have agency of their own and the internal and system-based resources to participate in ways that are appropriate to both their context and their own needs and capacities.

Inclusive participation recognizes that it is important to emphasize and draw from the strengths (rather than deficiencies) of actors in a system in interactions with other participants. This principle assumes, as the idea of positive deviance[19] argues, that the resources needed to change the system are already there in the system and that people in the system are intelligent, capable, and have knowledge and agency to act in their own best interests. These resources exist as strengths that can be tapped and need to be part of any decision making or changes that affect the system—and that is what the connecting and cohering processes work toward. Inclusive participation means that system participants themselves design their future rather than having it somehow imposed from "without." Following this principle, then T-systems need to be inclusive of the variety of stakeholders in the system. As Senge put it, they need to "get the system into the room"[20] where changes are being discussed. If key stakeholder groups are left out or not represented, then they could readily derail the transformation efforts once they are underway, because their voices have not been heard.[21]

### Generate Equitable Collaboration

The need to generate *equitable collaboration* as a design principle follows directly from the nature of transformation (T-) systems discussed at the outset of this section and from the principle of inclusive participation just discussed. Although some initiatives and efforts in a T-system may be competitive in some parts of their world (around funding, for example), it is important that they engage *collaboratively* and cocreatively (versus competitively) in the T-system.

While there are many possible definitions of collaboration,[22] one comprehensive definition is:

> Collaboration is a process in which autonomous or semiautonomous actors interact through formal and informal negotiation, jointly creating rules and structures governing their relationships and ways to act or decide on the issues that brought them together; it is a process involving shared norms and mutually beneficial interactions.[23]

That latter point speaks of inclusion and active engagement in T-system activities being particularly sensitive to traditionally marginalized or underrepresented groups and stakeholders. It also refers to maintaining *equitable* decision making, collaboration, and input processes for any given actor. Equitability ensures that the input of all actors is comparable to that of any other actors in the system, even when those actors are less powerful or resource rich. *Equitable collaboration* means including and really *hearing* people whose voice might not otherwise be heard. And it also means ensuring that their voices are *heard equitably*. In other words, status differences need to be carefully considered in meetings, planning sessions, and organized activities, and eliminated as much as possible.

Ensuring equitable collaboration may not be easy given very real status differences. Yet it is very important to ensuring that everyone feels part of the system, has sufficient input that their ideas are seriously considered, and that the efforts are truly collaborative rather than imposed by more powerful actors. The key here is to take a general orientation that every voice is equally important and equally deserves to be heard (in many respects following principles associated with numerous Indigenous peoples). This principle is integrally related to the next one: cocreative engagement.

### Engage CoCreatively

*Cocreative engagement* is part of the collaborative processes described in the previous section. It includes the recognition that actors in T-systems remain autonomous. Yet they need to jointly—or *cocreatively*—develop how their relationships, plans, and joint or collaborative activities evolve. In other words, "solutions" cannot be imposed on the whole by any one party (including the TC). Instead, they need to be codeveloped by and emerge from the interactive engagement of actors in the T-system. Cocreation is often understood as interactive engagement between businesses and their customers in which the customers produce some of the company's product (i.e., solar panels on a customer's roof contributing to the power supply of an elective company).[24]

In the context of T-system development, cocreativity is used not in its marketing, open source, or business sense. Rather it means actors engaging together to jointly understand and map the system of interest, make sense of it together, and mutually plan actions and activities for its transformation toward desired ends. In doing that, they are cocreating and emerging something new that it is very likely that none of them could have created alone. In other words, designing system transformation requires that actors come together in new ways, share their ideas, inputs, sometimes resources, and efforts to produce something novel that would not otherwise be possible. Such efforts can be compared to the music created jointly by a jazz band or at a jam session, which would not be possible without all of the musicians coming together to collectively and jointly cocreate that moment of music. Notably, in these settings, all players are equally needed and important. The same principle applies in developing T-systems.

Thus, participants in T-systems need to intentionally develop what has been called a collaborative mindset,[25] which allows for something new and unexpected to emerge from their mutual engagement. This means that "plans" cannot be set in advance by one person, group, or initiative, but rather (as discussed in the complexity section next), actually (need to) *emerge* from the interactions and engagement with others. Neither TCs nor the T-systems they are developing can be top-down leader driven, since there is no formal hierarchical structure. Indeed, as noted, it is the set of shared aspirations or other narratives that provides the "glue" that holds actors together in the T-system context. There may well be better- or worse-resourced initiatives and actors, as well as people with more or less dominant personalities and status, or other important differences. Here is where the principle of cocreative engagement, recognizing the reality that all exist in the same system with the same "voice," is vital.

## Take Complexity/Systems-Based Approaches

Taking a *complexity or systems-based approach to transformation* is also important because of the nature of socioecological systems of all sorts— underorganized, complex, and fraught with wicked problems. A complexity/systems approach acknowledges multiple facets of systemic complexity that need to be considered when designing transformational efforts: adopt holistic system perspectives; interconnected relationality; multilevel, -spatial, -strategy, -stakeholder diversity; and evolutionary self-organization.

### Adopt Holistic System Perspectives

Basically, the *holistic system perspectives* principle means understanding that systems are whole entities with their own integrity as those wholes. Given that reality, systems undergoing transformation have to be approached and transformed holistically, not just by breaking them into their subcomponents. Most conventional change efforts take a more atomistic approach that picks one or two aspects of a system, for example, policies, institutional structure, or reward systems, then work on those single components one by one. Then they later attempt to put the system back together into the whole. Such an approach, which is quite typical particularly in the industrialized "developed" world, assumes that fragmentation of a system into its parts or components is the way to approach problems. It assumes, in essence, that there is a bandage or plaster that can be placed on the system's wounds that will heal all the ills. System transformation does not work that way, because systems are wholes with integrity of their own that need to be taken into consideration in all change initiatives.

As psychiatrist and thought leader Iain McGilchrist argues in his pathbreaking books *The Master and His Emissary* and *The Matter with Things*,[26] the more analytical fragmentation approach just described is a very "left-brained" approach. Left-brained thinking, according to McGilchrist, now dominates developed Western parts of the world, to their detriment. Instead, McGilchrist argues that a more "right-brained" approach" is what is needed. Right-brained thinking, which he terms "master," has a holistic, process-oriented, creative understanding of the complexity of the real world and its systems. Indeed, McGilchrist amasses a huge body of evidence to make his point that a more holistic approach is needed to both understand and cope with today's many complex issues and crises.

Right-brained, holistic, process-oriented approaches are vital in the case of system transformation. Living systems need to be viewed with the holistic, process- and flow-oriented understanding of the right brain. McGilchrist's arguments applied to system change mean that an understanding of living systems as complex adaptive systems fraught with wicked problems—complexly wicked systems—is essential to any possibility of effective transformative change. System transformation, by its very name, is a whole systems approach that demands understanding social, human, ecological, political, and economic systems (what can be called socioecological systems for short) holistically—as whole and living systems. Thus, holistic (right-brain dominant) understandings and system change approaches that tackle multiple aspects of a system are needed because socioecological systems are complex adaptive systems,[27] with numerous highly complex, dynamic, and interrelated wicked problems[28] that intersect with that complexity.

Approaching transformative change through a complexity-based systems lens means thinking about the *whole system*, ensuring changes are contextually appropriate. Take too much away and ultimately, they die. Removing many pieces of a living system means it no longer has what architect Christopher Alexander called *the quality without a name*— aliveness,[29] discussed earlier.

### Recognize Interconnected Relationality and Contextual Uniqueness

Taking the complexly wicked systems approach seriously means recognizing that living (socioecological) systems are based in *relationships*. Indeed, they are based in *interconnected relational dynamism*. As noted earlier, many disciplines of modern science, from biology, to ecology, to physics, now recognize interconnectedness and this uniqueness as describing the reality of the world, when that world is viewed from the holistic, process-oriented, and more realistic "right-brain" perspective that is appropriately balanced with the more analytical thinking of the left brain (which tends to dominate today's modern societies).[30] Indeed, it is that connectedness, which is based in a sense of relationality among all different parts (or "holons"—whole/parts)[31] of the system, that constitutes an entity as a system. Many Indigenous cultures integrally recognize this relatedness and the responsibilities and need for reciprocity (symbiosis and mutual cultural evolution[32]) that goes with it.[33]

Indeed, the Native American first peoples, the Lakota, have a saying that reflects this understanding: *Mitákuye Oyás'iŋ*, which means "all are related" or "all are my relations." That "all" in their understanding includes not just other people, but other-than-human beings, that is, animals, plants, and the very land itself. Building in this sense of interconnectedness and relationality to transformation efforts and maintaining awareness of it is an important element of thinking holistically—and of becoming more aware of other possible "voices" even when they are unheard.[34] In Africa, a similar principle of *Ubuntu*, "I am because you are," reflects the same sense of interdependency and interconnectedness among people.[35] The Haudenosaunee peoples of North America have a related principle that takes future generations into account: all decisions should be made keeping seven future generations in mind.[36] Imagine transformation efforts keeping this core principle in mind for each system that they worked with!

### *Acknowledge Multilevel, -Spatial, -Stakeholder, and -Strategy Diversity*

The system characteristics and principles just discussed, particularly the aspect of contextual uniqueness, mean that recognizing the nature of the system in all of its complexity is central to transformation. It also means recognizing that each such interconnected context is unique because it has different stakeholders, resources, geographies, issues, and so on, which means that there is no one-size-fits-all approach to system transformation.

That recognition requires that change agents take *multilevel, multispatial, multistrategy, and multistakeholder approaches.* Socioecological systems, or for that matter any living systems, especially when they are healthy, are characterized by diversity[37]—at least sufficient or "requisite" diversity.[38] Socioecological systems are also multispatial in that there are different geographical or institutional contexts where change need to occur, each of which is unique. They also are multistakeholders in that there are numerous different stakeholders with differing perspectives, "stakes," opportunities, deficits, and resources whose interests are at play and need, at least to some extent, to be aligned.

Relatedly, healthy or thriving ecological (and transformation) systems necessarily incorporate sufficient *diversity*, which arises out of the introduction of new things (novelty) discussed earlier. That novelty reflects nature's propensity in flourishing systems to generate not scarcity but rather abundance.[39] The complexity of transformative change manifests itself in a diversity and variety of types of initiatives, contexts, locations, and stakeholders, as well as the strategies and processes different stakeholders will use to achieve results. As introduced earlier, living systems are multilevel in that there are nested layers of what Koestler called *holons*—whole/parts typically where whole/parts are nested within larger more expansive "wholes." Consider, for example, that families are "wholes" on their own, but also "parts" of whole communities, which themselves are "parts" of larger entities like states or provinces (and so on).

Because these differences are naturally present in any socioecological system, it is important to recognize that there will be no "one best way" or simple solution proposed or pathway forward. The nature of complex wickedness is that different stakeholders will bring different perspectives to bear on proposed problem definitions, ideas about pathways forward, and possible solutions. That is why a stewardship or process orientation, discussed in the next section, rather than top-down leadership is important.

The key to effectiveness is finding ways to come to *sufficient* (requisite) agreement on proposed strategies and actions that some can be collectively engaged, while others are implemented by individual actors—aligned with the overall or overarching set of goals that have been agreed. The multiple ("multi-") aspects of systems and T-systems means that there is unlikely to be any "central" authority—governance, action strategies, and leadership activities discussed as stewardship in the following and, in detail, in the next chapter. Leadership/stewarding activities will come from many different sources in the form of what has been called *polycentric* (multifaceted or multi-actor) *governance*[40] and operates from local to global levels through values of cosmopolitan localism.

### Encourage Evolutionary Self-Organization

Because they are living entities, socioecological systems have the potential for *evolutionary self-organization* and also sudden state changes or tipping points that can create collapse. In such systems, finding key leverage points for change is important to bring about the state change needed. Living systems (and, indeed, all systems) are never stable. They are constantly changing, evolving, or devolving. Newtonian physics, second law of thermodynamics states that energy in a system merely changes from one state to another. Actually, healthy *living* systems continually change, often as noted in a direction that generates greater diversity and abundance, which is itself a sign of a healthy system.[41] Similarly, organizing T-systems is an emergent—and inherently unpredictable—process largely because of the cocreative energy that is needed to make it happen.

All living systems evolve and change over time, and recognizing that reality allows for greater acceptance of change, in what biologists say is an epigenetic process in which both genes and the environment influence the evolutionary path.[42] Something similar is going on when actors in a system interact with each other—they are constantly influencing each other while at the same time retaining an ability to maintain their own core set of purposes and agendas, which could also begin to shift because of the interaction.[43] That means nurturing an ability to steward what is needed in the face of ongoing uncertainty. The skills and capacities needed to do just that are what we discuss in the next section: stewarding systems.

Living systems (and some that are considered inorganic as well) can undergo a process called *autopoiesis*, that is, self-creation or self-organization.[44] Autopoiesis is the process in a living system that allow it to maintain and renew itself in an emergent way. Acknowledging this process of self-organization, particularly in the context of T-system organizing, means that no one will have "control" over how things evolve or their outcomes, because those processes will be dependent on who acts, where, when, and how. The implications of these attributes of complexity are further elaborated in ideas about system stewardship and its principles in the next section and, with their implications for leadership in transformation in the next chapter.

## Steward Systemic Change

The final design guideline to be discussed is that of *stewarding systems*. Stewarding a system means taking not a leadership but rather a stewardship approach to designing transformation interventions and T-systems. Taken together the first two design guidelines and associated principles establish the values-driven change processes and complexity-based context for achieving transformative change and a related leadership approach (stewardship). The system stewardship design guideline and its associated principles acknowledges the highly fragmented, largely independent, and initially unconnected initiatives that come together in new relationships (while largely remaining independent) to form T-systems.

The whole point of the connecting, cohering, and amplification processes that TCs undertake is to bring these actors/system participants into greater alignment for transformative action. Doing that requires taking a *system stewardship* role to ensure that key capabilities and capacities are developed among and within system participants. The specifics of "leading" in a context of system stewardship are fully explored in Chapter 9. Here the focus is on how stewardship plays out in the designing of transformational efforts and activities.

Building on the complexly wicked system qualities already discussed, particularly qualities of emergence and self-organization, speaks to why the idea of systems *stewardship* is a central core guideline for system transformation. The very idea of stewardship has at its core the notion of caretaking for something that is not necessarily "owned" by the steward. It means, that is, taking responsibility for caring something that belongs to others. In the case of systems change, that "something" is the whole system with its purposes and own dynamics. TCs cannot in any sense "own" the transformation (T-) system they are attempting to help emerge, though their efforts can help bring it and its potential actions into being. But they can care for it and its emergence.

With respect to system transformation, the interconnected and interdependent "others" whose efforts are being stewarded are the initiatives that constitute the change agents in a given context and make up the T-system. The objectives of the system being transformed could involve helping other humans and their initiatives and institutions, including marginalized groups. Or they could involve other-than-humans, including animals, plants, and ecosystems, or even future generations. Here it is important to recognize once again that change agents too are part of the system and will themselves inevitably change, because they evolve right along with the system.

Caretaking or stewardship also means recognizing the importance of the driving aspirational values that help cohere different actors and allow them to make sense (sensemaking) of their activities. Connecting and cohering help ensure aspirational goals and values are widely shared and agreed, and consistent with the aspirations for the specifics of the system undergoing transformation. Stewardship in the context of transformative change involves considering the following core principles: structuring, stewarding, and resourcing relationships, processes, and practices; guiding, enabling, experimenting, and adapting; developing reflective awareness around action as well as communicative advocacy, learning, knowing, and doing.

## Structure, Steward, and Resource Relationships and Supportive Processes

Transformation efforts are all about *structuring, stewarding, and resourcing relationships* and processes that support those ongoing relationships. Since actors in a T-system are both interdependent and independent simultaneously, they will take some actions on their own, some with others in agreement, and some as a result of previous interactions that no one could have predicted. It is this emergent quality, a process or journey not a specific goal or outcome, that results from the interactions among stakeholders, contexts, and strategies. Because the situations, places, dynamics, and individuals involved are unique to each context, working to emerge T-systems is both difficult and rewarding. Something entirely new can emerge unexpectedly, creating what in complexity theory is known as a *state change* when people with different ideas, approaches, and insights come together. (Of course, collapse is also a possibility here when things do not go well.)

The key to stewarding systems is recognizing that system change is about building, maintaining, and fostering relationships—interrelatedness, and mutually agreed agendas, actions, and strategies—so that these unique connections and inspirations can be found. It is also about recognizing and helping to build needed capacities and resources within the system. This means helping participants find sufficient and innovative ways to codevelop and emerge those capacities within themselves without necessarily having to rely on others for the skills, attributes, and resources needed.

### Guide, Enable, Experiment, and Adapt as Needed

The emergent, self-organizing and independent-interdependent nature of transformation (T-) systems means that they are not really amenable to the kinds of activities typically thought of as leadership: planning, controlling, and directing. *How* the process of stewardship described takes place is through *guiding, experimenting, enabling, and adapting* with others to act in aligned and coherent ways. In other words, by helping others make sense together of what they are trying to do and how to do it, but not necessarily by being the entity that does the changes.

Guiding, experimentation, adaptive, enabling processes depend on T-system actors having or developing the shared narrative—a shared set of aspirations, visions, common agendas, somehow cogenerated and codefined discussed at length earlier. A shared narrative allows each participant to take both collective and individual strategies, agendas, and implementation actions. When the guidance provided by the narrative is strong and actions are aligned with it, that narrative becomes the glue that allows the T-system to cohere and, ultimately, amplify its transformative impact.

These transformative actions, however, cannot be set in stone or articulated in rigid plans that must be followed. Rather given the complexly wicked nature of transformative change, they need to be thought of as adaptive strategies and shared aspirations that allow for experimentation, try-outs, or "seeds" of change being planted. That is where experimentation and adaptation comes in. Participants can learn from those experiments, figure out what works and what does not. With that learning they can make changes when things do not work out as hoped. The key to success here is figuring out the underlying *principles* of the implemented actions that made for success or generated failure. Then it means taking those learnings, and figuring out what is reasonable to apply in other contexts—and continuing that type of learning process iteratively. Thus, the combined processes of guiding the emergence of transformative aspirations, enabling participants to figure out what the best pathways forward individually and collectively are.

### Generate Self- and System-Awareness

The whole process of guiding, enabling, experimenting, and learning is why the principle of *action-oriented self- and system-awareness* is needed. The work of connecting and cohering actors in T-systems demands that people in initiatives working as TCs maintain (or develop) both self- and system-awareness. Simultaneously, it means attempting to foster awareness of the T-system *as* a system among its participating members so that effective actions can be taken and amplified. As introduced in Chapter 4, humans, unlike most other beings that we know of, have self-awareness or consciousness with attendant reflective capacities that need to be nurtured and fostered as part of system transformation. Part of what gives life to systems is that very awareness or *reflective consciousness*, here called *self- and system-awareness*.

Awareness is the capacity of humans to be aware of how the system itself is emerging or changing, the interdependencies that exists among its elements. That awareness means that improvements can be made when problems arise. Importantly, it means people can reflect on their own and others' positive and not-so-positive roles in making those changes happen. Mistakes will be made. Self-awareness and reflective capacity provide the capacity for acknowledging both what is working—and what is not. Self-awareness provides for making changes accordingly, including how individuals in interaction need to shift, how group dynamics might need to change, and how the system as a whole is and needs to transform. All of that is part of recognizing that T-systems and the socioecological systems they work with are living systems, as are change efforts themselves. They are dynamic, living, growing, and evolving entities with self-reflective capacities because people are involved.

What these principles mean in practice is that part of the work of the TC is to help the T-system to become aware of itself as a whole, connected entity working in aligned ways (cohered) toward shared (yet still independent) aspirations. In other words, the T-system needs to become aware of possibilities, and to make whatever adjustments are needed so that its full potential can be realized. To accomplish that means bringing in a wide array of diverse perspectives to ensure that the whole system is represented in some way while acknowledging the well-being of the "whole." It also means ensuring that key participants in the change activities have the requisite level of self-, other-, and system awareness to be reflective, learn, and change when necessary. Figure 8.2 synthesizes the design guidelines and associated design principles discussed here.

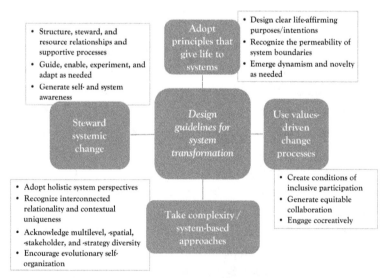

*Figure 8.2 Design guidelines with principles for transformative change*

## An Ongoing Process of Change

As this chapter makes clear, systems level TCs need to take up the challenge of continually adapting to the T-systems, values-based, holistic, changing, and evolutionary dynamics using a process of stewardship that supports all the various actors to achieve their own ends simultaneously with agreed collective aspirations. The design guidelines and associated principles discussed provide an initial framework on which potential success rests. But of course, each system also needs to discover what is unique to it and how it operates.

The reality is that active system participants and change agents come and go, patterns of interaction and engagement change, and conflicts do occur. Particularly as T-system infrastructure is established and needed capacities within the transformation (T-) system are built, the system itself changes, including its boundaries, experiments, and activities that become redefined in an evolutionary way.

That is why there is a need for ongoing catalytic function *within* the T-system to ensure that its efforts to continually evolve understanding of the system, changes needed, transformative impact, and who relevant actors are at different moments of time matters. Understanding these design guidelines and principles, T-system participants can form their own, (sub-)system specific TCs in different sectors, geographies, or issues—or at different levels of scale as appropriate. Subsystem TCs can then continually work to understand and, when needed, shift what is happening in the system accordingly within their own contexts.

Even though there can be long periods of relative stability in the type of adaptive transformation cycle that Holling calls *panarchy* in which systems go through cycles of conservation, release, exploitation, and reorganization,[45] living systems have these characteristics of constant change and evolution. As noted, when healthy, living systems tend to evolve toward greater complexity, connectedness, and diversity[46]—or potentiality that Holling calls *wealth*,[47] which can be thought of well-being and flourishing. That, in the end, of course, is the goal of system transformation. How individual change agents in positions of leadership, more accurately stewardship, do that is the subject of the next chapter.

# Takeaways From Chapter 8

- Design guidelines (as used here) frame how system can successfully design transformation interventions and actions. They serve as a compass to orient change agents how to act and interact most effectively in the context of systemic change, and how processes, relationships, interactions, and system dynamics ought to work.
- Design principles (as used here) are basic truths or beliefs about what works best to help change agents achieve effective systemic transformation.
- Adopt principles that give life to systems:
  o Design clear, life-affirming purposes and intentions;
  o Recognize the permeability of system boundaries and the need for constant change;
  o Emerge dynamism and novelty as needed.
- Use values-driven change processes that:
  o Create conditions of inclusive participation;
  o Generate equitable collaboration;
  o Enable participants to engage cocreatively.
- Take complexity/systems-based approaches:
  o Adopt holistic system perspectives;
  o Recognize interconnected relationality and contextual uniqueness;
  o Acknowledge multilevel, multispatial, multistakeholder, and multistrategy diversity;
  o Encourage evolutionary self-organization.
- Steward systemic change:
  o Structure, steward, and resource relationships and supportive processes;
  o Guide, enable, experiment, and adapt as needed;
  o Generate self- and system-awareness.

# CHAPTER 9

# Stewarding and Catalyzing Systemic Change

Stewarding transformational change efforts, particularly through the work of TCs and transformation (T-) systems, is not the same as leading in conventional organizations. Considerably different skills are needed, because the hierarchical—or even network—structure of conventional organizations can be lacking in underorganized TCs and T-systems. T-systems are generally organized in loosely coupled rather than tightly coupled[1] or hierarchical ways, meaning that actors, initiatives, and efforts stay largely independent even while becoming more connected. "Leading" in these types of contexts is a *stewardship* function rather than a conventional leadership one.[2] Further, stewards in these contexts can come from anywhere in the system, sometimes functioning or acting without any specific authority to lead. Their efforts may come to the fore by virtue of their insights, abilities, or ideas, or their capacity to influence others mostly through informal channels.

Contextually (and conceptually), T-systems consist of many different, largely independent initiatives and institutions with their own agendas and sets of activities that are trying to cohere and align their efforts in new ways. Most of those activities probably never have been attempted before. TCs' members and participants in T-systems have to figure out what will help initiatives in such "underorganized" contexts align. That requires quite an array of collaborative and other types of stewardship skills, including the ones needed for coping with the VUCA (volatile, uncertain, complex, ambiguous) and BANI (brittle, anxious, nonlinear, incomprehensible) characteristics of today's world. Because initiatives in T-systems overlap around transformational efforts, however, that means that they likely already share values and aspirations that can potentially help them codefine shared transformation agendas.

Further, while there may be people who assume more prominence than others during transformation activities, no one individual is likely to have all the requisite skills for doing the array of activities involved to connect, cohere, and amplify T-systems' work. Thus, stewardship is likely to be shared and distributed among many system participants. Different people will step into different roles as needs and opportunities arise through what has been called heterarchy[3] or leaderfulness.[4] Heterarchy and leaderfulness mean that leadership—here, stewardship—exists throughout a system, arising emergently where it is needed. Stewardship can be initiated by anyone depending on when it is needed in a given context and circumstances. Stewardship is (or needs to be) "distributed" in such transformation contexts.

This idea of distributed stewardship is particularly relevant in TCs and T-systems, because of their loose structures, informal if any hierarchies, and orientation toward cocreation and emergence. T-systems exist in a context that is underorganized,[5] which catalysts are attempting to give some shape to. Still, initiatives and actors will likely remain somewhat independent in their activities and actions even when they are willing to connect, cohere, and amplify their transformative impacts collectively. Whoever assumes stewardship in such contexts may well fluctuate depending on the particular context, issues, and needs in a given time and space. Letting that emergent process happen is not so easy for many people. And it also means that people with important skills and capacities need to be in place in key parts of the T-system—and certainly in TCs.

As a result of these factors, catalysts for system transformation need to be stewards or caretakers of the system as a whole (at all the levels—the TC, the transformation system, and the system itself)—and wise stewards at that. Change stewards are (whatever their age) in a very real sense wise elders who integrate three key capacities: awareness or moral imagination, systems understanding, and aesthetic sensibility in the interests of purposes beyond self-interest and for the greater good[6] of the system. They then apply these capacities or sensibilities to their catalytic activities of connecting, cohering, and amplifying the work of transformation agents in the system—in the interests of achieving their aspirations through coemerging an effective and purposeful transformation system. The rest of this chapter will explore how that stewarding work gets done.

## Wisdom Needed for Stewarding Transformation

As just noted, catalyzing transformation requires wisdom. In earlier writings, I defined wisdom as "the capacity to integrate three capabilities—moral imagination (the good), systems understanding (the true), and aesthetic sensibility (the beautiful) into (future-oriented) actions and decisions focused on the greater good."[7] In the following, each of these three capacities is briefly discussed. In other words, wisdom involves a mix of three core personal attributes or capacities—awareness, particularly of ethical issues, the capacity to think about and understand systems holistically, and a sense of beauty that integrate purpose beyond the self and for the system[8] (see Figure 9.1). The following sections briefly discuss these capacities and capabilities—essential for the wise elder stewarding transformative change.

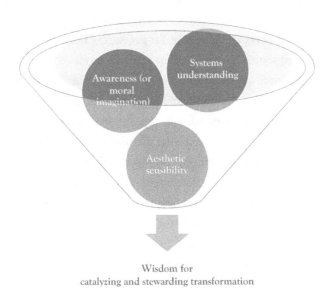

Wisdom for
catalyzing and stewarding transformation

*Figure 9.1 Wisdom for catalyzing and stewarding transformation*

### Awareness (or Moral Imagination)

Wisdom demands awareness of and attention to the ethical issues inherent in efforts to change a system—or what is sometimes called *moral imagination* (or "the good").[9] Moral imagination relates directly to the capacity for "seeing" and understanding a system, which demands both self- and system-awareness, which in turn is closely associated with reflective practices of various kinds. Systems thinking demands what the adult development literature calls postconventional ways of reasoning, cognitively, morally,[10] and emotionally[11] that allow for the understanding of multiple paradigms simultaneously and the capacity to think systemically—across boundaries and borders of all sorts. It is clearly a "beyond the self" orientation that allows awareness to expand to the greater good of the whole—in the case of TCs—of the whole system of interest. It also explicitly involves awareness of and capacity to see the ethical or moral issues that are deeply embedded in a context, especially with respect to systems change.[12]

One recent comprehensive review of links between internal and external change by Wamsler and colleagues (i.e., of change agents and their transformation efforts) identified numerous capacities associated with awareness: presence, attentiveness, self-awareness, and self-reflection.[13] Five sets of attributes are important for generating transformative capacities according to this review and they arguably result in the capacity for moral imagination: awareness, connection, insight, purpose, and agency.[14]

Awareness includes the ability to be mentally and psychologically flexible, to think in big pictures (that is, right-brained, holistic, process-oriented ways of thinking and perceiving the world[15]) or what Wamsler and colleagues labeled metacognition, emotional processing, and regulation, and qualities of equanimity, discernment, and openness, among others.[16] Added to these, are attributes associated with emotional intelligence (EQ) or the ability to manage your own emotions and understand the emotions and perspectives of other people.[17]

Connection involves the capacity for compassion, empathy, kindness, and generosity. This capacity is closely tied to the idea of stewardship of the whole system, as it links to integrating humans into nature, emerging strong ethics, and being humble.[18] Insight is related to what

adult development theorists call postconventional stages of development,[19] which involves a capacity for "seeing" broader systems. Creating a sense of purpose involves developing and articulating values and
purpose, as well as taking a future orientation,[20] which we have already
seen to be essential in shaping transformative action. Agency involves the
capacity for taking (effective) action, cocreating meaning, and doing so
inspirationally—with optimism, courage, and hope.[21] Stewarding transformation wisely, however, also requires ways of thinking and conceptualizing that go beyond these personal abilities to build capabilities for
thinking in systems.

### Systems Understanding

Systems understanding is a way of "seeing" that involves understanding
the complexity of the whole system and being able to view the system as
a whole rather than in its fragmented parts or entities (the "true"). That
means understanding, for example, a T-system through a complexity or
systems thinking lens, that is, using what McGilchrist points out in great
detail is holistic, right-brained ways of thinking. While no one can ever
fully understand the complex wickedness of human socioecological systems undergoing transformation, systems understanding, the capacity to
understand systems and their dynamics,[22] is vital to determining where
key leverage points for transformation might be, how different actors
might and do interact, and where to push forward—and hold back—on
transformative actions. It also means recognizing when more analytical
approaches associated with left-brained ways thinking are valuable, particularly when engaging mapping processes requiring technical detail,
input, and analysis.[23] Holistic systems understanding helps stewards in
different capacities to understand who needs to come together, how, and
what initiatives might need to be connected to start building an effective
T-system.

Systems thinking, then, involves an ability to focus on and understand
the whole system—and purposes beyond the self that access a greater good
for that whole. One approach to systems thinking argues that four fundamental patterns enhance this capacity[24]: making distinctions between
self and others (or the system), recognizing the existence of the system as

a system (and defining its boundaries, as discussed earlier), emphasizing relationality or connectedness of the different parts and elements in a system and their contribution to the whole, and the ability to differentiate among different perspectives. These capabilities allow for the capacity to integrate across differences and boundaries, weaving together many different perspectives into a coherent whole, a key aspect of the connecting and cohering functions of the transformation steward as catalyst.

### Aesthetic Sensibility Including Purpose Beyond Self

Aesthetic sensibility (or "the beautiful") in the context of transformative change involves a capacity to see the design and aesthetic implications in the change processes. Having such a sensibility helps to address questions about the impact or effectiveness of proposed pathways forward and actions from a holistic design perspective. It engages the emotional, inspirational, and motivational aspects of transformation. Aesthetic sensibility offers the creative element of transformative change that is needed to bring people together.[25] This aesthetic sensibility brings balance and harmony to the aspirations and purposes that are developed, allowing for new emergences and recognition when those emergences have potential to work, in part because there is a certain "beauty", harmony, or integrity to them.[26]

## Wisdom and Stewarding Transformative Change

Integrating these three aspects of wisdom, we can see that stewardship in the context of system transformation is not about managing and controlling as conventionally understood. The processes of connecting, cohering, and amplifying transformative impact require a complex array of skills and capacities that can be developed and enhanced, sometimes in one person and more often in multiple system participants. Most of these skills and capacities are needed for all three activities, reflecting different aspects of what has been called collective[27] or shared (lateral) leadership, here called *stewardship*. In the following subsections, the three lenses of connecting, cohering, and amplifying highlight relevant stewardship capacities in each type of activity, fully recognizing that all or most of these skills and capacities are needed across transformation efforts.

### Connecting

Connecting is all about fostering and facilitating relationships among key actors in a context so that they can emerge as a purposeful transformation system that is working effectively on bringing transformation about in a given system. Connecting means bringing actors in a given system together in new ways to codefine common and individual strategies that can make their transformation efforts more effective, by figuring out who is in the system doing what. The point is to define the system through "seeing" processes that include approaches like system mapping and identification of stakeholders to help actors and initiatives come together in collective sensemaking and actions planning in new ways. Sensemaking activities then help system participants codevelop broadly shared aspirations and agendas, so they can act collectively and individually in new ways toward their emergent shared aspirations.

Key skills needed for connecting include relationship management and emotional intelligence; cocreating shared purpose, visions, agendas, and values; narrative and story development; seeing and visioning complexity, leverage points, and possibilities; weaving diverse values, perspectives, and possibilities together; curiosity, listening, hearing, and inquiring; and taking collective and stewardship (caretaking) orientations, including around conflict management (Figure 9.2).

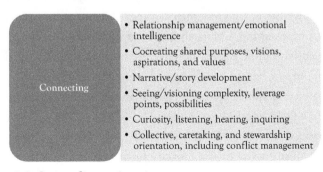

*Figure 9.2  Stewarding connecting*

*Relationship Management and Emotional Intelligence.* The connecting activity clearly involves relationship management and use of emotional intelligence. Connecting is the first step of bringing diverse actors and initiatives together into alignment around shared aspirations for transformation. Four key attributes are essential to the transformation steward as catalyst, which are explicitly associated with emotional intelligence (EQ).[28] One is self-awareness or the ability to read your own emotions and recognize impacts while simultaneously using gut feelings to guide decisions. A second is self-management or controlling one's own emotions and impulses and being adaptable as needed in the circumstances. A third is social awareness or a capacity for sensing, understanding, and reacting to others' emotions especially in the context of a social network. Finally, EQ involves relationship management, which is the ability to inspire, influence, and develop others while also managing conflict.[29]

*Cocreating Shared Purposes, Visions, Agendas, Aspiration, and Values.* In attempting to connect diverse initiatives and actors into a transformation system, one of the first priorities that stewards need to undertake is understanding and developing pathways for *how* to develop a collective or shared sense of purposes, agendas, values, and aspirations that will engage the attention of key actors and initiatives. That involves setting forth a very broad agenda and rationale for coming together—and then providing incentives around coemerging shared purposes so that actors are willing to start working together. Such purposes and visions need to be emotionally engaging and inspirational, as well as broadly shared. So, a capacity for seeing the potential for a clear and compelling potential shared purpose, along with a sense of shared or common values among relevant initiatives, is important to getting initial T-system actors to begin to work together at all. Only then can they codevelop their shared aspirations, purposes, and, ultimately action strategies. Because the purposes developed have to be shared, however, stewards have to hold their own sense of purpose lightly—to allow for the group to emerge its own cocreated shared aspirations, visions, purposes, and agendas. Aligned with that capacity is the next one—storytelling.

*Narrative and Story Development.* Aligned with cocreating shared purposes, just discussed, is a capacity for narrative and story development or storytelling. Broadly conceived as shared purposes, aspirations, agendas, visions, values, and the like, inspirational stories and narratives (which might also be images, art, or other ways of presenting a vision) help actors in a transformation system get buy in and agreement on their shared aspirations. Stewards thus need to have some degree of visioning capacity, as well as a willingness to let the vision emerge not from them or any one individual or initiative, but from the group as a whole. They need an attendant capacity for "telling the story", whether in words, phrases, or images in compelling, inspiring, and emotionally engaging and connecting ways. Some articulation of a shared aspirational narrative, a story, around building a better world together, what I have labeled *ecological civilization*, can provide the inspiration that brings initiatives together into working on T-system development. But it will need to be developed so that it specifically *speaks* to the system or context that is undergoing transformation. And any shared story or narratives needs to be composed of core ideas, memes, that can be used in multiple ways, to still give participants room, in a sense, to evolve their own yet related visions.

Thus, organizing the T-system into action strategies requires storytelling capacities to cocreate and disseminate compelling purposes, shared values, and common agendas,[30] or engaging meaning-making processes[31] that galvanize system participants into collaborative and collective action and realign individual actions to be consistent with the shared aspirations.

Cocreating shared agendas means evolving a shared new social imaginary or future perspective for the system that is inspirational and aspirational for most participants. The new social imaginary, to be powerful, needs to be jointly owned and accessible to many, demanding a collective orientation. Hence too the need for outstanding storytelling or narrative development skills, even marketing abilities, somewhere in the T-system and TC.

*Seeing and Visioning Complexity, Leverage Points, and Possibilities*: Seeing is about possibilities and potential or the ability to imagine different futures and engage others in bringing about new social imaginaries. It is also about the visioning processes associated with cohering. Seeing involves finding and describing possibilities that are inspiring, aspirational, and emotionally engaging. That is why the skill of creating compelling stories and developing shared inspirational narratives about a future that may not yet exist in a world where people might be discouraged is so important to stewarding change. It is also about employing another skill—the capacity and willingness not to "own" any given potential or possibility. Rather, stewards allow futures to be cocreated or coemerged from the interactions of T-system partners, allies, and collaborators not from any one individual or perspective, that envision new possibilities and potentialities.

Thus, while visions and aspirations need to be powerful and compelling, they cannot be too tightly held or they will fail to bring others needed to make transformation efforts successfully on board. People generally need to see their "part" in the vision, whether from alignment or input, to become truly engaged and buy-in to any vision. Stewards of transformation also need to understand a variety of techniques associated with participative visioning and group dynamics processes. They need to know when different approaches and techniques are useful and either know how to facilitate such processes or find and engage people who do.

*Weaving Diverse Values, Perspectives, Possibilities Together.* Along much the same lines, cocreating common and shared agendas demands a capacity to understand and integrate diverse perspectives, worldviews, and points of view. Stewards need to do so without alienating people in the process or leaving out important perspectives. In turn, that requires an openness to others' ideas, an ability to "hold" multiple perspectives simultaneously even when they apparently conflict. That often means that transformation stewards need a sense of profound curiosity and interest in differing perspectives, plus a capacity to weave together in new ways those perspectives, without losing any important ones. It means having a willingness to hear out numerous points of view, somehow integrating across many different possibilities and ideas. It means finding the common ground in such diversity, like a woven tapestry, and figuring out aspirational ways to move forward jointly. In a sense, that is a collectivist rather than an individualistic orientation. And the outcomes, that is, new visions, stories, narratives, or social imaginaries, will then be a collective product with no single owner. That potentiality stands in contrast to much of what the conventional leadership literature says about visioning, which is often thought to be held in the mind of the (or *a*) leader.[32]

*Curiosity, Listening, Hearing, and Inquiring.* Collective stewardship goes well beyond the most common forms of "top-down" leadership, though there may be instances in which that form of stewarding is also necessary. Shared, collaborative, and collective stewardship demand a combination of top-down, bottom-up, and "lateral" leadership, or "integrated" capacities.[33] Particularly important, there are six types of processes (called *dimensions*) important to implementing collective leadership, or stewardship: inquiring, connecting, engaging, strategizing, empowering, and reflecting.[34] These processes are vitally important in working on system transformation.

Generally speaking, top-down styles of leadership assume a hierarchical organizing arrangement, which despite innovations still exist in many businesses and governmental agencies. Leading (stewarding) in top-down ways is not likely to be suited to the collaborative dynamics of connecting, cohering, and amplifying the transformational capacity of multiple actors. That is because no individual or organizational entity is in control or has the ultimate decision-making capacity as, for example, a CEO in a company might be.[35] Instead, stewardship in T-systems is *across* the entities involved and therefore is shared, emergent, and fluctuating. The *context* in which stewarding T-systems occurs is itself complex, emergent, and fluctuating as different entities enter into conversations and alliances, goals emerge, and changes take place. This context is quite different from a structured organization with specified decision-making authority, which is where most traditional ideas about leadership derive from.

*Collective, Caretaking, and Stewardship Orientation, Including Conflict Management.* Obviously, many different skills and capacities will be called for in transformation contexts, which are collective,[36] shared, and collaborative processes. According to Caviglia-Harris, collaborative leadership involves multiple characteristics and abilities, some of which have already been discussed earlier: shared vision and values, interdependence and shared responsibility, mutual respect, empathy and vulnerability, ambiguity, communication through dialogical processes, and the emergence of synergy.[37] Further, collaborative leadership or stewardship means engaging with diversity and differences and creating inclusive environments, nurturing relationships, a nonhierarchical approach to stewardship, and capacity to deal with resistance.[38] All these stewardship activities are necessary for transformation systems to emerge and be effective. They are unlikely to be found in a single individual, so sharing stewardship responsibilities also becomes important.

Again, though, it is important to note that no one person likely has all these requisite skills. It truly, as the saying goes, takes a village to bring about transformational change.

## Cohering

Cohering was defined in Chapter 7 as bringing actors identified in the connecting process into alignment, that is, coherence, to create action plans that are both joint and independent through action planning and cocreating transformation capacities for the system as a whole. Stewarding cohering activities helps participants in a system move their collective agenda forward through visioning processes and collective action planning that involves both individual and joint strategies for transformative change. It also requires avoiding duplications and overlaps. Sometimes this aspect of stewardship means sharing projects, resources, and insights for greater impact, including figuring out how to collectively govern T-system initiatives, efforts, and other actors. In addition to the skills noted for connecting, cohering involves key capacities for: stakeholder netweaving and trust building; engaging dialogue and conversation; boundary-spanning and translating; generating collaboration and alignment; and having and using relevant technical skills (Figure 9.3).

*Stakeholder Netweaving and Trust Building.* Key to the cohering process, once potential T-system participants have been identified in the seeing and sensemaking processes, is what transformation scholar Bruce

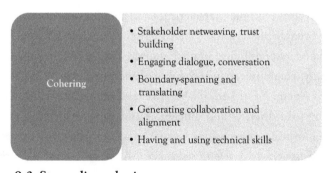

*Figure 9.3 Stewarding cohering*

Goldstein calls *netweaving*. Netweaving involves skilled facilitation of diverse initiatives in a network or aligned set of initiatives, bringing them together to encourage idea sharing, development of powerful linkages that help facilitate information sharing, coemergence of ideas, and the ability to develop a common voice.[39] As the Netweaver Network, which Goldstein facilitates, states, "Netweavers knit their networks together to develop collective capacity to overcome resistance to systems change."[40] Netweaving, or network development, is a process of aligning different initiatives within the context of a T-system that requires intense skills of stakeholder engagement, collaboration, and conflict management. It involves figuring out what will draw and keep different initiatives, groups, and efforts together in the distributed yet linked networks woven together. Stewardship is thus distributed, too.

The idea of distributed stewardship is particularly relevant in TCs and T-systems, because of their loose structures, informal if any hierarchies, and orientation toward cocreation and emergence. That is, as noted earlier, T-systems exist in a context of underorganization,[41] and initiatives and actors will likely remain somewhat independent in their activities and actions even when they are willing to connect, cohere, and amplify their transformative impacts collectively. Whoever assumes stewardship in such contexts may well fluctuate depending on the particular context, issues, and needs in a given time and space. Letting that emergent process happen is not so easy for many people. Yet it also means that people with important skills and capacities need to be in place in key parts of the T-system—and certainly in TCs.

*Engaging and Translating Dialogue and Conversation.* Cohering further demands an orientation toward dialogical processes, mutual engagement, and facilitated conversation rather than top-down, do-what-I-say approaches. That is because cohering is an emergent process that depends on the interactions among participants. Throughout the emerging T-system the capacity for co- or collective envisioning important, along with the skills to elicit those visions through a wide range of possible processes, is vital. Importantly, stewards in such systems, using participative, fully engaged approaches have to "take off their power hats" (or maybe drop their egos and need for being important). Doing so, they can let the power, empowerment, reside in the process and in the group, rather than trying to control processes and outcomes, which is impossible in any case given the complexly wicked context. Sharing power, resources, ideas, insights, and the like needs to become a norm, rather than an unusual occurrence.

*Boundary-Spanning and Translating.* All of this integrative activity stewarding coherence and aligning widely different initiatives means that stewards need to have skills in boundary spanning. Such skills involve speaking the different "languages" of different types of initiatives, organizations, disciplines, issues, and sectors. "Translation" skills that enable people to understand each other across such boundaries are vital. So too, as noted, is a willingness not to always be in the limelight. Stewards do not always need to take credit for positive outcomes; they can let others share the glory of successes. This set of skills demands that stewards willingly acknowledge failures and show a capacity for letting go and moving on. Key to ensuring successful T-system emergence is the capacity to integrate and synthesize diverse ideas, inputs, powers, resources, and abilities so that commitment from key stakeholders can be engaged that span across widely different types of boundaries, i.e., sectors, disciplines, organizations and institutions, geographies, and even languages to name a few.

*Having and Using Technical Skills.* Finally, technological sophistication is needed in both the connecting and cohering activities for using tools, methods, and approaches associated with connecting and cohering. These methodologies, used to bring people together and ensure that everyone's voice is heard, ensure that important parts of the system are all represented, and that there is alignment on visions and action plans. If key individuals do not themselves have this type of expertise, it is important that they are willing to acknowledge that gap and bring in people who do have those skills. Because there are many such possible approaches and tools, somewhere in the emerging T-system, there need to be people with the skills to facilitate and engage multiple stakeholders in action planning and forwarding those plans *into* action.

## Amplifying

Amplifying involves ensuring that action plans are implemented and modified as necessary, that experiments are undertaken, learning happens, and new experiments generated when needed, and that additional transformative capacities and capabilities are added where they are needed, typically in subsystems or specific local contexts. Amplifying involves ensuring that the transformation infrastructure needed to ensure ongoing efforts in the T-system is developed over time. Key stewardship capacities associated with amplifying are: guiding and "allowing," letting be, and letting come; building infrastructure, capacities, ideas, and innovations where needed; risk-taking, experimentation, and reflexive learning; adaptability, flexibility, and openness; accountability; and strategizing and taking action (Figure 9.4).

*Guiding and "Allowing," Letting Be/Letting Come.* Transformative change can at best be guided in stewarding system transformation. As a result, the capacity to coemerge visions and then in a very real sense "let go" to allow those visions, shared agendas, and common aspirations to emerge and develop in their own ways to guide change is centrally important. This means that individual actors and initiatives, which still have their own agendas, will likely engage with action plans and implementation in their own way, rather than the way that some other initiative or system steward might have done things. That kind of process has to be okay, but it takes capacity to "allow" or "let come" (as change theorist Otto Scharmer puts it)[42] rather than trying to make things happen.

*Building Infrastructure, Capacities, Ideas, and Innovations.* Implementation activities also involve developing capabilities to build new infrastructure, institutions as needed for the system to thrive into the future, continuing to evolve and change as circumstances shift. Recognizing what is needed and getting that done is a quite different skills set than needed in the visioning and connecting processes. It is impossible to

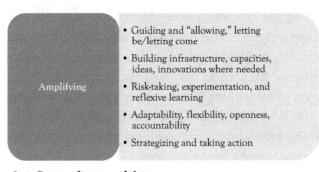

*Figure 9.4 Stewarding amplifying*

know in advance what innovations and new infrastructure will be needed in a given context. That will emerge from the collaborative undertakings stewarded by the TC. It is not that the stewards need to know everything about new innovations or technologies. Rather, they need to have the self-awareness and stewarding capacity to find sources of those innovations, invent them where necessary, and disseminate them as needed. In other words, they need to know the system well enough to understand where necessary innovations are emerging and be willing to tap the individuals creating them, bring them into the T-system, and engage them in the collective enterprise that a T-system is.

*Risk-Taking, Experimentation, and Reflexive Learning.* If stewarded properly and guided, systems-based TCs and the T-system will become stronger, and more centrally relevant to the given context. That might mean the original TCs and their stewards will need to step back, or try some new things that is, take risks, to continue to move the system forward. In a sense, the transforming system eventually and its T-system will eventually begin to go its own way. Although they will hopefully retain the guiding aspirations, visions, and values that enabled actors to come together in the first place, there needs to be a certain amount of "trust the system" or "trust the process" mindset in place. All of that requires experimentation to acknowledge the risks that these evolution and maturation processes involve. If system transformation is about anything, it is about experimentation and risk. Not everything will succeed, so willingness and ability to accept failure is a must, along with celebrating successes. Stewarding those processes of experimentation necessarily means trusting participants in the T-system to act in good faith and taking the associated risks of doing that.

Learning and associated processes of reflection and mindfulness are vital to any steward of transformative change. Because the ground of transformation is inevitably new, untrodden territory, it not only requires the risk-taking attitude just discussed, but also an orientation toward ongoing, constant learning from the experiments and innovations that are tried. It helps stewards to take a nonzero-sum orientation to ensure this learning process works and enable the experimentation that necessary, as success in one part of a system or context does not guarantee (or preclude) successes in others. The whole will become better when good ideas, approaches, insights, and processes are shared, reflected upon, and learned from. Thus, constant reflection on how things are going, holistic approaches to evaluation and learning from those evaluation efforts can help. There is much yet to be learned about stewardship around the roles of TCs in developing transformation systems. Further, there is plenty that needs to be learned about how such systems become successful and what causes them to fail, as well as about the processes or stages of development they go through over time. For now, though, this short book has attempted to distill what is already known or conceptualized into a framework, synthesized in Chapter 10 that can potentially transform approaches and processes of system transformation.

*Adaptability, Flexibility, Openness, and Accountability.* All of the demands of system transformation mean that stewards need to be adaptive to changing circumstances, flexible, open to change, and, importantly, willing to give up power when the system evolves and matures. T-systems and all socioecological systems are living things. Living things constantly change. That's what makes them alive. Still, ensuring that there is accountability for implementation, for outcomes, impacts, and processes is important, especially in a context where some failures are inevitable, not for blame but for learning. Ongoing learning from the experiences in the T-system, the experiments, risks, and failures and, of course, successes, and sharing that learning is vital to stewarding long-term transformation. That learning should be shared with others, so that they do not need to repeat mistakes and can identify the stages of evolution and what kinds of different skills, capacities, and stewardship are needed during those different stages. Since the idea of T-systems is new, however, there is still much to be learned about what those stages are, how long they take to evolve, and how to steward within them.

*Strategizing and Taking Action.* Transformation is about strategizing for change, of course. More importantly, it is about taking concerted and often collective action to make desired changes. Necessary learning in these transformational contexts can be done by drawing out key lessons from experiences that are context specific in one sense. Recognizing that generalizable lessons helpful to others are also possible is key to the ongoing learning needed. That is especially true when looking for patterns that result in successes and figuring out what worked in various "seeds" of innovation and change. Because transformational efforts can be not replicated but rather propagated, like seeds, finding ways to grow them in their own ways in their specific contexts, while learning from the past, is key.

## Stewarding Transformation

Figure 9.5 synthesizes the important leadership activities most needed in each of the three main activities of connecting, cohering, and amplifying the work of T-systems as discussed earlier. None of this work is easy. No one person has all of these skills, so shared stewardship (collective leadership[43]), is vital. Process of connecting, cohering, and amplifying transformative action with a diverse mix of stakeholders, initiatives, and efforts is hard work and, as must be evident, demands a variety of capacities and skills of the stewards. Because no one person has all the needed skills, it is important to find a number of stewards who can work together effectively, know how to collaborate and compromise,

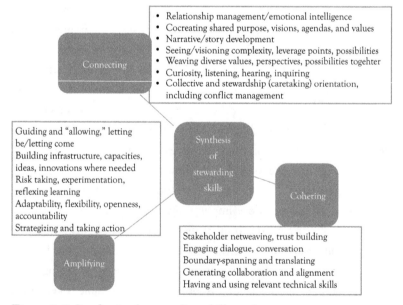

*Figure 9.5 Synthesis of stewarding skills and processes*

can manage conflicts both within their own group, and at the other two levels of the system, that is, the transformation system and the whole system undergoing transformation.

So, we have largely reached the end of our journey, identifying an innovative set of processes and activities for *how* to bring transformational change about. The next and last chapter provides a synthesis of this whole approach, putting the pieces together into one place.

## Takeaways From Chapter 9

- Transformational change needs to be stewarded rather than "led" because of the underorganized and emergent nature of the systems to be changed, and that initiatives and actors will likely remain independent, even though they are willing to some extent to connect, cohere, and amplify their efforts toward transformative impact.

- Connecting involves fostering and facilitating relationships. Key skills needed for connecting include relationship management and emotional intelligence; cocreating shared purpose, visions, agendas, and values; narrative and story development; seeing and visioning complexity, leverage points, and possibilities; weaving diverse values, perspectives, and possibilities together; curiosity, listening, hearing, and inquiring; and having collective and stewardship (caretaking) orientations, including conflict management skills.

- Cohering additionally involves key capacities for: stakeholder netweaving and trust building; engaging dialogue and conversation; boundary-spanning and translating; generating collaboration and alignment; and having and using relevant technical skills.

- Amplifying additionally involves ensuring that action plans are implemented and modified as necessary, that experiments are undertaken, learning happens, and new experiments generated when needed, and that additional transformative capacities and capabilities are added where they are needed, typically in subsystems or specific local contexts. Key stewardship capacities associated with amplifying are: guiding and "allowing," letting be, and letting come; building infrastructure, capacities, ideas, and innovations where needed; risk-taking, experimentation, and reflexive learning; adaptability, flexibility, and openness; accountability; and strategizing and taking action.

# CHAPTER 10

# Synthesis

## Transforming System Transformation

This chapter synthesizes the approach to catalyzing transformation developed throughout this book. In a sense, it provides a roadmap or set of pathways to guide transformational change agents, transformation catalysts or TCs, in their efforts to bring about systemic change. This approach acknowledges both the wicked complexity of whole system change processes, and the need to steward them carefully, using core design principles that emphasize values of inclusion, participation, and equity around achieving a flourishing world for people and nature (ecological civilization). This approach also acknowledges the need for catalytic work at three levels of change in developing these pathways: the work of the *TC(s)* who *organize* and facilitate connection, coherence, and amplification of the work of actors in *transformation systems*, who collectively work to transform *the system of interest* holistically and in positive, aspirational directions. In this chapter, we revisit our original holistic image that illustrates the three levels of change needed to bring about purposeful catalyzed system transformation: the work of TCs weaving together initiatives and actors working toward similar transformational aspirations to collectively bring about whole system transformation toward what for short has been labeled *ecological civilizations* (Figure 10.1).

*Catalyzing Transformation* is a process that iteratively emerges from the connecting, cohering, and amplification work of *TCs*, who work to organize purposeful and self-aware *transformation systems* comprised of actors oriented to shared transformational aspirations that can effectively achieve *whole system transformation* in a given context.

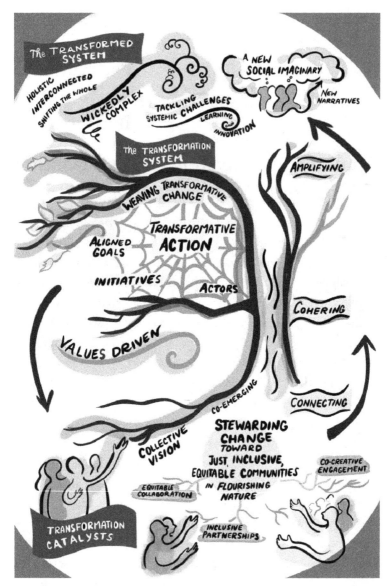

*Figure 10.1  The catalyzing transformation process*

Image: Patricia Kambitsch, https://playthink.com.

## The Whys and Hows of System Transformation

There is a lot of discussion these days in many quarters about the need for whole system transformative change to cope with the many increasingly daunting intersecting crises, polycrisis, that the world is facing.

Inequality, climate change, biodiversity loss, political and cultural divides, ecosystem endangerment, overpopulation, deforestation, desertification, food scarcity in some places and obesity epidemics in others, energy security, and gender disparities, are only a few of the potentially civilizational threats facing the world today. These crises demand that things be done differently in the future than they have been done in the past. They demand new ways of organizing and fostering transformative change, and new visions and social imaginaries that propel change agents and everyone else in directions that foster just, inclusive, equitable societies in a flourishing natural world, that is, or ecological civilizations. Purposeful whole-system change goes far beyond tinkering around the edges of systems to achieve the depth, breadth, and scale of change that is needed. And the urgency of achieving that type of change is only increasing.

Transformative change grapples with shifting the fundamentals that keep current systems in place and bringing shared aspirations for a better world into reality. Catalyzing transformation through the connecting, cohering, and amplifying work of TCs aiming to emerge powerful transformation systems potentially offers leverage and the very real potential to achieve desired change. But it is not and will not be easy. Such transformation will not take place unless ways can be found to shift *whole systems*, not just pieces of them. Incrementalism and even reform are not sufficient, yet transformation is scary because it is so fundamental. That is why *whole systems*, here called transformation (T-)systems, need to be *involved in generating the desired changes*, to generate widespread buy-in for the changes. And that is why people working as TCs focus on emerging effective transformation systems.

*Catalyzing Transformation* requires a lot of creative energy and innovative thinking from people and initiatives willing to work as TCs in self-aware and effective transformation systems. TCs need to be willing and able to *steward* processes that bring people and initiatives together to *collectively emerge ideas* about what will work in their specific context. Then they need to be willing to *share the credit* for changes that take place, working *collaboratively in innovative new ways* with others, bringing them together into *aligned and powerful transformation systems*. Ultimately, though, it is the *transformation systems participants who do the work* of transformation, each in their own way. So, they too need to be willing and able to come together in shared aspirations, agendas, strategies, and actions. When transformation works, transformation system participants can emerge shared values, principles, and visions to guide the whole system toward a world where all can flourish.

*Catalyzing Transformation* builds on the work of numerous "transformers" over many years, and, in particular, synthesizing ideas developed in the context of the Bounce Beyond initiative since the global pandemic began in 2020, has tried to lay out a framework for effective whole system transformation. This final chapter synthesizes the processes involved in catalyzing transformation, fully recognizing that ideas will evolve as we learn more. Given the context of today's crises, which pose civilizational threats, it seems clear that transformational processes and practices need to center explicitly on the well-being of both humanity and nature, forwarding the idea of what I've called *ecological civilizations*, that is, socially just, equitable, inclusive societies in a flourishing natural world.

Despite the urgency, there have been few systemic change approaches articulated to date that actually offer ways of thinking about and, more importantly, *doing* whole system change that actually deals with those fundamentals. Lots of theories, articles, and initiatives point to the reality that today's socioeconomic, political, and approaches to ecological systems need to change drastically. Frequently, they offer wonderful visions about what those transformations, once achieved, would look like and what values they reflect. Few, however, offer any kind of integrative template for getting there. That is what *Catalyzing Transformation* (with all its limitations) has tried to do.

Although it may seem that this template for catalyzing transformation is still sketchy, that is partly because of the uniqueness of each context. What *Catalyzing Transformation* does offer is an *integrated framework for approaching and organizing for transformational change*. In doing so, it provides a sense of *what* needs to change, identified here as purpose, paradigms, performance metrics, practices, and power relations/structures. Importantly, it also offers approaches for *how* to achieve desired change through connecting, cohering, and amplifying the emergence of action strategies that evolve with the development of transformation systems through the work of TCs.

Though the bones of the needed whole systemic approach to transformation are here, clearly there is still much to be learned. It will be learned as different TCs put these ideas into practice, reflect on their learning, and make needed changes (and, hopefully, write them up to share with others). Transformational change by its nature is an evolutionary process that demands an openness to learning, to adaptation and change when necessary, and to ongoing reflection about what works and what does not. This framework/approach is no different. What *Catalyzing Transformation*\* ultimately offers is a much-needed whole system change approach based on a theory of *how* whole system change can be fostered and facilitated by TCs organizing purposeful transformation systems.

## Catalyzing Change: An Integrated Process for Whole System Transformation

What follows is a synthesis of this catalyzing transformation approach, using the ideas developed throughout this book. This chapter speaks directly to any readers who have made it this far into the book, offering an overview of "how" TCs working with transformation systems bring about system change. Readers should recognize that many efforts, activities, and initiatives will be experimental. Some efforts will fail. As powerful as these ideas are, they are still ahead of common practice and require different capacities and skills of people who would steward change than are common. Hence, they need to be implemented with care and some degree of openness to needed changes, adaptations, as the process progresses. Both successes and failures provide opportunities for your own learning, particularly about bringing the transformative change you are seeking if you got this far into being.

It is important not to think of the following outline as rigidly or prescriptively dictating an ordered set of steps. Many of these processes, all of which are important, occur simultaneously. That said, the order in the following outline does provide an ordered template for thinking about some necessary step-based processes.

---

\* Here again I want to acknowledge the contributions to this thinking of the entire Bounce Beyond team (www.bouncebeyond.global) without whose collaboration these ideas would not be in the shape that they currently are in: Steve Waddell (in particular), Ian Kendrick, Peter Jones, Indra Adnan, Jonny Norton, Zenda Ofir, Lesley Southwick-Trask, plus, at various points in time numerous others including: Karen Downes, Jasper Kenter, Jean-Louis Robadey, Meenakshi Goonj, Ned Daly, and Stuart Cowan.

## Understanding the Complexly Wicked Nature of System Transformation

A transformative systems-change approach demands understanding the nature of socioecological contexts as complex adaptive systems that include numerous wicked problems. That is, they are wickedly complex or complexly wicked. As human systems, they are also living systems, therefore open-ended, interconnected, integrated wholes with interdependent elements, and permeable boundaries. Issues in such systems are intertwined and emergently nonlinear. They have no easily identifiable beginnings or endings, multiple pathways to solutions, and numerous stakeholders with varying perspectives. Outcomes too tend to be emergent, dependent on the actions taken and pathways chosen that coevolve, and nonlinear. Thus, outcomes of actions taken are inherently unpredictable, though patterns can be and often are evident and helpful to system changers. Thus, change, transformative or otherwise, in such contexts cannot be controlled or planned. Instead, it needs to be guided by shared aspirations, visions, and values.

Essential to bringing about transformative change is recognizing its fundamental nature. In *transformation* of socioecological (shorthand for social, economic, political, and ecological human systems as living entities) systems, key elements or aspects of the relevant system may all need to change:

- *Purposes* or the fundamental reasons for existence of the system;
- *Paradigms* or mindsets used to understand the system and different beings' place in it and relationship to it;
- *Performance metrics* that enable assessment and evaluation to occur;
- *Practices* that define day-to-day operations and activities of the system; and
- *Power structures* and relationships that determine status and resource flows.

All of these Ps will differ depending on the system and figuring out what the status quo is, to the extent possible, is important if that status quo is to be changed. They all, however, can be reframed to provide needed guidance to change makers once their importance is understood. Guidelines for thinking about these aspects of transformative change include understanding the following:

- *Recognizing and dealing with the realities of complex wickedness*: Recognize the characteristics of complexly wicked socioecological systems and the need for *guiding* change strategies, which will be inherently emergent and unpredictable. That means paying attention to emerging shared aspirations, agendas, visions, values, and beyond.
- *Understanding system purposes, paradigms, performance metrics, practices, power structures and shifting them as needed*: Identify the system's current purposes, which could be multiple, both stated and unarticulated, paradigms, or the mindsets/ perspectives of key system participants, performance metrics, which are used to measure, evaluate, and assess performance but may be misguided, practices and which determine how the system actually operates, and power relationships that structure relationships and resource flows. Think about how each of these core system aspects needs to change to achieved a desired end state—or transformed system.
- *Being catalytic not prescriptive:* Take a catalytic, coemergent, cocreative, interactive, and stewardship approach to transformation, recognizing that there will be no one "leader" in the conventional sense, but rather numerous actors stewarding change, aspiration development, and emergence of action strategies as things evolve and the system begins to change.

### Emerge a Shared New Social Imaginary—A Values-Based Narrative/Vision

In these complexly wicked contexts, taking a *catalytic stewardship* approach is necessary, because planned change is not really possible. The best that change makers can hope for, given the array of largely independent yet ultimately connected actors, is to guide change. That guidance best occurs through reshaping, rearticulating, and redefining core narratives and stories that shape how people view the world or their system.

Such narratives include shared and codeveloped, powerfully resonant, emotionally engaging, and inspirational aspirations, values, visions, and agendas or strategies (aspirations for short). These aspirations provide needed guidance for implementation and broad agendas, like a touchstone that one can always return to, to check if things are on the right track. Thus, a good early step toward transforming approaches to transformative system change is collectively envisioning the world or the system that you want to bring into being, that is, the new social imaginary. What does it look like? What are its core values? How do people relate to each other and to nature? This visualization can be done in any number of ways. The key is generating something that is generally agreed to by participants. Processes employed to get to shared narratives need to be inclusive and equitable, ensuring that all voices are heard, and fair. And processes need to recognize and acknowledge both "voiced" (people and views represented) and "unvoiced" or marginalized interests, including marginalized peoples, future generations, and nature.

When the new social imaginary becomes widely shared, it can provide the basis for emerging the new cultural mythologies that shape understanding of how we humans relate to the world, why, and for what purposes. For example, if we envision a world that works for all, one where social justice, equity, and flourishing of all life are dominant values, where all can participate as they wish, operating in balance and harmony between humans and nature. That is a very different approach from neoliberalism's emphasis on (monetary) wealth creation and continual economic growth. Think about the particular systems that interest you: what is your vision for how they would look, be, and do things if they could be transformed to a desired state?

Steps for emerging your own system-relevant social imaginary (future vision) involve ensuring participatory approaches that begin to align different actors and initiatives through a variety of core processes and steps in contextually appropriate ways:

- *Collective visioning to create a new social imaginary for the system*: Articulate what you want the system to look like, be, and do. How *should* it be functioning? Consider what would be the ideal state for this system that inspires people to work toward change? Consider whose interests have been incorporated into the narrative and how both voiced and unvoiced interests are being heard/represented. Ensure that new narratives, the new social imaginary, are compelling, emotionally resonant, inspirational and aspirational, and collectively understood and agreed.

- *Values articulation*: Identify what are the core values that support both changes needed and the desired end state for the *relevant system*? Ensure that there is collective agreement about core values and that they inform the new social imaginary or vision so that they provide guidance for change strategies and change makers.

- *Narrative development and dissemination*: Identify the current narratives and cultural mythologies that hold the system in place. Analyze the current dominant narrative to determine where and why it is problematic. Develop new narratives that reflect the desired end state, the new social imaginary, as aspirational, inspirational, and emotionally compelling. Then use whatever means are available to widely share and disseminate this new vision or social imaginary to get as widespread buy-in, as well as related transformative actions, as possible.

### Recognize That Wicked Complexity Demands Values-Based Design Principles

Designing systemic change strategies involves recognizing the wickedly complex nature of socioecological system, particularly because in most cases the current state of transformation systems is one of fragmentation or blessed unrest: separate initiatives each doing their own things. The whole point of working to catalyze transformation is to bring these separated initiatives into self-aware alignment of their activities, aspirations, agendas, and actions. There are certain "how to's" that are important in designing systemic change interventions, based on the nature of the systems to be changed. Wicked complexity means that *transformative change approaches* need to be developed with certain design principles kept firmly in mind. Just as the aspirations and goals for the relevant system need to be based on core values kept firmly in mind, so do the *processes* for bringing change about. Three sets of principles can help change makers design interventions for transformation.

The recognition that actors attempting systemic change are largely independent yet need to work interactively means that they need to be drawn together or stewarded by some sort of shared aspirations, that is, *values-driven change processes* and potential benefits. The complex wickedness of the systems means that approaches based on understanding the *complexly wicked systemic nature* of what is to be changed is important. In such contexts, the best "leaders" are stewards, or catalytic change makers. And the best they can hope for is to *steward the desired changes*, since actors remain largely independent even when connected and cohered into transformation systems to amplify their collective work. While each transformational change effort needs to identify its own context-specific design principles, they should also use the following as process guides:

- *Adopt principles that give life to systems*: Design clear, life-affirming purposes, intentions, and aspirations. Recognize the permeability of system boundaries and the need for constant change. Emerge dynamism and novelty as needed.
- *Develop values-driven change processes* that inspire life-centered purposes and values. Create conditions of inclusive participation. Generate equitable collaboration. Enable participants to engage cocreatively.
- *Take complexity/systems-based approaches* that recognize the complexly wicked nature of transformative change. Adopt holistic system perspectives. Acknowledge interconnected relationality, multilevel, -spatial, -stakeholder, and -strategy diversity. Encourage evolutionary self-organization.
- *Lead through system stewardship* that recognizes the first two set of values. Structure, steward, and resource relationships and supportive processes. Guide, enable, experiment, and adapt as needed. Generate self- and system-awareness.

### Be, Become, or Work With a Transformation Catalyst: Connecting, Cohering, and Amplifying

Because of the nature of complexly wicked systems with many change initiatives in them, the transformational change approach we advocate operates through new types of entities we call TCs or transformation catalysts. *TCs* are a new way of *organizing change* that brings together numerous actors that are attempting change in a given context, that is, the *transformation (T-) system*, enabling them to cocreatively and collectively connect, cohere, and amplify their impacts.

*Connecting* involves helping a range of initiatives begin to understand themselves as a transformation system working toward shared aspirations around systemic change. One key set of processes here involves *seeing* the system, or mapping out who is doing what, where, why, and how with respect to systemic change in that context, which can work through various mapping, stakeholder analysis, and related approaches. A second set of processes engages *sensemaking* or jointly developing and articulating shared visions, agendas, values, and other aspirations, including new social imaginaries, that help align initiatives on common pathways and provide guidance for action.

*Cohering* involves actually bringing key change-making actors together (in person, virtually, or through various collaborative technologies) so that they can cocreatively develop and emerge a set of action plans and transformation capacities that enable them to begin recognizing their interactions as those of a transformation system. *Action planning* is a cocreative process of developing ideas, strategies, and implementation strategies and actions for bringing about transformative change. Cocreating transformation capacities means developing capabilities and infrastructure needed to bring about and sustain change within the relevant system, including governance mechanisms based on core principles for managing commons.

*Amplifying* is the process of *implementing* the action plans developed through the cohering processes, testing and experimenting with them, and modifying them as necessary. It also means developing needed *transformation infrastructure*, including connective mechanisms, ongoing dialogues, collaborations, and other engagements among system participants. As well, it means sharing knowledge, processes, and resources among system participants to enhance everyone's transformative potential. Amplifying also involves determining whether there is a need for one or more system-level TCs in different subsystems to continue to evolve and maintain the transformational work and enabling that to happen if the need exists.

Transformation catalysts:

- *Become or work with a TC* that works to *organize purposeful, self-aware, and impactful transformation system*s through processes of connecting, cohering, and amplifying the work of change makers in a given context, so that they understand themselves as and gel into a coherent transformation system that can work toward impactful change.
- *Connect*: Establish ways for system change agents to see and understand their systems as a transformation system and jointly sensemake to develop shared aspirations and common agendas through seeing and sensemaking:
  - o Help participants in a potential purposeful transformation system "see" and understand their system. Seeing involves describing and understanding the system, stakeholder and initiative identification, and mapping processes that outline who is doing what, where, and how.
  - o Sensemaking involves engaging in processes that emerge and agree on shared meanings, visions, values, agendas, and aspirations with respect to purposeful systemic change.
- *Cohere*: Enable participants to cocreatively develop transformational strategies and plans, and how to implement them, while also developing needed capabilities and capacities within the system to support purposeful transformational efforts in an ongoing way.
  - o Develop coevolved action planning strategies, including shared ideas about what needs to change and how it might be changed. Work to align the actions strategies, and

activities of various actors and initiatives in the emerging
transformation system to collectively achieve their desired
impacts.

o  Cocreate transformation capacities, which means
developing the ability of numerous actors in a context to
undertake connecting and cohering processes themselves,
that is, become subsystem TCs, to establish a platform
for ongoing systemic change so that collectively and
independently actors can deal with systemic challenges.

- *Amplify*: Engage change makers in implementing the action
plans that they have jointly developed, and help them emerge
the necessary infrastructure within their context to support,
maintain, and enhance ongoing transformative efforts over
time, including sharing insights, knowledge, and processes.

### Develop Transformation (T-) Systems That Can Work With Core Systemic Challenges

Using the processes of connecting, cohering, and amplifying, TCs work
to coemerge *transformation (T-) systems* out of typically fragmented, independent, and unaligned initiatives. The T-system consists of all those
actors engaged in attempting to bring about systemic change toward
shared aspirations or agendas. The work of the TC, just described, is to
help them come into connection and alignment with each other, becoming aware of themselves *as* a T-system, so they can begin to work for transformation in aligned, collectively more powerful and impactful ways.

Once they begin to align, T-system participants can work in new ways
to tackle at least the following six common types of challenges facing system change makers plus others arising in their specific context, which typically stand in the way of transformative change. One is developing new
*narratives* and stories that articulate shared assumptions, visions, values,
aspirations, agendas, and understandings of purposes needed for transforming that context toward ecological civilizations. Another is creating
*innovations* that are transformative in their impact and implementation
and aligned with the values and aspirations articulated around system
change. Creative approaches to *governance* need to pick up on the core

design principles articulated for the system also need to be coevolved by T-system participants working with principles for governing commons. *Financing* and resourcing mechanisms that support systemic change (versus keeping the old system in place, which most current financing mechanisms do) are also needed.

All these challenges create a need for *collaboration* among key actors that involves evolving system-level consciousness and awareness and dropping personal in favor of collective agendas. Importantly, *holistic evaluation and assessment criteria* (performance metrics) need to be established for determining how well both the TC and the transformation system are doing, how transformative their efforts actually are, and what needs to be learned so that needed changes can be made. Thus, the final common or shared systemic challenge is that of *creating measurement and learning approaches* that support the holistic, evolutionary, and emergent approaches that are at the foundation of systemic change.

- *Recognize and evolve an effective transformation (T-) system*: Tap transformation catalysts to help connect, cohere, and amplify the existing and potential new work of transformation agents within the system into a more impactful and effective transformation system, and ensure that actors are aware of themselves as a T-system.
- *Support the transformation system to tackle at least six systemic challenges collectively* and identify any context-specific challenges that need to be tackled collectively and independently.
  - *Narratives*: Coidentify and coemerge new aspirational and functionally "fit-for-purpose" narratives and stories that articulate shared aspirations for the system.
  - *Innovation*: Develop innovations in products, processes, and services that reflect cogenerated systemic aspirations and important values.
  - *Governance*: Develop innovative governance approaches that reflect the shared aspirations and design principles codeveloped by system participants enabling the emergence

of shared directions and aligned actions. Govern using
principles associated with governing commons.

o *Financing and resourcing*: Emerge and use innovative
financing and resourcing mechanisms that support desired
systemic changes, treating money as a means to achieving
shared aspirations (rather than as end in itself).

o *Collaboration*: Develop and implement new methods
of collaborating among relatively independent actors to
coemerge initiatives and interventions at multiple system
levels that achieve shared aspirations.

o *Measurement and learning*: Cocreate and implement
holistic ways of evaluating, assessing, and measuring
system effectiveness, changes, learning, and outcomes as
they relate to shared aspirations.

### Steward Transformative Change

Achieving whole system transformation is unconventional: it involves
processes of *stewardship* or caretaking rather than "leadership" as normally
understood. Because of the nature of T-systems and TCs, the stewardship
role is necessarily shared and one of guidance—and it can come from anywhere in the system. That is because in the context of complex wickedness
that is system transformation, there is little capacity for anyone to dictate,
plan, or control outcomes. Systemic forces, collaborative interactions,
and emergent coevolutionary processes mean that the shared aspirations
and agendas developed by system participants are what guide actions, not
the willful dictate of a conventional leader.

Processes that TCs and others in T-systems use are necessarily collaborative, involving the connecting processes of bringing people together to
cocreatively evolve *their own* agendas. The process is one of netweaving or
knitting together previously unaligned initiatives by finding and coevolving share aspirations, or cohering them in new ways. The amplification
processes that are stewarded, including implementation and development
of system infrastructure, need to be "held lightly" rather than tightly controlled as new developments will necessarily be experimental and system

participants need to learn from them as they go (akin to the metaphor of repairing the airplane while it flies). Stewarding transformative change involves numerous skills and a holistic understanding.

- *Steward (don't "lead") change*: Develop core skills that engage the processes of connecting, cohering, and amplifying the work of participants in transformation systems, working as a TC.
- *Steward connecting*: Develop skills for cocreating shared purposes and agendas, new narratives, seeing systems, social imaginaries, and possibilities, integrating diverse perspectives, being inquiring and curious, and taking a collective orientation.
- *Steward cohering*: Develop skills for netweaving, stakeholder engagement, dialogue and engagement, visioning, listening, sharing power, being emotionally intelligent, spanning boundaries, aligning others, collaborating, moving on from failures, integrating and synthesizing, and using necessary tools, methods, and approaches.
- *Steward amplification*: Develop skills for guiding and "allowing" change and emergence, building capacities, risk-taking, adaptation, accountability, strategizing, action learning, a nonzero-sum orientation, and reflexive learning.

## Coemerge Necessary Transformative and System Infrastructure

Recognizing that *transformative change is an ongoing process* is important. Very likely system change will never be "complete" in the sense of being finished. Systems have a way of going on and continually evolving, whether or not their direction is being guided. Thus, it is important to view transformative change through a lens that suggests that even when changes are being made in the desired, purposeful direction, it is likely that there will be fits and starts, side paths and misdirections. Some change efforts will work. Others will not. Some will be transformative and others will not be. The important thing is to create a collective or shared sense of possibility through the creation of a shared social imaginary that appeals to many (and discourages naysayers) because it is based on broadly shared values, principles, and aspirations.

Key is to maintain your perspective about *shifting the whole system*, not just pieces of it. That also means holding on to hope in the face the difficulties that inevitably arise and sharing that hope with others. Transformative change agents need passion, a sense of (shared) purpose and an openness to cocreating those purposes, and a holistic perspective to help them through the rough spots. Successes will be worth it. People can begin to live better, socially just, more equitable, inclusive lives in a world where they and nature flourish together (i.e., in ecological civilizations). Transformational change agents who keep such aspirations in mind and structure efforts along the lines outlined, adapting them as necessary to conditions, play an important role in the regenerative process that brings life to socioecological systems, even though the task was difficult and probably sometimes seemed overwhelming.

- *Take a long-term system perspective:* Recognize that system transformation toward ecological civilization is a long-term, ongoing process that will require iterative and sometimes evolving narratives, strategies, and actions over time. Taking the core ideas of TCs and transformation (T-) system seriously means understanding that each system will need to develop its own catalysts and T-systems coherence to thrive long term. That means putting in place ways to develop and ensure the continuity of these structures over time and emerging transformation infrastructure relevant to the particular context.
- *Emerge system-level transformation infrastructure:* Allow and plan for the development and emergence of system- and subsystem-level TCs and infrastructure as needed to ensure continuity of transformation efforts over time.

## Catalyzing Whole System Transformation: Jamming Together for a Better Future

I hope that the approach developed in this book helps you *in catalyzing purposeful whole system transformation.* Here is a metaphor that may be helpful as you continue on your system transformation journey. Think of transformative change as a jam session, that is, a group of folks making music together, collaboratively, joyfully, and cocreatively.[†] The music might be jazz, bluegrass, rock, folks, blues, any number of other genres, of which there are many. Choosing the type of music depends on the skills of the musicians and context in which the jam is being held, just as system transformation is contextually specific. The tune or song selected provides a framework that all the musicians share, which could be a chord structure, a tune, and possibly a set of lyrics. A music jam is about taking that core framework, that is, the central structure, and playing it together, then allowing changes to be made to it that transforms it into something else that everyone is cocreating together.

Jamming allows for some people to take leads sometimes, when they desire, so they can improvise something new, while others hang back and play the basic chords or structure. In that, it relies on everyone in the group to do their part to support the lead musician, who then backs away from the lead when his or her turn is done, so that others can, if they wish, step forward. That means that musicians need to listen carefully to each other, understand the bigger picture of what they are playing and when it makes sense for one person to do something different and when not. When a jam goes really well, musicians "riff" off each other. They build on what has gone before in new ways that will likely not be repeated should that tune or song be played again by a different group or even by the same group. So too with system transformation. Each "production", whether a song, tune, or transformation effort, will be unique to the setting, players, and interactions that take place in the moment. Yet, when done well, it creates a joyful noise that is an "attractor" in the complexity sense, something emotionally engaging and inspirational that draws others around it to listen and sometimes participate themselves.

---

[†] The inspiration for this metaphor came from an e-mail from Shelagh Aitkin, Managing Editor of *AI Practitioner* describing the *Appreciative Inquiry* process developed by David Cooperrider and colleagues, July 2022. As a note the author is a folk musician who loves to jam with other musicians. When this chapter was being written she had just returned from an amazing week of music-making with others, where informal jams on the porch were the highlight of the week, including one that took place after a massive thunderstorm that knocked the power out and left players in the dark for several hours. The analogy is very real.

The "attractors" in system change are the visions or aspirations that are, hopefully, jointly held and accessible to anyone interested in the change dynamics and processes, or in improving the system at hand, just as the musical form and structure attracts a certain set of musicians. When that vision or set of aspirations deeply affirm life in its unique way, many people will be attracted to it, shaping it and changing in their own unique ways. Attractors like that can draw people into active engagement, attentional observation, and possibly new actions can support the transformation.

So too with system transformation. It is an improvisation built on a framework, which hopefully has been provided. This framework offers structure, guidance, and a core set of approaches that anyone can build on, and it can be used in any number of different settings and contexts, by people coming from many different backgrounds and orientations. It is not meant to be prescriptive. Rather it presents a *framework or approach for guiding transformative actions*. Still, catalyzing whole system transformation demands close attention to and cooperation among actors in the transformation system. The outcomes of catalytic transformation efforts, however well planned, are not predictable because of the complex wickedness involved. But the basic pattern, the framework of the system and the change processes, remains intact. Riffing off of others means learning from others and then creating something new, building on that. New participants can join, and ones who feel like they have done what they could may leave, providing fresh energy for the effort. The pace of change may speed up or slow down according to circumstances, and the stewarding roles will change accordingly, depending on the urgency of changes needed.

May you have the best of luck in joining in on this journey toward a world that works for all. I hope that this short book makes that journey a bit easier, more understandable, and, ultimately, more transformative.

# Notes

## Chapter 1

1. IMAGINE (2016).
2. Taylor (2002), pp. 91–124.
3. Ibid.
4. Masson-Delmotte et al. (2021); Ripple et al. (2021), pp. 1–5.
5. "The Most Urgent Refugee Crises Around the World" (2022).
6. Guterres (2020); Zucman (2019), pp. 109–138.
7. Diaz, Settele et al. (2020).
8. Markard and Rosenbloom (2020), pp. 53–60.
9. Bollier and Helfrich (2019).
10. RADAR (2022).
11. Ibid.
12. Abram (2012).
13. Korten (2021).
14. Caniglia et al. (2021), pp. 93–100.
15. Waddock (2021), pp. 165–182.
16. Rockström et al. (2009a) p. 32; Seitzinger et al. (2012), pp. 787–794; O'Neill, Fanning, Lamb, and Steinberger (2018), pp. 88–95.
17. Capra (1997).
18. Hawken (2007).
19. Waddock (2021), pp. 165–182.
20. Ibid.
21. Waddock and Waddell (2021a), pp. 1–41.
22. Korten (2017), pp. 17–24; Korten (2021).

## Chapter 2

1. Graeber and Wengrow (2021).
2. Weisdorf (2005), pp. 561–586.
3. Graeber and Wengrow (2021).
4. Waddock, Waddell, and Gray (2018).

5. Waddock and Waddell (2021a), pp. 1–41.
6. Korten (2017), pp. 17–24.
7. Waddell (2011, 2016).
8. Waddock and Waddell (2021a); Leadbeater and Winhall (2021).
9. Waddock and Waddell (2021a), pp. 1–41.
10. Lee and Waddock (2021); Waddock and Waddell (2021b), pp. 165–82.
11. Hawken (2007).
12. Ibid.
13. Ackoff and Gharajedaghi (1996), pp. 13–23.
14. Koestler (1968), pp. 45–48.
15. Holling (2001), pp. 390–405.
16. Ibid, p. 394.
17. Ackoff and Gharajedaghi (1996), pp. 13–23.
18. Ibid.
19. Waddock et al. (2015), pp. 993–1012.
20. Waddock et al. (2015); Conklin (2006); Capra (2005), pp. 33–44; Grobman (2005), pp. 350–382; Kauffman (1995); Mason and Mitroff (2010), p. 27.
21. Conklin (2006), pp. 33–44; Batie (2008), pp. 1176–1191; Finegan (2003), pp. 35–45; Rittel and Webber (1973), pp. 155–169; Churchman (1967).
22. Allen et al. (2014), pp. 578–589.
23. Meadows (1999).
24. Waddock et al. (2015), pp. 993–1012.
25. Holling (2001), pp. 390–405.

# Chapter 3

1. Dow (1986), pp. 56–69.
2. Lent (2021).
3. Capra (1997); Senge (2006).
4. Laszlo et al. (2021); O'Brien (2021).
5. Goodchild (2022), pp. 53–76; Goodchild (2021), pp. 75–103.
6. Kimmerer (2013); Harris and Wasilewski (2004), pp. 498–503; Arrows (2016).

7. McGilchrist (2021).
8. McDonald and Patterson (2007), pp. 169–192.
9. Catton and Dunlap (1978), pp. 41–49.
10. McDonald and Patterson (2007), p. 171.
11. Rockström et al. (2009b), pp. 472–475.
12. Atkins, Wilson, and Hayes (2019).
13. *UN News* (2022).
14. Jiménez (2022).
15. Maturana and Varela (1987).
16. Harris and Wasilewski (2004), pp. 498–503; Arrows (2016); Kimmerer (2013).
17. Masson-Delmotte et al. (2021).
18. IPBES (2019).
19. Waddock (2016); pp. 91–105; Monbiot (2016); Riedy (2020), pp. 100–112; Lovins et al. (2018); Pirson (2017).
20. Kenter et al. (2021).
21. Lovins et al. (2018).
22. Eisler (2008).
23. Waddock (2016), pp. 91–105.
24. Waddock (2020), p.7553.
25. Blackmore (2000); Blackmore (1997), pp. 43–49.
26. Dawkins (1976).
27. Blackmore (2000).
28. Lent (2021).
29. Waddock (2016), pp. 75–90.
30. Meadows (1999).
31. Blackmore (2000).

## Chapter 4

1. Lovins et al. (2018).
2. Meadows (1999).
3. Alexander (1977, 1979); Finidori, Borghini, and Henfrey (2015).
4. Jacobs (1961, 2002).
5. Capra (2015), pp. 242–249; Capra (2005), pp. 33–44; Capra (1995).

6. Maturana and Varela (1987, 2012).

7. Weber (2013).

8. Swanson and Miller (2009), pp. 136–148.

9. Fullerton (2015).

10. McDonough and Braungart (2010); Hawken, Lovins, and Lovins (2013).

11. Harris and Wasilewski (2004), pp. 498–503; Arrows (2016); Kimmerer (2013).

12. Kuenkel and Waddock (2019); Waddock and Kuenkel (2020).

13. Blackmore (2000).

14. Alexander (1977).

15. Weber (2013).

16. McDonough and Braungart (2010).

17. Alexander (1977).

18. Weber (2013); Fullerton (2015).

19. Jacobs (1961).

20. De Waal (1996).

21. Atkins, Wilson, and Hayes (2019).

22. Wilber (2001); Torbert and Cook-Greuter (2004); Kegan (2002); Kohlberg (1981); Gilligan (1982).

23. Capra and Luisi (2014).

24. Heinrich (2017); Atkins, Wilson, and Hayes (2019).

25. Weber (2016).

26. Capra and Luisi (2014).

27. Weber (2013).

28. Koestler (1968), pp. 45–48.

29. Alexander (1977); Bohm (2002).

30. Alexander (1977).

31. Kuenkel and Waddock (2019), pp. 14–38; Waddock and Kuenkel (2020), pp. 342–358.

32. Maturana and Varela (1987).

33. Lovins et al. (2018).

34. Waddock (2016), pp. 91–105; Monbiot (2016); Lovins et al. (2017); Lent (2017).

35. Eisler (2008); Eisler and Fry (2019); Francis (2015).

36. O'Neill et al. (2018), pp. 88–95; Chapin et al. (2011), pp. 44–53; Rockström et al. (2009a, 2009b), pp. 472–475.
37. Lovins et al. (2018); Kenter et al. (2015), pp. 86–99; Raworth (2017); Max-Neef (2010), pp. 200–210.
38. Capra (2015), pp. 242–249; Capra (2005), pp. 33–44; Capra and Luisi (2014); Bohm (2002); Costanza et al. (2014), p. 283; Dasgupta (1995), pp. 91.
39. Harris and Wasilewski (2004), pp. 498–503; Arrows (2016); Kimmerer (2013).
40. Lent (2017); Atkins, Wilson, and Hayes (2019); Heinrich (2017).
41. Pirson (2017), pp. 553–565; Pirson and Lawrence (2010), pp. 553–565; Melé (2016), pp. 33–55.
42. Levy and Spicer (2013), pp. 659–678; Kossoff (2019), pp. 51–66; Nussbaum (2003), pp.33–59; Sen (2014), pp. 525–547.
43. Waddock (2020), p. 7553.
44. Ostrom (2010), pp. 155–166; Ostrom (2000), pp. 137–158.
45. Raworth (2017); Chapin et al. (2011), pp. 44–53; O'Neill et al. (2018); Rockstrom et al. (2018), pp. 88–95; Rockstrom et al. (2009a), p. 32.
46. Donaldson and Walsh (2015), pp. 181–207.
47. Max-Neef (2010), pp. 200–210; Sen (1999); Nussbaum (2003), pp. 33–59.
48. Pirson (2017), pp. 553–565; Hicks (2013).
49. Kossoff (2019), pp. 51–66.
50. Ibid.
51. Capra (2005), pp. 242–249; Capra and Luisi (2014); Laszlo et al. (2021).
52. Capra (2005), pp. 242–249.
53. Chapin et al. (2011). pp. 44–53.
54. Kimmerer (2013); Lipton and Bhaerman (2009).
55. Atkins, Wilson, and Hayes (2019); Heinrich (2017).
56. Eisler (2008).
57. Max-Neef (2010), pp. 200–210; Turner and Fisher (2008), pp. 1067–1068.
58. Pio et al. (2013), pp. 195–219; Pio and Waddock (2020).

59. McDonough and Braungart (2010).

60. Robert (2002).

61. Harris and Wasilewski (2004), pp. 498–503; Arrows (2016); Kimmerer (2013).

62. Benyus (1997).

63. Hawken (2021).

64. McDonough and Braungart (2010).

65. Davis (2016); Davis (2009), pp. 27–44.

66. Backlund (2000), pp. 444–451.

# Chapter 5

1. Waddock and Waddell (2021a), pp. 1–41.

2. Ackoff and Gharajedaghi (1996), pp. 13–23.

3. Cederlof and Hornborg (2021), pp. 111–123.

4. Ibid.

5. Ibid.

6. Weber (2013).

7. Donaldson and Walsh (2015), pp. 181–207.

8. Meadows (1999).

9. Kimmerer (2013); Arrows (2016).

10. Korten (2015).

11. Cederlof and Hornborg (2021), pp. 111–123.

12. Costanza et al. (2014), p. 283; Costanza et al. (2009).

13. Boarini and D'Ercole (2013), pp. 289–314; Eisler (2008); Hoff and Stiglitz (2016), pp. 25–57.

14. Durand (2015), pp. 4–17; Costanza, Fioramonti, and Kubiszewski (2016), p. 59; Costanza (2001), pp. 459–468.

15. Durand (2015), pp. 4–17; Boarini and D'Ercole (2013); Mizobuchi (2014).

16. Thinley and Hartz-Karp (2019), p. 11.

17. Talberth and Weisdorf (2017), pp. 1–11.

18. Patton (2019).

19. Meadows (1999).

20. Abram (2012).

# Chapter 6

1. Wadell (2018), pp. 40–45.
2. Kjell (2007), pp. 487–504.
3. Geels (2011), pp. 24–40; Dahle (2007), pp. 487–504.
4. Waddell (2011).
5. Geels (2011), pp. 24–40.
6. Holling (2001), pp. 390–405; Allen et al. (2014), pp. 578–589.
7. Geels (2011), pp. 24–40.
8. Holling (2001), pp. 390–405.
9. Waddock and Waddell (2021b), pp. 165–182; Lee and Waddock (2021), p. 9813.
10. Adapted from Waddock and Waddell (2021b), p. 168.
11. Ibid., p. 169.
12. Ibid.
13. Lee and Waddock (2021), p. 9813.
14. Ibid.
15. Jones and Ael (2022).
16. Jones and Bowes (2016); Jones and Bowes (2017), pp. 229–248.
17. Capra (1997).
18. Meadows (1999, 2008).
19. Weick, Sutcliffe, and Obstfeld (2005), pp. 409–421.
20. Blackmore (2000).
21. Sharpe (2015), pp. 4–6.
22. Cooperrider (2001); Cooperrider and Whitney (1999); Whitney and Cooperrider (2000), pp. 13–26.
23. Scharmer and Kaufer (2013); Scharmer (2007).
24. Jones and Ael (2022).
25. Lee and Waddock (2021), p. 9813.
26. Ibid.
27. Patton (2019).
28. Isaacs (1999).
29. Cooperrider and Whitney (1999).
30. Sharpe et al. (2016).
31. Scharmer (2007).

32. Weisbord and Janoff (1995, 2010).
33. Brown (2010).
34. Owen (1997a, 1997b).
35. Senge (2006).
36. Geels and Schot (2007), pp. 399–417.
37. Geels (2012), pp. 471–482.

## Chapter 7

1. Waddock et al. (2022), pp. 77–100.
2. Ibid.
3. Meadows (1999).
4. Isaacs (1999).
5. Torbert and Cook-Grueter (2004).
6. Schön (1983).
7. Senge et al. (2004).
8. Patton (2019).
9. Ibid.
10. Gates et al. (2022), pp. 9–11.
11. Ostrom (1990, 2000).
12. Ostrom (2010a).
13. Kimmerer (2013); Arrows (2016); Harris and Wasilewski (2004).
14. Laszlo et al. (2021).
15. Ostrom (2000).
16. Waddell et al. (2021).
17. Waddell et al. (2022).

## Chapter 8

1. Fundamental Design Principles (2022).
2. Alexander (1977).
3. Jacobs (1961).
4. Iversen, Halskov, and Leong (2012), pp. 87–103.
5. Brown (1980), pp. 181–208.
6. Orton and Weick (1990), pp. 203–223; Weick (1976), pp. 1–19.
7. Brown (1980).

8. Popp et al. (2014).

9. Weber and Khademian (2008), pp. 334–349.

10. Popp et al. (2014).

11. Ibid.

12. Kuenkel and Waddock (2019); Waddock and Kuenkel (2020).

13. Ibid.

14. Schwartz (2012), pp. 3–4.

15. Ibid., p. 4.

16. Cooperrider (2001).

17. Scharmer (2007).

18. Weisbord and Janoff (1995).

19. Cooperrider and Whitney (2001), pp. 611–630; Hoffman and Haigh (2010), pp. 1–37; Marsh et al. (2004), pp. 1177–1179.

20. Senge (1994).

21. Division for Diversity, Equity, and Inclusion (2020).

22. Wood and Gray (1991), pp. 139–162.

23. Thomson, Perry, and Miller (2009), pp. 23–56.

24. Ind and Coates (2013), pp. 86–95.

25. Linden (2010), pp. 57–62; Paxton and Stralen (2015), pp. 11–25.

26. McGilchrist (2019, 2021).

27. Holling (2001); Waddock et al. (2015), pp. 993–1012; Capra and Luisi (2014).

28. Rittel and Webber (1973), pp. 155–169; Churchman (1967).

29. Alexander (1977).

30. McGilchrist (2021); Ehrenfeld (2008).

31. Koestler (1968).

32. Atkins, Wilson, and Hayes (2019).

33. Arrows (2016); Harris and Wasilewski (2004), pp. 498–503; Kimmerer (2013).

34. Arrows (2016); Kimmerer (2013).

35. Pio et al. (2013), pp. 195–219.

36. Kimmerer (2013).

37. Weber (2013).

38. Kuenkel and Waddock (2019), pp. 14–38.

39. Fullerton (2015).

40. Ostrom (2010b); Skelcher (2005).

41. Fullerton (2015).

42. Lipton and Bhaerman (2009).

43. Fullerton (2015).

44. Maturana and Varela (2012).

45. Holling (2001).

46. Kuenkel and Waddock (2019); Waddock and Kuenkel (2020).

47. Holling (2001).

# Chapter 9

1. Weick (1976).

2. Caniglia et al. (2021), pp. 93–100.

3. Rosile, Boje, and Claw (2018), pp. 307–328.

4. Raelin (2003).

5. Brown (1980).

6. Waddock (2013), pp. 129–147; Waddock (2010), pp. 177–196.

7. Waddock (2010), p. 131.

8. Waddock (2010, 2013).

9. Werhane (2008), pp. 463–474.

10. Kegan (2002).

11. Goleman (1995).

12. Abowitz (2007), pp. 287–298.

13. Wamsler (2020), pp. 112–130.

14. Ibid.

15. McGilchrist (2019, 2021).

16. Wamsler (2020).

17. Goleman (1995); Goleman, Boyatzis, and McKee (2013).

18. Wamsler (2020).

19. Kegan (2002).

20. Wamsler (2020).

21. Ibid.

22. Senge (1994).

23. McGilchrist (2019, 2021).

24. Cabrera, Colosi, and Lobdell (2008), pp. 299–310.

25. Dewey (1980).

26. Waddock (2010).

27. Caviglia-Harris et al. (2021); Fairhurst et al. (2020), pp. 598–614.

28. Goleman, Boyatzis, and McKee (2013).

29. Ibid.

30. Denning (2021), pp. 26–31; Goldstein et al. (2015). pp. 1285–1303.

31. Bentz, O' Brien, and Scoville-Simonds (2022).

32. Pearce, Conger, and Locke (2007), pp. 281–288; Locke (2003).

33. Pearce, Conger, and Locke (2007).

34. Caviglia-Harris et al. (2021); Fairhurst et al. (2020).

35. Locke (2003).

36. Raelin (2016), pp. 1–18; Raelin (2017), pp. 215–221; Raelin (2016).

37. Lawrence (2017), pp. 89–96.

38. Ibid.

39. Netweaver Network (2022).

40. Netweaver Network (2022); Goldstein (2021).

41. Brown (1980), pp. 181–208.

42. Scharmer and Kaufer (2013); Scharmer (2007).

43. Raelin (2016b).

# References

Abowitz, K.K. 2007. "Moral Perception Through Aesthetics Engaging Imaginations in Educational Ethics." *Journal of Teacher Education* 58, no. 4, pp. 287–298.

Abram, D. 2012. *The Spell of the Sensuous: Perception and Language in a More-Than-Human World.* Knopf Doubleday Publishing Group.

Abram, D. July 22, 2012. "On Being Human in a More-than-Human World." https://humansandnature.org/to-be-human-david-abram/ (accessed July 17, 2022).

Ackoff, R.L. and J. Gharajedaghi. 1996. "Reflections on Systems and Their Models." *Systems Research* 13, no. 1, pp. 13–23.

Alexander, C. 1977. *A Pattern Language: Towns, Buildings, Construction.* Oxford, UK: Oxford University Press. https://global.oup.com/academic/product/a-pattern-language-9780195019193?cc=us&lang=en& (accessed July 21, 2023).

Alexander, C. 1979. *The Timeless Way of Building.* New York, NY: Oxford University Press.

Allen, C.R., D.G. Angeler, A.S. Garmestani, L.H. Gunderson, and C.S. Holling. June 1, 2014. "Panarchy: Theory and Application." *Ecosystems* 17, no. 4, pp. 578–589. https://doi.org/10.1007/s10021-013-9744-2.

António, G. 2020. "Tackling Inequality a New Social Contract for a New Era. Nelson Mandela Annual Lecture 2020." United Nations. www.un.org/en/coronavirus/tackling-inequality-new-social-contract-new-era (accessed July 21, 2023).

Arrow, K., B. Bolin, R. Costanza, P. Dasgupta, C. Folke, C.S. Holling, J. Bengt-Owe, et al. 1995. "Economic Growth, Carrying Capacity, and the Environment." *Ecological Economics* 15, no. 2. pp. 91.

Arrows, F. 2016. *Point of Departure: Returning to Our More Authentic Worldview for Education and Survival.* Charlotte, NC: IAP.

Atkins, P.W.B., D.S. Wilson, and S.C. Hayes. 2019. *Prosocial: Using Evolutionary Science to Build Productive, Equitable, and Collaborative Groups.* Oakland: New Harbinger Publications.

Backlund, A. January 1, 2000. "The Definition of System." *Kybernetes* 29, no. 4, pp. 444–451. https://doi.org/10.1108/03684920010322055.

Batie, S.S. 2008. "Wicked Problems and Applied Economics." *American Journal of Agricultural Economics* 90, no. 5, pp. 1176–1191. https://doi.org/10.1111/j.1467-8276.2008.01202.x.

Bentz, J., K. O'Brien, and M. Soville-Simonds. 2022. "Beyond 'Blah Blah Blah': Exploring the 'How' of Transformation." *Sustainability Science.* https://doi .org/10.1007/s11625-022-01123-0.

Benyus, J.M. 1997. *Biomimicry.* New York, NY: William Morrow.

Blackmore, S. 1997. "The Power of the Meme." *Skeptic* 5, no. 2, pp. 43–49.

Blackmore, S. 2000. *The Meme Machine,* vol. 25. Oxford, UK: Oxford Paperbacks.

Boarini, R. and M.M. D'Ercole. 2013. "Going Beyond GDP: An OECD Perspective*." *Fiscal Studies* 34, no. 3, pp. 289–314. https://doi.org/10 .1111/j.1475-5890.2013.12007.x.

Bohm, D. 2002. *Wholeness and the Implicate Order.* London: Routledge. https:// doi.org/10.4324/9780203995150.

Bollier, D. and S. Helfrich. 2019. *Free, Fair, and Alive.* Gabriola, BC, Canada: New Society Publishers. https://newsociety.com/products/9780865719217.

Brown, L.D. 1980. "Planned Change in Underorganized Systems." In *Systems Theory for Organization Development,* ed. T.G. Cummings, pp. 181–208. Chichester, UK: Wiley.

Brown, J. 2010. *The World Café: Shaping Our Futures Through Conversations That Matter.* ReadHowYouWant.com.

Cabrera, D., L. Colosi, and C. Lobdell. 2008. "Systems Thinking." *Evaluation and Program Planning* 31, no. 3, pp. 299–310.

Caniglia, G, C. Luederitz, T. von Wirth, I. Fazey, B. Martín-López, K. Hondrila, A. König, H.V. Wehrden, et al. February 2021. "A Pluralistic and Integrated Approach to Action-Oriented Knowledge for Sustainability." *Nature Sustainability* 4, no. 2, pp. 93–100. https://doi.org/10.1038/s41893-020-00616-z.

Capra, F. 1995. *The Web of Life.* New York, NY: Anchor Doubleday.

Capra, F. 1997. *The Web of Life: A New Scientific Understanding of Living Systems.* Anchor.

Capra, F. 2005. "Complexity and Life." *Theory, Culture & Society* 22, no. 5, pp. 33–44.

Capra, F. October 25, 2015. "The Systems View of Life: A Unifying Conception of Mind, Matter, and Life." *Cosmos and History: The Journal of Natural and Social Philosophy* 11, no. 2, pp. 242–249.

Capra, F. and P.L. Luisi. 2014. *The Systems View of Life: A Unifying Vision.* Cambridge University Press.

Catton, W.R. and R.E. Dunlap. 1978. "Environmental Sociology: A New Paradigm." *The American Sociologist* 13, no. 1, pp. 41–49.

Caviglia-Harris, J., K.E. Hodges, H. Brian, E.M. Benett, G. Kathleen, K. Margaret, L. Karen, L. Meg, et al. August 5, 2021. "The Six Dimensions of Collective Leadership That Advance Sustainability Objectives: Rethinking What It Means to Be an Academic Leader." *Ecology and Society* 26, no. 3. https://doi.org/10.5751/ES-12396-260309.

Cederlof, G.V. and A. Hornborg. March 15, 2021. "System Boundaries as Epistemological and Ethnographic Problems: Assessing Energy Technology and Socio-Environmental Impact." *Journal of Political Ecology* 28, no. 1, pp. 111–123. https://doi.org/10.2458/jpe.2303.

Chapin, F.S., S.T.A. Pickett, M.E. Power, R.B. Jackson, D.M. Carter, and C. Duke. 2011. "Earth Stewardship: A Strategy for Social–Ecological Transformation to Reverse Planetary Degradation." *Journal of Environmental Studies and Sciences* 1, no. 1. pp. 44–53.

Churchman, C.W. 1967. "Wicked Problems." *Management Science.* http://search .ebscohost.com/login.aspx?direct=true&db=bth&AN=7124291&site=bsi-live.

Conklin, J. 2006. *Wicked Problems & Social Complexity.* USA: CogNexus Institute Napa.

Cooperrider, D.L. 2001. *Appreciative Inquiry: An Emerging Direction for Organization Development.* Champaign, IL: Stipes.

Cooperrider, D.L. and D.K. Whitney. 1999. *Appreciative Inquiry.* San Francisco: Berrett-Koehler.

Cooperrider, D.L. and D. Whitney. 2001. "A Positive Revolution in Change: Appreciative Inquiry." *Public Administration and Public Policy* 87, pp. 611–630.

Costanza, R. June 1, 2001. "Visions, Values, Valuation, and the Need for an Ecological Economics: All Scientific Analysis Is Based on a 'Preanalytic Vision,' and the Major Source of Uncertainty about Current Environmental Policies Results from Differences in Visions and World Views." *BioScience* 51, no. 6, pp. 459–468. https://doi.org/10.1641/0006-3568(2001)051[0459: VVVATN]2.0.CO;2.

Costanza, R., L. Fioramonti, and I. Kubiszewski. 2016. "The UN Sustainable Development Goals and the Dynamics of Well-Being." *Frontiers in Ecology and the Environment* 14, no. 2, p. 59.

Costanza, R, I. Kubiszewski, E. Giovannini, H. Lovins, J. McGlade, K.E. Pickett, K.V. Ragnarsdóttir, D. Roberts, et al. 2014. "Development: Time to Leave GDP Behind." *Nature News* 505, no. 7483, p. 283.

Costanza, R., H. Maureen, J. Talberth, and S. Posner. 2009. "Beyond GDP: The Need for New Measures of Progress." *The Pardee Papers* 4.

Dahle, K. June 1, 2007. "When Do Transformative Initiatives Really Transform? A Typology of Different Paths for Transition to a Sustainable Society." *Futures* 39, no. 5, pp. 487–504. Transformative Initiatives. https://doi.org/10.1016/ j.futures.2006.10.007.

David, B. and H. Silke. 2019. *Free, Fair, and Alive.* Gabriola, BC, Canada: New Society Publishers. https://newsociety.com/products/9780865719217.

Davis, G.F. 2009. "The Rise and Fall of Finance and the End of the Society of Organizations." *Academy of Management Perspectives* 23, no. 3, pp. 27–44. https://doi.org/10.5465/AMP.2009.43479262.

Davis, G.F. 2016. *The Vanishing American Corporation: Navigating the Hazards of a New Economy*. Berrett-Koehler Publishers.

Dawkins, R. 1976. *The Selfish Gene*. Oxford, UK: Oxford University Press.

Delmotte, M., V.P. Zhai, A. Pirani, S.L. Connors, C. Péan, S. Berger, N. Caud, Y. Chen, et al. 2021. "IPCC 2021: Summary for Policymakers." In: *Climate Change 2021: The Physical Science Basis. Contribution of Working Group I to the Sixth Assessment Report of the Intergovernmental Panel on Climate Change.*

Denning, S. January 1, 2021. "Effective Storytelling: Leadership's Magic Motivational Methodology." *Strategy & Leadership* 49, no. 3, pp. 26–31. https://doi.org/10.1108/SL-03-2021-0029.

De Waal, F.B.M. 1996. *Good Natured*. Cambridge, MA: Harvard University Press.

Dewey, J. 1980. *Art as Experience*. New York, NY: Perigee Books.

Division for Diversity, Equity, and Inclusion. 2020. "Toolkit for Equity-Minded Decisions & Policies." *Inclusive Excellence*. Charlottesville, VA: University of Virginia. https://dei.virginia.edu/.

Donaldson, T. and J.P. Walsh. 2015. "Toward a Theory of Business." *Research in Organizational Behavior* 35, pp. 181–207.

Dow, J. 1986. "Universal Aspects of Symbolic Healing: A Theoretical Synthesis." *American Anthropologist* 88, no. 1, pp. 56–69.

Durand, M. 2015. "The OECD Better Life Initiative: How's Life? And the Measurement of Well-being." *Review of Income and Wealth* 61, no. 1, pp. 4–17.

Ehrenfeld, J. 2008. *Sustainability by Design: A Subversive Strategy for Transforming Our Consumer Culture*. New Haven: Yale University Press.

Eisler, R. 2008. *The Real Wealth of Nations: Creating a Caring Economics*. San Francisco: Berrett-Koehler Publishers.

Eisler, R. and D.P. Fry. 2019. *Nurturing Our Humanity: How Domination and Partnership Shape Our Brains, Lives, and Future*. Oxford University Press.

Fairhurst, G.T., B. Jackson, E.G. Foldy, and S.M. Ospina. April 1, 2020. "Studying Collective Leadership: The Road Ahead." *Human Relations* 73, no. 4, pp. 598–614. https://doi.org/10.1177/0018726719898736.

Finegan, A. 2003. "Wicked Problems, Organisational Complexity and Knowledge Management: A Systems Approach." *International Journal of Knowledge, Culture and Change Management* 3, pp. 35–45.

Finidori, H., S.G. Borhini, and T. Henfrey. 2015. "Towards a Fourth Generation Pattern Language: Patterns as Epistemic Threads for Systemic Orientation." In *Proceedings of the Purplsoc (Pursuit of Pattern Languages for Societal Change) Conference 2015.*

Francis, P. 2019. "Laudato Si': On Care for Our Common Home." In *Ideals and Ideologies*, pp. 503–510. Routledge.

Fullerton, J. 2015. "Regenerative Capitalism: How Universal Principles and Patterns Will Shape Our New Economy." Capital Institute [Online]. URL:

http://Capitalinstitute.Org/Wp-Content/Uploads/2015/04/2015-Regene
rative-Capitalism-4-20-15-Final.Pdf.

"Fundamental Design Principles." 2022. *Engineering Design.* www.mcgill.ca/
engineeringdesign/step-step-design-process/design-principles-and-laws/
fundamental-design-principles (accessed June 30, 2022).

Gabriel, Z. 2019. "Global Wealth Inequality." *Annual Review of Economics* 11,
pp. 109–138.

Gates, E.F., G. Page, J.M. Crespo, M.N. Oporto, and J. Bohórquez. October 25,
2022. "Ethics of Evaluation for Socio-Ecological Transformation: Case-Based
Critical Systems Analysis of Motivation, Power, Expertise, and Legitimacy."
*Evaluation.* https://doi.org/10.1177/13563890221129640.

Geels, F.W. June 1, 2011. "The Multi-Level Perspective on Sustainability Transitions:
Responses to Seven Criticisms." *Environmental Innovation and Societal Transitions*
1, no. 1, pp. 24–40. https://doi.org/10.1016/j.eist.2011.02.002.

Geels, F.W. September 1, 2012. "A Socio-Technical Analysis of Low-Carbon
Transitions: Introducing the Multi-Level Perspective into Transport
Studies." *Journal of Transport Geography* 24, pp. 471–482. Special Section on
Theoretical Perspectives on Climate Change Mitigation in Transport. https://
doi.org/10.1016/j.jtrangeo.2012.01.021.

Geels, F.W. and J. Schot. 2007. "Typology of Sociotechnical Transition Pathways."
*Research Policy* 36, no. 3, pp. 399–417.

Gilligan, C. 1982. *In a Different Voice: Psychological Theory and Women's
Development.* Cambridge, MA: Harvard University Press.

Goldstein, B.E. March 4, 2021. "System Weaving During Crisis." *Social
Innovations Journal* 5. https://socialinnovationsjournal.com/index.php/sij/
article/view/710.

Goldstein, B.E., A.T. Wessells, R. Lejano, and W. Butler. May 1, 2015.
"Narrating Resilience: Transforming Urban Systems Through Collaborative
Storytelling." *Urban Studies* 52, no. 7, pp. 1285–1303. https://doi.org/10
.1177/0042098013505653.

Goleman, D. 1995. *Emotional Intelligence.* New York, NY: Bantam Books.

Goleman, D., R.E. Boyatzis, and A. McKee. 2013. *Primal Leadership: Unleashing
the Power of Emotional Intelligence.* Harvard Business Press.

Goodchild, M. February 25, 2021. "Relational Systems Thinking: That's How
Change Is Going to Come, From Our Earth Mother." *Journal of Awareness-Based
Systems Change* 1, no. 1, pp. 75–103. https://doi.org/10.47061/jabsc.v1i1.577.

Goodchild, M. May 31, 2022. "Relational Systems Thinking: The Dibaajimowin
(Story) of Re-Theorizing 'Systems Thinking' and 'Complexity Science'."
*Journal of Awareness-Based Systems Change* 2, no. 1, pp. 53–76. https://doi
.org/10.47061/jabsc.v2i1.2027.

Graeber, D. and D. Wengrow. 2021. *The Dawn of Everything: A New History of
Humanity.* New York, NY: Farrar, Strauss and Giroux.

Grobman, G.M. 2005. "Complexity Theory: A New Way to Look at Organizational Change." *Public Administration Quarterly* 20, no. 3, pp. 350–382.

Guterres, A. 2020. *Tackling Inequality: A New Social Contract for a New Era. Nelson Mandela Annual Lecture 2020.* United Nations. https://www.un.org/en/coronavirus/tackling-inequality-new-social-contract-new-era.

Harris, L.D. and J. Wasilewski. 2004. "Indigeneity, an Alternative Worldview: Four R's (Relationship, Responsibility, Reciprocity, Redistribution) vs. Two P's (Power and Profit). Sharing the Journey towards Conscious Evolution." *Systems Research and Behavioral Science: The Official Journal of the International Federation for Systems Research* 21, no. 5, pp. 489–503.

Hawken, P. 2007. *Blessed Unrest: How the Largest Movement in the World Came Into Being, and Why No One Saw It Coming.* New York, NY: Viking.

Hawken, P. 2021. *Regeneration: Ending the Climate Crisis in One Generation.* New York, NY: Penguin Books.

Hawken, P., ed. 2017. *Drawdown: The Most Comprehensive Plan Ever Proposed to Reverse Global Warming.* New York, NY: Penguin Books.

Hawken, P., A.B. Lovins, and L.H. Lovins. 2013. *Natural Capitalism: The Next Industrial Revolution.* Routledge.

Heinrich, J. 2017. *The Secret of Our Success: How Culture Is Driving Human Evolution, Domesticating Our Species, and Making Us Smarter.* Princeton, NJ: Princeton University Press.

Hicks, D. 2013. *Dignity: Its Essential Role in Resolving Conflict.* Reprint edition. Yale University Press.

Hoff, K. and J.E. Stiglitz. June 1, 2016. "Striving for Balance in Economics: Towards a Theory of the Social Determination of Behavior." *Journal of Economic Behavior & Organization* 126, pp. 25–57. Thriving through Balance. https://doi.org/10.1016/j.jebo.2016.01.005.

Hoffman, A.J. and N. Haigh. 2010. "Positive Deviance for a Sustainable World: Linking Sustainability and Positive Organizational Scholarship." *Working Papers (Faculty)—University of Michigan Business School,* pp. 1–37.

Holling, C.S. August 1, 2001. "Understanding the Complexity of Economic, Ecological, and Social Systems." *Ecosystems* 4, no. 5, pp. 390–405. https://doi.org/10.1007/s10021-001-0101-5.

Humberto, R.M. and F.J. Varela. 1987. *The Tree of Knowledge: The Biological Roots of Human Understanding.* Boston, MA: New Science Library/Shambhala Publications.

IMAGINE. 2016. *(Ultimate Mix, 2020)—John Lennon & The Plastic Ono Band (with the Flux Fiddlers) HD.* www.youtube.com/watch?v=YkgkThdzX-8.

Ind, N. and N. Coates. January 1, 2013. "The Meanings of Co-creation." *European Business Review* 25, no. 1, pp. 86–95. https://doi.org/10.1108/09555341311287754.

IPBES. 2019. In *Summary for Policymakers of the Global Assessment Report on Biodiversity and Ecosystem Services of the Intergovernmental Science-Policy Platform on Biodiversity and Ecosystem Services*, eds. S. Díaz, J. Settele, E.S. Brondízio, H.T. Ngo, M. Guèze, J. Agard, A. Arneth, P. Balvanera, K.A. Brauman, S.H.M. Butchart, K.M.A. Chan, L.A. Garibaldi, K. Ichii, J. Liu, S.M. Subramanian, G.F. Midgley, P. Miloslavich, Z. Molnár, D. Obura, A. Pfaff, S. Polasky, A. Purvis, J. Razzaque, B. Reyers, R. Roy Chowdhury, Y.J. Shin, I.J. Visseren-Hamakers, K.J. Willis, and C.N. Zayas, 56 pages. Bonn, Germany: IPBES secretariat. https://doi.org/10.5281/zenodo.3553579.

Isaacs, W. 1999. *Dialogue and the Art of Thinking Together: A Pioneering Approach to Communicating in Business and in Life*. New York, NY: Currency.

Iversen, O.S., K. Halskov, and T.W. Leong. June 1, 2012. "Values-Led Participatory Design." *CoDesign* 8, no. 2-3, pp. 87–103. https://doi.org/ 10.1080/15710882.2012.672575.

Jacobs, J. 1961. *The Death and Life of Great American Cities*. New York, NY: Vintage.

Jacobs, J. 2002. *The Nature of Economies*. Toronto, Canada: Vintage.

Jiménez, J. July 18, 2022. "U.N. Chief Warns That Humanity Faces 'Collective Suicide' Over Climate Crisis." *The New York Times*. www.nytimes.com/2022/ 07/18/world/europe/un-chief-suicide-warning-climate-change.html.

Jones, P. and K.V. Ael. 2022. *Design Journeys through Complex Systems Practice Tools for Systemic Design*. Amsterdam, The Netherlands: BIS Publishers. www .bispublishers.com/design-journeys-through-complex-systems.html?source= facebook.

Jones, P. and J. Bowes.2016. "Synthesis Maps: Systemic Design Pedagogy." In *Narrative, and Intervention*, pp. 1–13. RSD5 Symposium.

Jones, P. and J. Bowes. September 1, 2017. "Rendering Systems Visible for Design: Synthesis Maps as Constructivist Design Narratives." *She Ji: The Journal of Design, Economics, and Innovation* 3, no. 3, pp. 229–248. https:// doi.org/10.1016/j.sheji.2017.12.001.

Kauffman, S.A. 1995. *At Home in the Universe: The Search for Laws of Self-Organization and Complexity*. USA: Oxford University Press.

Kegan, R. 2002. *In Over Our Heads: The Mental Demands of Modern Life*. Cambridge, MA: Harvard University Press.

Kenter, J.O., L. O'Brien, N. Hockley, N. Ravenscroft, I. Fazey, K.N. Irvine, M.S. Reed, M. Christie, et al. 2015. "What Are Shared and Social Values of Ecosystems?" *Ecological Economics* 111, pp. 86–99.

Kenter, J., S. Waddock, S. Martino, S. Buckton, and S. Waddell, April 22, 2021. "Emerging Insights From GANE: The Global Assessment for a New Economics." Presentation, SUSTEX2021, Virtual. www.tamuct.edu/coba/ sustex.html.

Kimmerer, R.W. 2013. *Braiding Sweetgrass: Indigenous Wisdom, Scientific Knowledge and the Teachings of Plants.* Milkweed Editions.

Koestler, A. 1968. "The Ghost in the Machine." *Psychiatric Communication* 10, no. 2. pp. 45–48.

Kohlberg, L. 1921. *The Philosophy of Moral Development: Moral Stages and the Idea of Justice,* 1. San Francisco: harper & row.

Korten, D. 2015. *Change the Story, Change the Future: A Living Economy for a Living Earth.* San Francisco: Berrett-Koehler Publishers.

Korten, D. 2017. "Ecological Civilization and the New Enlightenment." *Tikkun* 32, no. 4, pp. 17–24.

Korten, D. 2021. "Ecological Civilization: From Emergency to Emergence." New York, NY: Club of Rome. www.clubofrome.org/publication/ecological-civilization-from-emergency-to-emergence/.

Kossoff, G. 2019. "Cosmopolitan Localism: The Planetary Networking of Everyday Life in Place." *Centro de Estudios En Diseño y Comunicación* 73, pp. 51–66.

Kuenkel, P. and S. Waddock. 2019. "Stewarding Aliveness in a Troubled Earth System," *Cadmus* 4, no. 1, pp. 14–38.

Laszlo, C., S. Waddock, A. Maheshwari, N. Giorgia, and J. Storberg-Walker. November 24, 2021. "Quantum Worldviews: How Science and Spirituality Are Converging to Transform Consciousness for Meaningful Solutions to Wicked Problems." *Humanistic Management Journal.* https://doi.org/10.1007/s41463-021-00114-0.

Lawrence, R.L. 2017. "Understanding Collaborative Leadership in Theory and Practice." *New Directions for Adult and Continuing Education* 156, pp. 89–96. https://doi.org/10.1002/ace.20262.

Leadbeater, C. and J. Winhall. November 2021. *System Innovation on Purpose.* Copenhagen, Denmark: Rockwool Foundation. www.systeminnovation.org/s/SII_SystemInnovationOnPurpose_2021.pdf.

Lee, J.Y. and S. Waddock. 2021. "How Transformation Catalysts Take Catalytic Action." *Sustainability* 13, no. 17, p. 9813.

Lent, J. 2017. *The Patterning Instinct: A Cultural History of Humanity's Search for Meaning.* Amherst, NY: Prometheus.

Lent, J. 2021. *The Web of Meaning: Integrating Science and Traditional Wisdom to Find Our Place in the Universe.* Gabriola, BC, Canada: New Society Publishers.

Levy, D.L. and A. Spicer. September 1, 2013. "Contested Imaginaries and the Cultural Political Economy of Climate Change." *Organization* 20, no. 5, pp. 659–678. https://doi.org/10.1177/1350508413489816.

Linden, R. 2010. "Developing a Collaborative Mindset." *Leader to Leader* 2010, no. 58, pp. 57–62. https://doi.org/10.1002/ltl.443.

Lipton, B.H. and S. Bhaerman. 2009. *Spontaneous Evolution: Our Positive Future and a Way to Get There from Here.* Hay House, Inc.

Locke, E.A. 2003. "Leadership: Starting at the Top." In *Shared Leadership: Reframing the Hows and Whys of Leadership,* eds. C.L. Pearce and J.A. Conger. Thousand Oaks, CA: Sage.

Lovins, H. 2016. "Needed: A Better Story." *Humanistic Management Journal* 1, no. 1, pp. 75–90.

Lovins, L.H., S. Wallis, A. Wijkman, and J. Fullerton. 2018. *A Finer Future: Creating an Economy in Service to Life.* Gabriola Island, BC, Canada: New Society Publishers.

Markard, J. and D. Rosenbloom. December 31, 2020. "A Tale of Two Crises: COVID-19 and Climate." *Sustainability: Science, Practice and Policy* 17, no. S1, pp. 53–60. https://doi.org/10.1080/15487733.2020.1765679.

Marsh, D.R., D.G. Schroeder, K.A. Dearden, J. Sternin, and M. Sternin. November 11, 2004. "The Power of Positive Deviance." *BMJ* 329, no. 7475, pp. 1177–1179. https://doi.org/10.1136/bmj.329.7475.1177.

Mason, R. and I. Mitroff. 2010. "Complexity: The Nature of Real World Problems." *Strategy: Process, Content, Context, an International Perspective,* p. 27. Cengage.

Masson-Delmotte, V., P. Zhai, A. Pirani, S.L. Connors, C. Péan, S. Berger, N. Caud, Y. Chen, L. Goldfarb, M.I. Gomis, M. Huang, K. Leitzell, E. Lonnoy, J.B.R. Matthews, T.K. Maycock, T. Waterfield, O. Yelekçi, R. Yu, and B. Zhou, eds. 2021. "IPCC 2021: Summary for Policymakers." In *Climate Change 2021: The Physical Science Basis.* Contribution of Working Group I to the Sixth Assessment Report of the Intergovernmental Panel on Climate Change. Cambridge University Press. www.ipcc.ch/report/ar6/wg1/downloads/report/IPCC_AR6_WGI_SPM.pdf.

Maturana, H.R. and F.J. Varela, 1987. *The Tree of Knowledge: The Biological Roots of Human Understanding.* Boston, MA: New Science Library/Shambhala Publications.

Maturana, H.R. and F.J. Varela. 2012. *Autopoiesis and Cognition: The Realization of the Living,* eds. R.S. Cohen and M.W. Wartofsky, vol. 42. Boston Studies in the Philosophy of Science. New York, NY: Springer Science & Business Media.

Max-Neef, M. 2010. "The World on a Collision Course and the Need for a New Economy." *Ambio* 39, no. 3. pp. 200–210.

McDonald, G.W. and M.G. Patterson. June 1, 2007. "Bridging the Divide in Urban Sustainability: From Human Exemptionalism to the New Ecological Paradigm." *Urban Ecosystems* 10, no. 2, pp. 169–192. https://doi.org/10.1007/s11252-006-0017-0.

McDonough, W. and M. Braungart. 2010. *Cradle to Cradle: Remaking the Way We Make Things.* Albany, NY: North Point Press.

McGilchrist, I. 2019. *The Master and His Emissary.* New Haven, CT: Yale University Press.

McGilchrist, I. 2021. *The Matter With Things: Our Brains, Our Delusions, and the Unmaking of the World, Vol. 1 and 2.* London: Perspectiva Press. https://channelmcgilchrist.com/the-matter-with-things/.

Meadows, D. 1999. *Leverage Points: Places to Intervene in a System.* https://donellameadows.org/archives/leverage-points-places-to-intervene-in-a-system/ (accessed July 21, 2023).

Meadows, D.H. 2008. *Thinking in Systems: International Bestseller*, ed. D. Wright, Illustrated edition. Chelsea Green Publishing.

Melé, D. September 1, 2016. "Understanding Humanistic Management." *Humanistic Management Journal* 1, no. 1, pp. 33–55. https://doi.org/10.1007/s41463-016-0011-5.

Mizobuchi, H. 2014. "Measuring World Better Life Frontier: A Composite Indicator for OECD Better Life Index." *Social Indicators Research* 118, no. 3, pp. 987–1007.

Monbiot, G. 15 April, 2016. "Neoliberalism: The Ideology at the Root of All Our Problems." *The Guardian*. www.theguardian.com/books/2016/apr/15/neoliberalism-ideology-problem-george-monbiot.

"The Most Urgent Refugee Crises Around the World." 2022. www.worldvision.ca/stories/refugees/refugee-crises-around-the-world (accessed March 3, 2022).

"Netweaver Network." n.d. *Netweaver Network.* www.netweavernetwork.org (accessed April 29, 2022).

Nussbaum, M. 2003. "Capabilities as Fundamental Entitlements: Sen and Social Justice." *Feminist Economics* 9, no. 2-3, pp. 33–59.

O'Brien, K. 2021. *You Matter More Than You Think: Quantum Social Change for a Thriving World.* eChange Press. www.youmattermorethanyouthink.com.

O'Neill, D.W, A.L. Fanning, W.F. Lamb, and J.K. Steinberger. 2018. "A Good Life for All within Planetary Boundaries." *Nature Sustainability* 1, no. 2, pp. 88–95.

Orton, J.D. and K.E. Weick. April 1990. "Loosely Coupled Systems: A Reconceptualization." *Academy of Management Review* 15, no. 2, pp. 203–223. https://doi.org/10.5465/amr.1990.4308154.

Ostrom, E. 1990. *Governing the Commons: The Evolution of Institutions for Collective Action.* Cambridge, UK: Cambridge University Press.

Ostrom, E. 2010a. "Analyzing Collective Action." *Agricultural Economics* 41, no. s1, pp. 155–166. https://doi.org/10.1111/j.1574-0862.2010.00497.x.

Ostrom, E. 2010b. "Beyond Markets and States: Polycentric Governance of Complex Economic Systems." *The American Economic Review*, pp. 641–672.

Ostrom, E. September 2000. "Collective Action and the Evolution of Social Norms." *Journal of Economic Perspectives* 14, no. 3, pp. 137–158. https://doi.org/10.1257/jep.14.3.137.

Owen, H. 1997a. *Expanding Our Now: The Story of Open Space Technology.* San Francisco: Berrett-Koehler Publishers. http://catdir.loc.gov/catdir/enhancements/fy0715/97017806-d.html.

Owen, H. 1997b. *Open Space Technology: A User's Guide,* 2nd ed. San Francisco: Berrett-Koehler Publishers. http://catdir.loc.gov/catdir/enhancements/fy0715/97017807-d.html.

Patton, M.Q. 2019. *Blue Marble Evaluation: Premises and Principles.* Guilford Publications.

Paxton, D. and S.V. Stralen. 2015. "Developing Collaborative and Innovative Leadership: Practices for Fostering a New Mindset." *Journal of Leadership Education* 14, no. 4. pp. 11–25.

Pearce, C.L., J.A. Conger, and E.A. Locke. June 1, 2007. "Shared Leadership Theory." *The Leadership Quarterly* 18, no. 3, pp. 281–288. Destructive Leadership. https://doi.org/10.1016/j.leaqua.2007.03.009.

Pio, E. and S. Waddock. October 28, 2020. "Invoking Indigenous Wisdom for Management Learning." *Management Learning.* https://doi.org/10.1177/1350507620963956.

Pio, E., S. Waddock, M. Mangaliso, M. McIntosh, C. Spiller, H. Takeda, J. Gladstone, H. Marcus, et al. 2013. "Pipeline to the Future: Seeking Wisdom in Indigenous, Eastern, and Western Traditions." *Handbook of Faith and Spirituality in the Workplace,* pp. 195–219. Springer.

Pirson, M. 2017. *Humanistic Management: Protecting Dignity and Promoting Well-Being.* Cambridge, UK: Cambridge University Press.

Pirson, M. and P. Lawrence. 2010. "Humanism in Business—Towards a Paradigm Shift?" *Journal of Business Ethics* 93, no. 4, pp. 553–565. https://doi.org/10.1007/s10551-009-0239-1.

Popp, J.K., H.B. Milward, G. MacKean, A. Casebeer, and R. Lindstrom. 2014. "Inter-Organizatinal Networks: A Critical Review of the Literature to Inform Practice." Literature Review, Collaborating Across Boundaries. Calgary, Canada; Tucson AZ; Victoria, Canada: The IBM Center for the Business of Government. www.businessofgovernment.org/sites/default/files/Inter-Organizational%20Networks.pdf.

RADAR. 2022. "RADAR Futures Report—A Future in Sync." A Radar Future Report. https://futureinsync.radardao.xyz/.

Raelin, J.A. 2003. *Creating Leaderful Organizations: How to Bring out Leadership in Everyone.* Berrett-Koehler Publishers.

Raelin, J. 2016a. *Introduction to Leadership-as-Practice,* pp. 1–18. https://doi.org/10.4324/9781315684123-1.

Raelin, J.A. May 1, 2016b. "It's Not About the Leaders: It's About the Practice of Leadership." SSRN Scholarly Paper. Rochester, NY: Social Science Research Network. https://papers.ssrn.com/abstract=2777186.

Raelin, J.A. Apri l, 2017. "Leadership-as-Practice: Theory and Application— An Editor's Reflection." *Leadership* 13, no. 2, pp. 215–221. https://doi .org/10.1177/1742715017702273.

Raworth, K. 2017. *Doughnut Economics: Seven Ways to Think Like a 21st-Century Economist.* White River Junction, VT: Chelsea Green Publishing.

Riedy, C. August 1, 2020. "Discourse Coalitions for Sustainability Transformations: Common Ground and Conflict beyond Neoliberalism." *Current Opinion in Environmental Sustainability, Open Issue 2020, Part A: Technology Innovations and Environmental Sustainability in the Anthropocene,* no. 45, pp. 100–112. https:// doi.org/10.1016/j.cosust.2020.09.014.

Ripple, W.J., C. Wolf, T.M. Newsome, J.W. Gregg, T.M. Lenton, I. Palomo, J.A.J. Eikelboom, B.E. Law, S.Huq, P.B. Duffy, and J. Rockström. 2021. "World Scientists' Warning of a Climate Emergency 2021." *Bioscience,* pp. 1–5. https://doi.org/10.1093/biosci/biab079.

Rittel, H.W.J. and M.M. Webber. 1973. "Dilemmas in a General Theory of Planning." *Policy Sciences* 4, no. 2, pp. 155–169.

Robèrt, K.-L. 2002. *The Natural Step Story: Seeding a Quiet Revolution.* Bllomington, IN: Indiana University Press.

Rockström, J., W. Steffen, K. Noone, Å. Persson, F.S. Chapin III, E. Lambin, T.M. Lenton, M. Scheffer, et al. 2009a. "Planetary Boundaries: Exploring the Safe Operating Space for Humanity." *Ecology and Society* 14, no. 2. p. 32.

Rockström, J.,W. Steffen, K. Noone, Å. Persson, F.S. Chapin III, E.F. Lambin, T.M. Lenton, et al. 2009b. "A Safe Operating Space for Humanity." *Nature* 461, no. 7263, pp. 472–475.

Rosile, G.A., D.M. Boje, and C.M. Claw. June 1, 2018. "Ensemble Leadership Theory: Collectivist, Relational, and Heterarchical Roots from Indigenous Contexts." *Leadership* 14, no. 3, pp. 307–328. https://doi.org/ 10.1177/1742715016652933.

Scharmer, C.O. 2007. *Theory U: Leading From the Future as It Emerges.* Cambridge: Society for Organisational Learning.

Scharmer, O. and K. Kaufer. 2013. *Leading From the Emerging Future: From Ego-System to Eco-System Economies.* Berrett-Koehler Publishers.

Schön, D.A. 1983. *The Reflective Practitioner: How Professionals Think in Action.* New York, NY: Basic Books. http://catdir.loc.gov/catdir/enhancements/ fy0832/82070855-d.html.

Schwartz, S.H. 2012. "An Overview of the Schwartz Theory of Basic Values." *Online Readings in Psychology and Culture, Unit 2: Theoretical and Methodological Issues* 2, no. 1, pp. 1–20. http://dx.doi.org/10.9707/2307-0919.1116.

Seitzinger, S.P., U. Svedin, C.L. Crumley, W. Steffen, S.A. Abdullah, C. Alfsen, W.J. Broadgate, F. Biermann, N.R. Bondre, et al. 2012. "Planetary Stewardship in an Urbanizing World: Beyond City Limits." *Ambio* 41, no. 8, pp. 787–794.

Sen, A. 2014. "Development as Freedom (1999)." In *The Globalization and Development Reader: Perspectives on Development and Global Change*, eds. J.T. Roberts, A.B. Hite, and N. Chorev, vol. 2, pp. 525–547. Hoboken, NJ: Wiley Balckwell Sussex.

Senge, P.M. 1994. *The Fifth Discipline Fieldbook: Strategies for Building a Learning Organization*. New York, NY: Currency.

Senge, P.M. 2006. *The Fifth Discipline: The Art and Practice of the Learning Organization*. New York, NY: Doubleday/Currency. www.loc.gov/catdir/ enhancements/fy0703/2006281125-d.html. http://www.loc.gov/catdir/enhan cements/fy0703/2006281125-s.html. http://www.loc.gov/catdir/enhancements/ fy0703/2006281125-b.html.

Senge, P.M., C.O. Scharmer, J. Jaworski, and B.S. Flowers. 2004. *Presence: Human Purpose and the Field of the Future*. Cambridge, MA: SoL.

Sharpe, B. 2015. "Three Horizons: The Patterning of Hope." *Journal of Holistic Healthcare* 12, no. 1 (Spring), pp. 4–6.

Sharpe, B., A. Hodgson, G. Leicester, A. Lyon, and I. Fazey. 2016. "Three Horizons: A Pathways Practice for Transformation." *Ecology and Society* 21, no. 2. http://www.jstor.org/stable/26270405.

Skelcher, C. 2005. "Jurisdictional Integrity, Polycentrism, and the Design of Democratic Governance." *Governance* 18, no. 1, pp. 89–110.

Swanson, G.A. and J.G. Miller. 2009. "Living Systems Theory." *Systems Science and Cybernetics* 1, pp. 136–148. Systems Theories.

Talberth, J. and M. Weisdorf. December 1, 2017. "Genuine Progress Indicator 2.0: Pilot Accounts for the US, Maryland, and City of Baltimore 2012–2014." *Ecological Economics* 142, pp. 1–11. https://doi.org/10.1016/j.ecol econ.2017.06.012.

Taylor, C. 2002. "Modern Social Imaginaries." *Public Culture* 14, no. 1, pp. 91–124.

Thinley, J.Y. and J. Hartz-Karp. December 30, 2019. "National Progress, Sustainability and Higher Goals: The Case of Bhutan's Gross National Happiness." *Sustainable Earth* 2, no. 1, p. 11. https://doi.org/10.1186/s42055-019-0022-9.

Thomson, A.M., J.L. Perry, and T.K. Miller. January 1, 2009. "Conceptualizing and Measuring Collaboration." *Journal of Public Administration Research and Theory* 19, no. 1, pp. 23–56. https://doi.org/10.1093/jopart/mum036.

Torbert, W.R. and S. Cook-Greuter. 2004. *Action Inquiry: The Secret of Timely and Transforming Leadership*. San Francisco, CA: Berrett-Koehler. http:// catdir.loc.gov/catdir/enhancements/fy0715/2003063777-d.html. Materials specified: Publisher description http://catdir.loc.gov/catdir/enhancements/ fy0715/2003063777-d.html.

Turner, R.K. and B. Fisher. 2008. "To the Rich Man the Spoils." *Nature* 451, no. 7182, pp. 1067–1068.

*UN News.* March 21, 2022. "UN Chief Warns Against 'Sleepwalking to Climate Catastrophe.'" https://news.un.org/en/story/2022/03/1114322.

Waddell, S. 2011. *Global Action Networks: Creating Our Future Together.* Bocconi University on Management. Hampshire, UK: Palgrave-Macmillan.

Waddell, S. 2016. *Change for the Audacious: A Doer's Guide to Large Systems Change for Flourishing Futures.* Boston: Networking Action.

Waddell, S. 2018. "Four Strategies for Large Systems Change." *Stanford Social Innovation Review* 16, no. 2, pp. 40–45.

Waddell, S., S. Bowles, T. Carruthers, I. Kendrick, J. Nortin, and G. Singh. 2021. *An Investigation into Financing Transformation.* Boston, MA: Bounce Beyond, Cattail Strategy, Catalyst 2020.

Waddell, S., S. Waddock, S. Martino, and J. Norton. 2023. "Emerging Economic Operating Infrastructure to Support Wellbeing Economies." *Humanistic Management Journal* 8, no. 1, pp. 63–88.

Waddock, S. 2010. "Finding Wisdom Within—The Role of Seeing and Reflective Practice in Developing Moral Imagination, Aesthetic Sensibility, and Systems Understanding." *Journal of Business Ethics Education* 7, no. 1, pp. 177–196.

Waddock, S. 2013. "Wisdom and Responsible Leadership: Aesthetic Sensibility, Moral Imagination, and Systems Thinking." In *Aesthetics and Business Ethics,* eds. D. Koehn and D. El, pp. 129–147. Issues in Business Ethics. Berlin, Germany: Springer-Verlag.

Waddock, S. 2016. "Foundational Memes for a New Narrative About the Role of Business in Society." *Humanistic Management Journal* 1, no. 1 pp. 91–105.

Waddock, S. 2020. "Reframing and Transforming Economics Around Life." *Sustainability* 12, no. 18, p. 7553.

Waddock, S. 2021. "Wellbeing Economics Narratives for a Sustainable Future." *Humanistic Management Journal* 4, no. 4, pp. 165–182. https://doi.org/10.1007/s41463-021-00107-z.

Waddock, S. and P. Kuenkel. 2020. "What Gives Life to Large System Change?" *Organization and Environment* 33, no. 3, pp. 342–358.

Waddock, S. and S. Waddell. 2021a. "Five Core Dimensions of Purposeful System Transformation." *Journal of Management for Global Sustainability* 9, no. 2, pp. 1–41. https://doi.org/10.13185/JM2021.09203.

Waddock, S. and S. Waddell. 2021b. "Transformation Catalysts: Weaving Transformational Change for a Flourishing World for All." *Cadmus* 4, no. 4, pp. 165–182.

Waddock, S., G.M. Meszoely, S. Waddell, and D. Denton. 2015. "The Complexity of Wicked Problems in Large Scale Change." *Journal of Organizational Change Management* 28, no. 6, pp. 993–1012.

Waddock, S., S. Waddell, and P.S. Gray. 2018. "The Transformational Change Challenge of Memes: The Case of Marriage Equality in the United States." *Business & Society.* https://doi.org/10.1177/0007650318816440.

Waddock, S., S. Waddell, J. Peter, and K. Ian. May 31, 2022. "Convening Transformation Systems to Achieve System Transformation." *Journal of Awareness-Based Systems Change* 2, no. 1, pp. 77–100. https://doi.org/10.47061/jabsc.v2i1.2023.

Wamsler, C. January 1, 2020. "Education for Sustainability: Fostering a More Conscious Society and Transformation towards Sustainability." *International Journal of Sustainability in Higher Education* 21, no. 1, pp. 112–130. https://doi.org/10.1108/IJSHE-04-2019-0152.

Weber, A. 2013. "Enlivenment." *Towards a Fundamental Shift in the Concepts of Nature, Culture and Politics.* Berlin: Heinrich-Böll-Stiftung.

Weber, A. 2016. *The Biology of Wonder | Aliveness, Feeling, and the Metamorphosis of Science.* Gabriola, BC, Canada: New Society Publishers. https://biologyofwonder.org/.

Weber, E.P. and A.M. Khademian. 2008. "Wicked Problems, Knowledge Challenges, and Collaborative Capacity Builders in Network Settings." *Public Administration Review* 68, no. 2, pp. 334–349. https://doi.org/10.1111/j.1540-6210.2007.00866.x.

Weick, K.E. 1976. "Educational Organizations as Loosely Coupled Systems." *Administrative Science Quarterly* 21, no. 1, pp. 1–19. https://doi.org/10.2307/2391875.

Weick, K.E., K.M. Sutcliffe, and D. Obstfeld. 2005. "Organizing and the Process of Sensemaking." *Organization Science* 16, no. 4, pp. 409–421.

Weisbord, M. and S. Janoff. 1995. *Future Search: An Action Guide to Finding Common Ground in Organizations and Communities*, 1st ed. San Francisco: Berrett-Koehler.

Weisbord, M. and S. Janoff. 2010. *Future Search: Getting the Whole System in the Room for Vision, Commitment, and Action.* Berrett-Koehler Publishers.

Weisdorf, J.L. 2005. "From Foraging to Farming: Explaining the Neolithic Revolution." *Journal of Economic Surveys* 19, no. 4, pp. 561–586. https://doi.org/10.1111/j.0950-0804.2005.00259.x.

Werhane, P. 2008. "Mental Models, Moral Imagination and System Thinking in the Age of Globalization." *Journal of Business Ethics* 78, no. 3, pp. 463–474. https://doi.org/10.1007/s10551-006-9338-4.

Whitney, D. and D.L. Cooperrider. 2000. "The Appreciative Inquiry Summit: An Emerging Methodology for Whole System Positive Change." *OD PRACTITIONER* 32, no. 1, pp. 13–26.

Wilber, K. 2001. *A Theory of Everything: An Integral Vision for Business, Politics, Science, and Spirituality.* Dublin: Gateway.

Wood, D.J. and B. Gray. June 1, 1991. "Toward a Comprehensive Theory of Collaboration." *The Journal of Applied Behavioral Science* 27, no. 2, pp. 139–162. https://doi.org/10.1177/0021886391272001.

Zucman, G. 2019. "Global Wealth Inequality." *Annual Review of Economics* 11, pp. 109–138.

# About the Author

**Dr. Sandra Waddock**, Galligan Chair of Strategy, Carroll School Scholar of Corporate Responsibility, and Professor of Management at Boston College's Carroll School of Management, has published more than 180 papers and book chapters and 15 books to date. Her books include *Building the Responsible Enterprise* with Andreas Rasche (Stanford, 2012), *The Difference Makers* (Greenleaf, 2008), *Intellectual Shamans* (Cambridge, 2014), and, recently, *Transforming Towards Life-Centered Economies* (Business Expert Press, 2020). Waddock, a former steward in the Bounce Beyond Initiative, has received numerous lifetime achievement awards for her work, and holds her doctorate and MBA from Boston University's business school.

# Index

Accountability, 115, 161, 163
Action-oriented self-awareness,
 143–144
Adaptability, 163
Aesthetic sensibility, 148, 149, 152
Amplification, 92, 177–179
 stewarding transformation,
  160–164, 182
 transformative impact, 106
  collaborative capacities, 108–109
  emerging innovation capacities,
   117–118
  financing system transformation,
   115–117
  governance, 112–113
  holistic assessment, 109–112
  narrative challenge, 107–108
  Ostrom's principles, 113–115
  performance metrics, 109–112
  transformation infrastructure,
   118–120
Autopoiesis, 139–140
Awareness, 56–57, 150–151

Biodiversity loss, 3, 6
Blessed unrest, 15, 28, 88, 104, 175
Blue Marble evaluation, 75, 97, 110,
 111, 113–114
Boundary-spanning, 160
Boundedness, 54–55, 129
Brittle, anxious, nonlinear, and
 incomprehensible (BANI),
 4–5, 147
Butterfly effect, 31

Catalytic stewardship approach, 173
Change agent, 11, 17, 19, 22, 27–29,
 31, 35, 38, 52, 57–58, 65, 82,
 84, 86, 87, 94, 116, 124, 126,
 128, 138, 141, 183
Climate change, 21
Cocreative engagement, 133–135

Cohering process, 91–92, 97,
 158–160, 177–179
 action planning, 97–99
 cocreating transformation
  capacities, 99–101
 steward, 182
Collaboration, 132–133, 180, 181
Collaborative capacities, 108–109
Collaborative mindset, 134
Collective stewardship, 157
Collective suicide, 40
Collective value, 42, 59, 60, 110
Collective visioning, 174–175
Complexity/systems-based approach,
 TCs, 135
 contextual uniqueness, 136–137
 evolutionary self-organization,
  139–140
 holistic system perspectives,
  135–136
 interconnected relational
  dynamism, 136–137
 multilevel, multispatial,
  multistrategy, and
  multistakeholder approaches,
  137–139
Complexity visioning, 155–156
Connectedness, 53–54, 61, 64
Connecting process, 91–93, 177, 178
 seeing, 93–94
 sensemaking, 94–97
 stewarding, 153, 182
Contextual uniqueness, 136–137
Conventional economics, 8, 41,
 43–44
Conventional governance, 112–113
Cultural attractors, 43
Cultural myths, 35–36
 human exceptionalism, 39–41
 as narratives shaping mindsets,
  36–37
 neoliberalism, 41–43

reason for, 43–47
scientism, 37–39
shifting, 65

Diversity, 53–54, 138

Ecological civilizations, 2, 9, 12, 62,
    155, 170
Economics values proposition, 57–59
    cocreating collective value, 60
    connectedness, 61
    cosmopolitan-localist governance,
        60–61
    equitable markets and trade, 62–63
    regenerativity, reciprocity, and
        circularity, 61–62
    relationality, 61
    stewardship of the whole, 59–60
    subsidiarity, 60–61
Emotional intelligence, 154
Entrepreneur strategy, 82, 83
Equitable collaboration, 132–133
Evolutionary self-organization,
    139–140

Financing, 180, 181
Financing system transformation,
    115–117
Flexibility, 163
Flourishing, 2, 5–16, 23, 50, 73, 76,
    85, 112, 118, 131, 145, 167,
    174

Good life narrative, 8
Governance, 112–113, 179–181

Heterarchy, 148
Holistic system perspectives, 135–136
Holons, 29, 138
Human consciousness, 57
Human exceptionalism, 37, 39–41

Inclusive participation, 131–132
Innovation, 117–118, 179
Innovation capacities, 117–118
Intentionality, 129
Interconnected relational dynamism,
    136–137
Invisible hand, 62

Knowledge, 111

Leaderfulness, 148
Learning approach, 180, 181
Legitimacy, 111
Leverage, 31
Life-affirming values, 51–52
    awareness, 56–57
    boundedness, 54–55
    connectedness and diversity, 53–54
    novelty, 55
    purpose, 52
    wholeness, 55–56
Lover strategy, 82, 84

Mapping, 93
Measurement approach, 180, 181
Memes, 43, 46, 95
Mitákuye Oyás'iŋ, 62, 137
Moral imagination, 150–151
Motivation, 55, 110, 131
Multilevel perspective, 100

Narratives, 179
Neoliberal economics, 7
Neoliberalism, 37, 41–43
Netweaving, 158–159
New economics, 63–65
Novelty, 55, 130

Ontological reductionism, 38
Openness, 163
Ostrom's principles, 113–115

Panarchy, 29, 32, 86, 145
Paradigms, 44, 73–74, 172
Pathfinder strategy, 82–84
Patterns, 93–94, 126
Performance metrics, 109–112, 172
Permeability, 129–130
Permeable/porous boundaries,
    129–130
Planetary boundaries narrative, 8
Polycentric governance, 139
Polycrisis, 3, 85
Power, 110–111
Power relations, 75–76
Power structures, 75–76, 172
Practices, 76–77, 172

Proprioceptive consciousness, 56
Purpose, 52, 70–73, 129, 172
Purposeful system transformation, 22,
    23, 28
Purpose, paradigms, performance
    metrics, practices, and power
    relations (5Ps), 77–78

Reflective consciousness, 56–57
Reflexive learning, 162–163
Regenerativity, reciprocity, and
    circularity, 61–62, 64
Relationship management, 154
Resourcing, 180, 181
Risk-taking, 162–163

Scientism, 37–39
Self-awareness, 56, 143–144, 154
Self-management, 154
Sensemaking, 94–97, 177
7Vortex maps, 93
Shared narratives, 31
Sharing economy, 117
Social imaginary, 1–18
Socioecological systems, 28–29, 70,
    72, 138, 172
Stewarding systems, 140–141
    action-oriented self- and system-
        awareness, 143–144
    guiding, experimentation, adaptive,
        enabling processes, 142–143
    structuring, stewarding, and
        resourcing relationships,
        141–142
Stewarding transformation, 164–165
    aesthetic sensibility, 152
    awareness, 150–151
    moral imagination, 150–151
    systems understanding, 151–152
    wisdom and change, 147, 151–153
        amplifying, 160–164
        cohering, 158–160
        connecting, 153–158
    wisdom for catalyzing, 149–152
Stewardship, 59–60, 140–141,
    152–153
    amplifying, 160–164, 182
    change, 182
    cohering, 158–160, 182

connecting, 153–158, 182
stewarding transformation,
    164–165
transformative change, 181–182
Subsidiarity, 60–61
Sustainability, 6
System-awareness, 143–144
System infrastructure, 182–183
Systems thinking, 151–152
Systems understanding, 151–152
System transformation
    catalyzing, 183–185
    design guidelines for, 126–127
    integrated process for, 171
        connecting, cohering, and
            amplifying, 177–179
        system infrastructure, 182–183
        transformation (T-) systems,
            179–181
        transformative change, 182
        values-based narrative/vision,
            173–175
        wicked complexity, 175–176
        wicked problems, understanding,
            172–173
    need for, 168–171

Top-down leadership, 157
Transformational change, 81–82
Transformation catalysts (TCs),
    26–27, 81–82, 88–89,
    178–179
    cohering, 97
        action planning, 97–99
        cocreating transformation
            capacities, 99–101
        complexity/systems-based
            approach, 135
        contextual uniqueness, 136–137
        evolutionary self-organization,
            139–140
        holistic system perspectives,
            135–136
        interconnected relational
            dynamism, 136–137
        multilevel, multispatial,
            multistrategy, and
            multistakeholder approaches,
            137–139

connecting, 92–93
seeing, 93–94
sensemaking, 94–97
defined, 89
design guidelines, 123–125
for system transformation,
126–127
design principles, 125–126
principles, to support life, 128–130
values-driven change processes,
130–131
cocreative engagement, 133–135
equitable collaboration, 132–133
inclusive participation, 131–132
whole systems approach, 89–92
work of, 92
Transformation (T-) systems, 27–28,
179–181
amplifying impact, 106
collaborative capacities, 108–109
emerging innovation capacities,
117–118
financing system transformation,
115–117
governance, 112–113
holistic assessment, 109–112
narrative challenge, 107–108
Ostrom's principles, 113–115
performance metrics, 109–112
transformation infrastructure,
118–120
defining, 103–106
stewarding, 164–165
underorganized systems, 127–128
Transformative capacity, 113
Transformative system change, 77–78,
182
core system dimensions, 69–70

defined, 24–26
paradigms, 73–74
performance metrics, 74–75
power relations and structures,
75–76
practices, 76–77
purpose, 70–73
Transforming system transformation,
19–23, 85–87
catalytic approach, 26
transformation catalysts, 26–27
transformation (T-) systems,
27–28
complex wickedness, 30–32
defining, 24–26
socioecological systems, 28–29
transforming, 85–87
Translation skills, 160
Trust building, 158–159
T-system infrastructure, 145

*Ubuntu*, 61, 67, 137
Underorganized systems, 127–128

Values articulation, 175
Values-driven change processes,
130–131
Volatility, uncertainty, complexity,
and ambiguity (VUCA), 4,
147

Warrior strategy, 82, 83
Webcrawl, 93
Wholeness, 29, 53, 55–56, 59
Wicked complexity, 30–32, 35,
38, 54, 57, 71, 86–88, 91,
138, 151, 173, 175–176, 181,
185

Printed in the USA
CPSIA information can be obtained
at www.ICGtesting.com
LVHW051141021123
762339LV00010B/101